1999

W9-CMI-007

HOBBES
On the Citizen

CAMBRIDGE TEXTS IN THE
HISTORY OF POLITICAL THOUGHT

Series editors

RAYMOND GEUSS
Lecturer in Philosophy, University of Cambridge

QUENTIN SKINNER
Regius Professor of Modern History, University of Cambridge

Cambridge Texts in the History of Political Thought is now firmly established as the major student textbook series in political theory. It aims to make available to students all the most important texts in the history of Western political thought, from ancient Greece to the early twentieth century. All the familiar classic texts will be included but the series seeks at the same time to enlarge the conventional canon by incorporating an extensive range of less well-known works, many of them never before available in a modern English edition. Wherever possible, texts are published in complete and unabridged form, and translations are specially commissioned for the series. Each volume contains a critical introduction together with chronologies, biographical sketches, a guide to further reading and any necessary glossaries and textual apparatus. When completed, the series will aim to offer an outline of the entire evolution of Western political thought.

For a list of titles published in the series, please see end of book.

THOMAS HOBBES

On the Citizen

EDITED AND TRANSLATED BY

RICHARD TUCK
Harvard University and Jesus College, Cambridge

MICHAEL SILVERTHORNE
McGill University

CAMBRIDGE
UNIVERSITY PRESS

PUBLISHED BY THE PRESS SYNDICATE OF THE UNIVERSITY OF CAMBRIDGE
The Pitt Building, Trumpington Street, Cambridge CB2 1RP, United Kingdom

CAMBRIDGE UNIVERSITY PRESS
The Edinburgh Building, Cambridge, CB2 2RU, United Kingdom
40 West 20th Street, New York, NY 10011–4211, USA
10 Stamford Road, Oakleigh, Melbourne 3166, Australia

First published 1998

Printed in the United Kingdom at the University Press, Cambridge

Typeset in Ehrhardt 9.5pt [WV]

A catalogue record for this book is available from the British Library

ISBN 0 521 43204 9 hardback
ISBN 0 521 43780 6 paperback

Contents

Acknowledgements

The principal labour of this edition was by Michael Silverthorne, who provided a completely new translation of the Latin text and the notes on key words. Richard Tuck is primarily responsible for the introduction, the sketch of Hobbes's life and the suggestions for further readings, though each editor has commented on the other's work. Many other people have helped in the construction of this edition; we should pay a tribute first to the late Professor Howard Warrender, whose edition of the Latin text for Oxford University Press is the basis of our translation, and who began the modern scholarly study of Hobbes's texts. Richard Fisher of Cambridge University Press, Quentin Skinner and Raymond Geuss have been a constant source of support to both of us. In addition, Michael Silverthorne would like to thank Leszek Wysocki for careful criticism of an earlier draft; Stephen Silverthorne and Marcia Morris for secretarial assistance; and the Social Sciences and Humanities research Council of Canada for financial support. Richard Tuck would like to thank Noel Malcolm, Maurice Goldsmith, Lucien Jaume, Ian Harris, John Dunn, Jim Tully, David Johnston and Istvan Hont for their helpful comments during many years of working on Hobbes.

Introduction

Although Hobbes is known to most readers today primarily as the author of *Leviathan*, his first claim to fame was as the author of this work, *De Cive (On the Citizen)*. It had been known to a few intimates of Hobbes since 1641, but it was not known to a wider public until the famous Elzevir Company in Amsterdam picked it up and produced it in a generally available edition, which appeared in the bookshops in the early months of 1647, when its author was 59 and was about to begin working on *Leviathan*. It was entitled (in Latin) *Elementa Philosophica de Cive*, that is, 'Philosophical Elements of the Citizen' or, less literally but more felicitously, 'Philosophical Elements of Citizenship', by 'Thomas Hobbes of Malmesbury'.

It was an immediate best-seller – Elzevir's had sold out of its stock by the summer, and rushed out a reprint.[1] And it remained until the nineteenth century the major Hobbesian text for many readers on the Continent, partly because an authoritative French translation by Hobbes's friend Samuel Sorbière appeared in 1649, whereas *Leviathan* was not translated into French until our own time, and partly because it was kept in print throughout the late

---

[1] He had already published two books under his own name: his translation of Thucydides (*Eight Bookes of the Peloponnesian Warre* London, 1629), and his poem on the Peak District, *Ad Nobilissimum Dominum Guilierlmum Comitem Devoniae, &c. De Mirabilibus Pecci, Carmen* ([London, 1636?]). On the publishing history of the 1647 editions, see *De Cive: the Latin Version*, ed. Howard Warrender (Oxford University Press, 1983), pp. 8–13 and 300–15.

seventeenth and eighteenth centuries.[2] Hobbes himself never repudiated the book, despite having published *Leviathan* four years later, and he proudly reprinted it in his collected works (in Latin) in 1668, alongside a Latin translation of *Leviathan*.

Although it was so late in his life that Hobbes became known to the general public, he had been known to 'the choicer spirits' (as one of his friends put it)[3] for many years, and he had already printed (though one would hesitate to say published) *De Cive* five years earlier for circulation among them.[4] An English version of his ideas was also circulated widely in manuscript some years before that, which we know under the title of *Elements of Law, Natural and Politic*, while interesting anonymous works from his pen had been printed at various times from 1620 onwards – the most interesting, it now seems, being a discourse on the Roman historian Tacitus which appeared in that year (see below).

These works emerged from a life spent mixing with some of the most influential European politicians and writers. From 1608 until the outbreak of the Civil War Hobbes lived for much of the time in the household of the Cavendishes, earls of Devonshire, as a secretary to the successive heads of the family, tutor to its young men, and general adviser on all kinds of matters. His employers were among the richest men in England, with a corresponding political importance, and when they or their heirs travelled on the Continent they immediately had access to the highest ranks of European society. When Hobbes accompanied them to the English court or travelled abroad with them, as he often did, he too would often be introduced to the statesmen or authors whom his masters wanted to meet. Thus in the 1620s he was known to the duke of Buckingham, and was suggested by the Cavendishes to Sir Francis Bacon to act occasionally as his amanuensis; in the 1630s he made the acquaintance of the king's great minister Strafford, and of other politicians such as Edward Hyde, later Lord Clarendon. Abroad, in

---

[2] For the later editions, see *De Cive: the Latin Version*, pp. 66–7; the French translation of *Leviathan* is *Léviathan*, trans. and ed. François Tricaud (Editions Sirey, Paris, 1971).

[3] See the letter from Thomas de Martel in *De Cive: the Latin Version*, p. 300.

[4] This printing of 1642 is usually referred to, however inaccurately, as 'the first edition', and we follow this practice. Similarly we follow the usual practice of referring to the 1647 edition as 'the second edition'. For the details of the 1642 printing, see note 10 below.

Venice from 1614 to 1615 with the son of the earl, he encountered the leaders of the republic such as Paolo Sarpi, and continued to correspond with them on his master's behalf well into the next decade. On a voyage to France and Italy from 1634 to 1636 with the then earl (who was only 17), he dined with cardinals at Rome, met Galileo at Florence, and was introduced to the most advanced philosophers of Europe in Paris.

All this might seem very far removed from his origins in a provincial English town (Malmesbury in Wiltshire), the son of an obscure minor clergyman who had deserted his wife and children. Hobbes's education was paid for by his uncle, a tradesman in the town, who sent him to the town grammar school and then to a hall (the cheaper version of a college) at Oxford, where he graduated in 1608 at the age of 20. He was marked out as a young man by his remarkable linguistic skills: he was extremely fluent in Latin, Greek and French as well as English, and an accomplished prose stylist and versifier from an early age. These were the skills which the Renaissance education system valued above all others, principally because they could be put to public use in the service of princes or other great politicians, and Hobbes was nominated by the principal of his hall for just such a post in the Cavendish household soon after graduating; he became the tutor of Lord Cavendish's eldest son, and briefly joined him at Cambridge (where he incorporated a BA[5] at St John's College). He was only a couple of years older than his pupil, and quickly became more of a friend and secretary than tutor. From 1609 until 1640 he lived mostly with the Cavendish family at their houses in Derbyshire or London, though in 1640 he decided to flee into exile in France in order to escape the attack on the king's supporters.

His theoretical interests, when he took up his job and for some years to come, were largely in the humanities – in history, literature and the study and practice of rhetoric. It was this which led to his first publications; the very first (it is now quite convincingly established) was a group of three discourses in a collaborative volume of essays which appeared anonymously in 1620, entitled *Horae Subsecivae* ('Leisure Hours') (Hobbes's collaborator was probably his pupil and friend, Lord Cavendish's son William). The

---

[5] I.e. Hobbes was granted at Cambridge an equivalence for his Oxford BA.

most important of these discourses was a long commentary on the beginning of Tacitus' *Annals*, in which Hobbes revealed his deep knowledge of contemporary 'Tacitism', the literature of 'reason of state' which was popular across Europe in his generation.[6] In the mid-1630s he broadened his interests, to include what we would call science and the philosophy of science; but again, this was largely the result of his patrons' concerns. At this period he had come more into the service of the earl of Devonshire's cousin, the earl of Newcastle, who lived not far from the Devonshires' home. Newcastle, and his younger brother Sir Charles Cavendish, were extremely interested in modern optics and mathematics, largely because of their military applications: both brothers were prominent soldiers, and Newcastle became in effect the commander-in-chief of the royalist army during the Civil War. They corresponded with philosophers and mathematicians on the Continent, particularly those associated with the great intellectual entrepreneur Marin Mersenne, a friar who from his cell in the convent of the Minimes in Paris kept in touch with most of the leading philosophers of the day (above all with Descartes, whose work he constantly assisted and publicized). Deference to such prominent English aristocrats of this kind was so great that Hobbes was assured of a welcome in these circles when he arrived in 1634 bearing letters of introduction from them, though he seems not to have been very closely involved with these French philosophers until the 1640s.

Back in England in the late 1630s, he projected and drafted (more thoroughly than has usually been recognized) a large-scale work, in Latin, covering the whole area of traditional philosophy.[7] We may

---

[6] These discourses are now published separately from the rest of *Horae Subsecivae* with full introduction by Noel B. Reynolds and Arlene W. Saxonhouse, *Thomas Hobbes: Three Discourses. A Critical Modern Edition of Newly Identified Work of the Young Hobbes* (University of Chicago Press, 1995). For a discussion of Tacitism, and the location of Hobbes in that broad context, see Richard Tuck, *Philosophy and Government 1572–1651* (Cambridge University Press, 1993).

[7] What follows is largely a summary of an article of mine: Richard Tuck, 'Hobbes and Descartes', in *Perspectives on Thomas Hobbes*, ed. G. A. J. Rogers and Alan Ryan (Oxford University Press, 1988), pp. 11–42. There is an additional piece of evidence, not noted there, that by 1641 *De Homine* had already taken much the same form it was to have in 1658. This is provided by a remark in *De Cive* V.4 (*De Cive: the Latin Version*), that what counts as the agreement of many people had been defined 'praecedente sectione'. Hobbes always used the term *sectio* to refer to the three divisions of his *Elementa Philosophiae*, and the passage referred to here is presumably what later became *De Homine* XV.4, though in the context

assume that he already had in mind the title *Elementa Philosophiae*, 'The Elements of Philosophy', under which it eventually appeared in 1668, and we know that he had divided it into three *sectiones*, as he termed them, each one a (shortish) book-length work. The first section was entitled *De Corpore* ('Matter'), and dealt with metaphysics and physics; the second was *De Homine* ('Man'), which discussed the principles of perception and the passions; while the third was *De Cive*. The work was advanced enough by the spring of 1640 for Hobbes to circulate an English summary of the last two sections among a wide circle of friends, under the title *Elements of Law, Natural and Politic*. At about the same time he also began to circulate copies of the Latin drafts: we know that Lord Herbert of Cherbury and Sir Charles Cavendish were sent copies of *De Corpore*, and Mersenne seems to have been sent a version of *De Homine* to pass on to Descartes.

One of the purposes of the *Elements of Law, Natural and Politic* was to provide material which could be used by English politicians in defence of the policies of Strafford, as part of the struggle against the king's opponents in England. The political complexion of the two Parliaments which met in 1640, and the purge of Strafford and his supporters, understandably alarmed Hobbes, and in November 1640 he left England by himself for the first time, and settled in

of a discussion of *Fictitio* which Hobbes is likely to have added after writing *Leviathan*. (All references to *De Homine* and *De Corpore* are to *Thomae Hobbes . . . Opera Philosophica quae Latine scripsit Omnia*, ed. William Molesworth (5 vols., London, 1839–45), unless otherwise noted.) In a recent article, Noel Malcolm has argued that even though something like *De Corpore* and *De Homine* may indeed have been drafted by 1641, the existing fragments of *De Corpore* date from 1642–3 and not (as has been commonly supposed) from 1640. His reason for saying this is that the earliest fragment of *De Corpore* contains a sentence which also appears in Sir Thomas Browne's *Religio Medici*, which was not published until the end of 1642 (Malcolm, 'A summary biography of Hobbes', in Tom Sorell, ed., *The Cambridge Companion to Hobbes* (Cambridge University Press, 1996), p. 30). But the sentence, which is to be found on p. 449 of Hobbes's *Critique du 'De Mundo' de Thomas White*, ed. Jean Jacquot and Harold W. Jones (Vrin, Paris, 1973) in fact differs from the text in the published version of *Religio Medici* – see the critical edition by Vittoria Sanna (Cagliari, 1958), p. 42. *Religio Medici* was written in the 1630s and circulated widely in manuscript, with many variations between the existing copies (though none of them contains the variation found in the Hobbes fragment); as a young man, Browne had moved in the same Oxford circles as some of Hobbes's friends (Hobbes, *Correspondence*, ed. Noel Malcolm, Oxford University Press, 1994, p. 777). So Hobbes may perfectly well have known about *Religio Medici* before its publication.

relative poverty in Paris. Inspired by the political turmoil in England, he concentrated on finishing the third section of the *Elementa Philosophiae*, and by November 1641 he had a polished manuscript to present to his lord, the earl of Devonshire. Written on vellum, with a specially drawn title page bearing the title *Elementorum Philosophiae Sectio Tertia de Cive*, this manuscript was designed as an eye-catching and permanent record of Hobbes's ideas.[8] At the same time Hobbes arranged for 'a few examples' of the manuscript to be printed and distributed among his friends, so that they could comment on it; this seems to have been an extension of a system whereby Mersenne let visitors to his chamber consult a manuscript of the work, possibly the vellum copy itself.[9] The printed copies carry the date 1642 on their title pages.

There is no doubt that these copies were not put on sale at any bookseller: Hobbes himself said as much in the preface to the 1647 edition, and two of the recipients also remarked on the fact.[10] It should not be supposed that because the book was in print, it was significantly more widely known than the manuscript *Elements of Law, Natural and Politic*: more than ten copies of this manuscript still exist, which may be more than existing copies of the first edition of *De Cive*. If his remarks in the 1647 preface are to be believed,

---

[8] This was a life-long habit of Hobbes: *Elements of Law, Natural and Politic* was presented to its dedicatee, the earl of Newcastle, in a similar fashion, as was *Leviathan* itself, probably to the king – see my edition of *Leviathan* (2nd edn, Cambridge, 1996), p. lv.

[9] *De Cive: the Latin Version*, p. 300 (letter 2). The phrase 'a few examples' is from *Vitae Hobbianae Auctarium*, Hobbes, *Opera Latina*, p. xxxii. Mersenne also sent a copy of the printed text to Constantine Huygens in The Hague, requesting him to show it to his friends and colleagues (*ibid.*, p. 7). The printed copy has 1642 on its title page, and it was available to be sent to Huygens by May of that year (Hobbes, *Critique du 'De Mundo' de Thomas White*, p. 20). It is worth noting that in his own prose autobiography, Hobbes omitted the 1642 edition of *De Cive* completely (*Opera Latina*, I, p. xv), though he did mention it in his verse autobiography (*ibid.*, p. xc).

[10] '[T]here has appeared here, not indeed among the common sort, but among the choicer spirits a book *De Cive* by an anonymous author; ... it contains many paradoxes about the state and Religion, and so is not available to everyone ...': Thomas de Martel to Sorbière, 13 January 1643 (*De Cive: the Latin Version*, p. 300). 'I have seen the book *De Cive* ... I do not think the book is for sale, but I will find out [*Librum de Cive vidi ... Librum non puto venalem esse, sed inquiram*]' Hugo Grotius to Willem de Groot, 11 April 1643 (*Grotius, Epistolae quotquot reperiri potuerunt* (Amsterdam, 1687), pp. 951–2). The book also lacks any bookseller's imprint, telling the reader where it might be bought.

Hobbes saw the 1642 edition as a kind of draft, and intended to incorporate the comments of his friends into a final version: the long footnotes added in the 1647 edition represent the elucidations to which he was prompted by their remarks. Moreover, not only the title but a number of passages in the text of the 1642 work refer to the existence of other 'sections': for example, the work begins with the confident claim that

> In the previous section the whole of human nature has been described, comprising the faculties of both body and mind; they may all be reduced to four kinds; which are, Physical force, Experience, Reason and Passion. We shall begin the present section with a consideration of the human condition, namely, what attitude men have towards each other, being gifted with these natural endowments.[11]

Hobbes clearly intended the work to be read by people who were aware of what he had argued in the manuscripts of *De Corpore* and *De Homine*.[12]

This was of course not possible for the wider audience of 1647, and indeed Elzevir's resisted using the old title on the ground that it would prejudice sales; Hobbes accordingly excised these references to the earlier sections, and proposed that the title should simply be, as it has in fact always been called, *De Cive*.[13] Nevertheless, he still believed in 1646 that he could have the other sections ready for printing by the end of the year,[14] and if he could have managed this the three sections would after all have appeared together – this is probably why Elzevir's in the end made a gesture towards the idea of a larger work by calling their version *Elementa Philosophica de Cive*. Elzevir's keen commercial instincts are, incidentally, evident in another feature of the 1647 edition, which much annoyed Hobbes. Hearing that Hobbes had recently been appointed reader in mathematics to the prince of Wales, then living at the exiled English court at St Germain, they promptly had a portrait of Hobbes engraved as a frontispiece with the inscription 'Director of Studies for His Highness the Prince of Wales'. As Hobbes recog-

---

[11] *De Cive* (1642) I.1 in the first edition: see *De Cive: the Latin Version*, pp. 90–1. All passages from *De Cive (On the Citizen)* are quoted from the present translation.
[12] See also above note 7.
[13] *De Cive: the Latin Version*, p. 302.
[14] *Ibid.*

nized when he eventually received a copy of the book, this had the arresting implication that his ideas were officially accepted at the prince's court, so that when

> they see his name prefixed to a political theory so abhorrent to the views of almost everyone, his enemies will grandly and even offensively make a boast of the fact that it now seems to demonstrate in advance what sort of right of Sovereignty he expects and is likely to claim for himself.[15]

Hobbes had edgy enough relations with the prince's court,[16] and he was clearly very angry at this piece of tactlessness.

In the end, it took Hobbes many more years before he could bring himself to hand the other sections to a printer. Not until 1655 did *De Corpore* appear, while *De Homine* had to wait until 1658; both were in the end published by the English publisher of *Leviathan* and not by Elzevir's. The three works finally appeared together under their original title *Elementa Philosophiae* in Hobbes's Latin works of 1668, published by Elzevir's principal Dutch competitor, Blaeu's. This long period of tinkering with the texts undoubtedly damaged them: *De Homine*, in particular, is a mere shadow of what might have been expected by a reader of the early manuscript, though even so it does not deserve the neglect which it has suffered at the hands of modern readers.[17]

To understand *De Cive* fully, therefore, it is necessary first to consider (albeit briefly) the ideas of the first two sections of the *Elementa Philosophiae*. Both the early drafts of *De Corpore* and its final version begin with a striking image: in the words of one of those drafts,

> If we conceive the world annihilated except one man to whom there would remain ideas or images of all the things he had seen, or perceived by his other senses (that is) a memory and imagination of the *magnitudes*, *motions*, *sounds*, *colours* etc. and likewise of their *order* and *parts*: all which though in truth they would be only ideas and phantasms internally happening and

[15] Hobbes to Sorbière, 22 March 1647, translated in *De Cive: the Latin Version*, pp. 310–11. The Latin original is given at *Correspondence*, Malcolm, pp. 155–7.

[16] See my account of his eventual rupture with the prince in my edition of *Leviathan*, pp. xliii–xliv, lii–liii.

[17] Astonishingly, the first chapters have still not been translated – the only case of a major work by Hobbes which is not completely available in English.

falling to the imaginant himself, nevertheless they would appear as if they were external and *not depending upon the power or virtue of the mind . . .*[18]

This is an idea very similar to Descartes's celebrated 'hyperbolical doubt' about the existence of any material world corresponding to what we observe, and may have been influenced by it. Hobbes's essential thought, which governed all three sections of the *Elementa Philosophiae*, was that there is no way in which we can know anything specific about the external world. We cannot tell whether it contains objects possessing the properties which we think we detect in them, such as shape, size, colour and so on: for all we know, there is indeed *nothing at all* out there, and we are simply 'imagining' an external world of material objects.

An attack of this sort on most kinds of naive realism underpins all Hobbes's work. In the case of physics, he proposed that we should begin all scientific investigations from what we directly and indubitably apprehend, namely our own sense-impressions or internal 'phantasms'. The Cartesians believed the same, but they also believed that by themselves our sense-impressions could not be used as the basis for a true physics, precisely because they might have no correspondence to any real objects, but simply be some invention of our own. Instead, Descartes argued that there had to be an *a priori* proof of God's existence to vindicate the use of sense-impressions as a guide to the real world, for only if there was a benevolent God who would not deceive his creation could we have confidence in the general veracity of our senses. Hobbes deeply disliked this theistic argument, and insisted against Descartes that he had overlooked a vital feature of our sense-impressions. We have direct acquaintance not merely with shape, colour and so on, but also with *change* or *motion*: indeed, if our phantasms lacked this property, they could not be said to be sense-impressions. As Hobbes said in another striking passage,

> If we should suppose a man to be made with clear eyes, and all the rest of his organs of sight well disposed, but endued with no other sense; and that he should look only upon one thing,

[18] This is from the early version of *De Corpore* discussed above, note 7. Hobbes, *Critique du 'De Mundo' de Thomas White*, p. 449. Translation by the editor (Richard Tuck).

which is always of the same colour and figure, without the least appearance of variety, he would seem to me, whatsoever others may say, to see, no more than I seem to myself to feel the bones of my own limbs by my organs of feeling; and yet these bones are always and on all sides touched by a most sensible membrane. I might perhaps say he were astonished, and looked upon it; but I should not say he saw it; it being almost all one for a man to be always sensible of one and the same thing, and not to be sensible at all of anything. (*De Corpore* xxv.5)[19]

Our sense-impressions or phantasms themselves therefore exhibit all the properties of what we might term a 'ballistical' system: they have spatial properties and they display change of shape or location, which are features of material objects causally interacting with each other. We cannot conceive of such interactions except in terms of general laws of motion, such as the proposition that nothing can move itself; our thoughts and sense-impressions are thus (on Hobbes's account) to be understood as material objects being moved in accordance with these fundamental laws. This is as far as a well-founded physics can go, however, since there are any number of possible explanations for the movement of a particular body (just as a billiard player can (in theory) make a red ball go in a certain direction and at a certain velocity irrespective of where the cue ball starts on the table). We can make conjectures about the actual physical constitution of the outside world, and we know that it will have to be amenable to ballistical explanations, but it is a mistake to insist upon any particular account of the material world as being true.

According to Descartes, one can observe one's own sense-impressions, like someone in a cinema watching a film, and this observer is the 'I' which cannot be reduced to the material objects in front of it. Moreover, he believed, it is self-evident that this 'I' is free, precisely because it stands aloof from its experiences and is not causally determined by them.[20] Hobbes strenuously denied this: for him, the train of phantasms is all there is, and there is no separate observer. He rejected this notion of self-awareness: 'although

[19] *English Works*, ed. William Molesworth (London, 1839), I, p. 394.
[20] On this see for example, *Principles of Philosophy*, I.39, in *The Philosophical Writings of Descartes*, trans. and ed. John Cottingham, Robert Stoothoff and Dugald Murdoch (Cambridge, 1984), I, pp. 205–6.

someone may think that he *was* thinking (for this thought is simply an act of remembering), it is quite impossible for him to think that he *is* thinking, or to know that he is knowing. For then an infinite chain of questions would arise: "How do you know that you know that you know . . .?" '[21] And correspondingly, Hobbes always denied that human beings possessed in this sense a 'will' which was in principle 'free'.

On the other hand, one should not oversimplify the account of human action which he proposed as an alternative to Descartes's. The train of phantasms which constitutes our inner life can have any amount of self-reference, in which earlier phantasms are remembered *as phantasms*, as well as simply recalled; this is the subjective difference, after all, between dreaming and waking – the dream is recalled *as* a dream. Any account which we might want to give of the thought processes which led to a particular decision would be acceptable to Hobbes, as long as we did not suppose the existence somewhere of a disembodied and undetermined 'self'. In particular, it was not the case for Hobbes (as some of his critics asserted) that human beings are simply automata driven by a set of drives of which they are unaware.

He accepted that beneath human action and decision were funda-mental motives or appetites, which could not be altered by deliber-ation. But it is important to recognize that the scope of these funda-mental motives was actually, on Hobbes's account, rather small: most of what we conventionally regard as human motivation was, he believed, capable of intentional alteration. As he said in *De Corpore*,

> little infants, at the beginning and as soon as they are born, have appetite to very few things, as also they avoid very few, by reason of their want of experience and memory; and there-fore they have not so great a variety of animal motion as we see in those that are more grown. For it is not possible, without such knowledge as is derived from sense, that is, without experience and memory, to know what will prove pleasant or hurtful; only there is some place for conjecture from the looks or aspects of things . . . (XXV. 12)[22]

---

[21] This is from his *Objections* to Descartes's *Meditations, Philosophical Writings*, II, pp. 122–3.
[22] *English Works*, Molesworth, I, pp. 407–8.

Since the principal concern of man was with his own preservation, without the complex structures of belief produced by a mature mental life we would indeed still be like infants, or like animals (about whom Hobbes said something rather similar in *De Homine*). In particular, it was *speech* which made the crucial difference, giving us an organized and powerful inner life through its capacity to recall phantasms for us in a systematic and purposive way.

De Homine contains a powerful statement of Hobbes's convictions about the importance of speech. This was in part a parody of a theory commonly found in Roman writers such as Cicero about the importance of rhetoric. The Romans had claimed that only through the power of oratory had men been persuaded to become civilized; Hobbes apparently agreed with them. *Oratio* allowed men to use numbers and hence to create technologies – 'all of these proceed from numbering, but numbering proceeds from speech [*sermone*]'. It also enabled men to teach one another, and, most importantly, it allowed men to give and receive commands. This

> is a benefit of speech [*sermonis*], and truly the greatest. For without this there would be no society among men, no peace, and consequently no disciplines; but first savagery, then solitude, and for dwellings, caves. For though among certain animals there are seeming polities, these are not of sufficiently great moment for living well; hence they merit not our consideration; and they are largely found among defenseless animals, not in need of many things; in which number man is not included . . . From this it is easily understood how much we owe to *oratio*, by which we, having been drawn together and agreeing to covenants, live securely, happily, and elegantly; we can so live, I insist, if we will. (x.3)[23]

But Hobbes saw the dark side of oratory as clearly as its light side, and it was his sense of its pervasive power for evil which distinguished him from the Romans:

> *Oratio* also hath its disadvantages; namely because man, alone among the animals, on account of the universal signification of names, can create general rules for himself in the art of living just as in the other arts; and so he alone can devise errors and pass them on for the use of others. Therefore man errs more

---

[23] *Opera Latina*, II, p. 91 (translated Richard Tuck).

widely and dangerously than can other animals. Also, man if it please him (and it will please him as often as it seems to advance his plans), can teach what he knows to be false from works that he hath inherited; that is, he can lie and render the minds of men hostile to the conditions of society and peace; something that cannot happen in the societies of other animals, since they judge what things are good and bad for them by their senses, not on the basis of the complaints of others, the causes whereof, unless they be seen, they cannot understand. Moreover, it sometimes happens to those that listen to philosophers and Schoolmen that listening becomes a habit, and the words that they hear they accept rashly, even though no sense can be had from them (for such are the kind of words invented by teachers to hide their own ignorance), and they use them, believing that they are saying something when they say nothing. Finally, on account of the ease of speech, the man who truly doth not think, speaks; and what he says, he believes to be true, and he can deceive himself; a beast cannot deceive itself. Therefore by *oratio* man is not made better, but only given greater possibilities. (x.3)[24]

So an adult's judgement about what is pleasurable and therefore to be pursued, unlike an infant's, is critically determined by the descriptions he gives of his world. What appears to be a clash of desires or interests is very often, Hobbes believed, nothing more than a clash of beliefs: the passions themselves have an essentially cognitive component. In *Elements of Law, Natural and Politic*, he explained the passions in terms of 'conceptions of the future':

> Conception of the future is but a supposition of the same, proceeding from remembrance of what is past; and we so far conceive that anything will be hereafter, as we know there is something at the present that hath power to produce it. And that anything hath power now to produce another thing hereafter, we cannot conceive, but by remembrance that it hath produced the like heretofore. Wherefore all conception of future, is conception of power able to produce something; whosoever therefore expecteth pleasure to come, must conceive withal some power in himself by which the same may be attained. And . . . the passions whereof I am to speak next, consist in conception

---

[24] *Opera Latina*, II, pp. 91–2 (translated Richard Tuck).

of the future, that is to say, in conception of power past, and the act to come . . . (1.8.3)[25]

All human passions, according to Hobbes in *Elements of Law, Natural and Politic*, are fundamentally to do with power, and with *honour*, which is 'the acknowledgement of power' (1.8.5). But power is itself a matter of belief, as is shown by his discussion of the concepts of glory, false glory and vainglory in 1.9.1, in which glory or 'imagination of our power and worth' may be 'an assured and certain experience of our own actions', or it may 'proceed . . . from fame and trust of others, whereby one may think well of himself, and yet be deceived', or it may consist in 'the fiction (which also is imagination) of actions done by ourselves, which never were done' – i.e. vainglory. 'Imagination' thus constitutes these passions, as it does most of the others (such as pity, which is 'imagination or fiction of future calamity to ourselves, proceeding from the sense of another man's present calamity'). As we shall see presently, vainglory plays a key role in the political theory put forward in *De Cive*.

This cognitive element in passion would not be a great danger to human life, were it not for the naive realism which infects all human utterances: for there is in principle no conflict between my saying that I think something is bad and you saying that you think it is good, if the two descriptions are simply taken to be descriptions of our personal tastes. But as Hobbes said at the beginning of his account of vision, in chapter II of *De Homine*,

> It is implanted by nature in all animals that at first glance they think an image of something is the thing itself being seen, or at least that it is some material object exactly reproducing the thing itself in its spatial properties. And men definitely think that an image is the object itself (if we except the few who have corrected the judgement of their senses by reason), nor without instruction can they come to believe that the Sun and stars are larger and further away than they seem.[26]

[25] From *The Elements of Law, Natural and Politic*, ed. Ferdinand Tönnies, 2nd edn by M. M. Goldsmith (New York, Barnes and Noble, 1969).
[26] Translated by Richard Tuck. The original reads 'Natura autem insitum est omni animali, ut primo intuitu imaginem illam, ipsam rem visam esse putent, vel saltem aliquod corpus quod ipsam rem simili situ partium exacte referat. Imo homines (si valde paucos qui judicia sensuum ratione correxerunt, excipias) imaginem illam putant esse objectum ipsum, nec sine disciplina in animum inducere possunt Solem & Astras majora esse aut remotiora quam videntur.' (*De Homine*, II.1,

And since the first and most important function of speech is to assign names to the 'idea or concept' (*ideam sive conceptum*) (X.1), language itself immediately takes on this false realism. Throughout his discussion of moral matters Hobbes assumed that the actual moral language which human beings employ presupposes (wrongly) the real existence of the entities with which it is concerned, and therefore presupposes the possibility of conflict over the correct description of the entities.

Hobbes's general philosophy, as set out in this way in *De Corpore* and *De Homine*, was thus already very much attuned to the problem of moral conflict, even before the actual armed conflict of the English civil wars broke out. *De Cive* was written as his solution to the problem of moral conflict, a solution in which politics came to the rescue of ethics.

The book begins with an account of the sources of conflict in the state of nature, that is, in a situation without civil government. It has often been supposed that Hobbes believed that conflict arises from man's inherent selfishness, but as we have seen, that is a misleading interpretation. Selfishness or self-concern is a neutral principle: men in a well-functioning society are as selfish as those outside it. Hobbes made this point clear in replying to the comments of some readers of the first edition:

> it does not follow from this Principle that men are evil by nature. For we cannot tell the good and the bad apart, hence even if there were fewer evil men than good men, good, decent people would still be saddled with the constant need to watch, distrust, anticipate and get the better of others, and to protect themselves by all possible means. Still less does it follow that those who are evil were made so by nature. For although they have from nature, i.e. from their birth itself, from the fact that they are born animals, this characteristic, that they immediately want what pleases them and do whatever they can, in fear or anger, either to flee or to ward off the evils that threaten them, they are not normally thought to be evil on that account. For

Hobbes, *Opera Philosophica, quae Latine scripsit, Omnia* (Amsterdam, 1668), II, p. 8). The only English translation of *De Homine* (*Man and Citizen*, ed. Bernard Gert (Humanities Press, 1972)) omits the chapters on optics 'since they are irrelevant to Hobbes's moral and political philosophy' (p. 35n).

the passions [*affectus animi*] which arise from animal nature are not themselves evil, though the actions that proceed from them sometimes are, namely, when they are harmful and contrary to duty . . . Preface to *De Cive* [12]

Instead, Hobbes explained in 1.4–6 the sources of mutual aggression. 'In the state of nature there is in all men a will to do harm', but the desire arises in different ways. First, some might simply want to defend themselves in straightforward ways, while others might want unnecessary power over their fellow men; 'In his [i.e. the latter's] case, the will to do harm derives from conceit [*inanis gloria*, vainglory] and over-valuation of his strength. For the first man, it derives from the need to defend his property and liberty against the other.' But the vainglorious aggressor is, on Hobbes's account, motivated by a *belief* – the 'false esteeme' which is (as he said in the *Elements of Law, Natural and Politic*) an act of 'imagination'. The role of belief is quite explicit in the second case Hobbes discussed, 'intellectual dissension' such as wars 'between different sects of the same religion and factions of the same country [*respublica*], when the conflict is about doctrines or public policy'; and although Hobbes did not make it explicit in the third case, where 'many want the same thing at the same time, without being able to enjoy it in common or to divide it', nevertheless it is clear both from his discussion of appetite in *De Homine*, and from his treatment of the 'right to all things' later (see below), that he understood appetite here also to be mediated by belief. Hobbes was in fact very unwilling to suppose that, in the world as presently constituted, there could be a genuine struggle over scarce resources: throughout *De Cive* he assumed that contest over resources is unnecessary if a society is well ordered (see for example XII.9). In *Leviathan* he was to put the point graphically:

> The multitude of poor, and yet strong people still encreasing, they are to be transported into Countries not sufficiently inhabited: where neverthelesse, they are not to exterminate those they find there; but constrain them to inhabit closer together, and not range a great deal of ground, to snatch what they find; but to court each little Plot with art and labour, to give them their sustenance in due season. And when all the world is overcharged with Inhabitants, then the last remedy of

all is Warre; which provideth for every man, by Victory, or Death.[27]

Given the absence of any science which could give objective and generally accepted criteria for the truth or falsehood of a belief, in a state of nature it was up to each man to decide on what was true and what was false. There was one proposition which, Hobbes believed, no one even in the state of nature would deny:

> It is not therefore absurd, nor reprehensible, nor contrary to right reason, if one makes every effort to defend his body and limbs from death and to preserve them. And what is not contrary to right reason, all agree is done justly and of Right . . . (*De Cive*, I.7)

This is the single universal principle in Hobbes's theory. Its universality is not predicated on the idea that all men *will* actually preserve themselves from death by whatever means: Hobbes always recognized that there are cases where this is not so, such as a refusal to execute one's parent – 'a son may prefer to die rather than live in infamy and loathing' (*De Cive*, VI.13) – or martyrdom (XVIII.13). Instead, its universality rests on the fact that self-preservation is always *understandable*. It may be a fine thing to be a martyr, but no one can be condemned for refusing martyrdom. (Compare also Hobbes's remarks at II.19 about bearing witness against one's father – it is not wrong to refuse to do so, but equally it is not wrong under torture to accuse him, since in such a situation whatever we do we do 'by right'.) Hobbes nowhere gives any very systematic defence of the idea that self-preservation is universally acceptable, but he may have been encouraged in the idea by the similar claim, backed up with a wealth of historical and anthropological evidence, in Hugo Grotius' authoritative *De Iure Belli ac Pacis* of 1625.[28]

However, a universal principle of this kind does not go very far, since the circumstances for its application remain radically contested. We are entitled to do what is necessary for our preservation,

---

[27] Thomas Hobbes, *Leviathan*, ed. Richard Tuck (Cambridge University Press, 1991), p. 239. This is strikingly similar to the justification for the annexation of aboriginals' land provided by Locke: see J. H. Tully's 'Rediscovering America: the *Two Treatises* and aboriginal rights' in his *An Approach to Political Philosophy: Locke in Contexts* (Cambridge, 1993), pp. 137–76.

[28] For a full discussion of Grotius' ideas, and their similarity to Hobbes's, see Richard Tuck, *Philosophy and Government*, chapter 5.

but there is no objective criterion for what *is* necessary: each person 'has the right to do and to possess everything that he shall judge to be necessary to his self-preservation. In the judgement of the person actually doing it, what is done, is rightly done, even if it is a wrong, and so is rightly done' (I.10n). Anything may be seen as necessary, and in this sense we have a 'right to all things' in the state of nature; but it does not follow that whatever we do in the state of nature is legitimate, since legitimacy is given by the sincere belief of the agent that the act is necessary. 'A person may sin against the Natural Laws, . . ., if he claims that something contributes to his self-preservation, but does not believe that it does so' even in the state of nature, wrote Hobbes (*ibid.*), and he later gave a couple of examples:

> *there are some natural laws whose observance does not cease even in war. For I cannot see what drunkenness or cruelty (which is vengeance without regard to future good) contribute to any man's peace or preservation.* (III.27n)

It is in this sense also that a sovereign may break the laws of nature, as he may do something even though he is not confident that it is necessary for the well-being of his citizens (see VI.13n).

But what we can do legitimately in nature is far reaching enough to create unmanageable conflict, a state of affairs in which men (in words which anticipate the famous remark in *Leviathan*) are 'few, savage, short lived, poor and mean, and lacked all the comforts and amenities of life which *peace* and society afford' (I.13). Hobbes gave as an example of this, 'the Americans' of 'the present century', that is, the aboriginal peoples of North America; the importance to him of this example is underlined by the fact that the illustrated title page of both the manuscript and the first edition of *De Cive* depicts *Libertas* as the life of the Carolina Algonkians, a representation drawn from the famous sketches by John White in 1585.[29] Hobbes was very interested in the settlement of North America, and was even technically a landowner there (as an aide to the earl of

---

[29] They are presumably based on the engravings in Theodor de Bry's *Admiranda narratio, fida tamen, de commodis et incolarum ritibus Virginiae* (Frankfurt, Wechel, 1590), which were themselves based on White's paintings, now in the British Museum. See *The American drawings of John White 1577–1590*, ed. Paul Hulton and David Beers Quinn (London, Trustees of the British Museum and Chapel Hill, North Carolina, University of North Carolina Press, 1964), particularly plates 31, 35, 47, 123, 134, 135.

Devonshire).[30] His use here of this concrete example emphasizes that the state of nature was not, for Hobbes, quite the 'thought experiment' which it is sometimes supposed to have been: he believed that it was a possible state of affairs, though he did not believe that it was historically the case that all societies had to begin from such a condition. Indeed, if it were not possible – if it were the kind of avowedly impossible situation which John Rawls (for example) has postulated as an 'original position' – then it would lose much of its force as a threat, the contemplation of which should encourage us to obey our own sovereign.

The solution to this conflict is to be found in following the law of nature, which he defined in *De Cive*, II.I as 'the Dictate of right reason about what should be done or not done for the longest possible preservation of life and limb'. The relationship between the right of nature and the law of nature is one of the oldest puzzles in Hobbes's work, and is still a matter of great contention.[31] The difficulty in his theory at this point can be put as follows. He has just been at great pains to establish a version of moral relativism, in which whatever we think is right, is right for us. Is this not blatantly contradicted by the introduction of a principle of 'right reason' which is (apparently) an objective criterion for determining what is necessary for our survival? In particular, this fundamental law of nature is the basis for a whole string of derivative laws, of great specificity, of which the first seems to be directly opposite to the right of nature, since it decrees that '*the right of all men to all things must not be held on to*' (II.3).

The best way of understanding Hobbes's argument at this point is to see it as the development of a view which would not have been unfamiliar to his audience: that the wise man (that is, the man concerned with his own survival and well-being) should recognize that there is no objective truth to any of his beliefs, and should choose as practical principles to live by those opinions which were most convenient to him. This was the position taken (arguably) by the ancient sceptics, and it was certainly the view put forward both by Montaigne and (when voicing the sceptical attitude) Descartes.

---

[30] See Noel Malcolm, 'Hobbes, Sandys, and the Virginia Company', *Historical Journal*, 24 (1981), pp. 297–321.

[31] For examples of early queries about it, see Tuck, *Philosophy and Government*, p. 307.

For example, the former observed in his essay entitled 'That the taste of goods or evils doth greatly depend on the opinion we have of them' (essay 40 of book 1), that

> Men (saith an ancient Greeke sentence) *are tormented by the opinions they have of things, and not by things themselves.* It were a great conquest for the ease of our miserable humane condition, if any man could establish every where this true proposition. For if evils have no entrance into us, but by our judgement, it seemeth that it lieth in our power, either to contemne or turne them to our good ... If that which we call evill and torment, be neither torment, nor evill, but that our fancie only gives it that qualitie, it is in us to change it ...

Similarly Descartes, before he felt able to refute scepticism, imposed upon himself

> a provisional moral code consisting of just three or four maxims
> . . .
> The first was to obey the laws and customs of my country, holding constantly to the religion in which by God's grace I had been instructed from my childhood, and governing myself in all other matters according to the most moderate and least extreme opinions – the opinions commonly accepted in practice by the most sensible of those with whom I should have to live
> . . .
> My second maxim was to be as firm and decisive in my actions as I could, and to follow even the most doubtful opinions, once I had adopted them, with no less constancy than if they had been quite certain ...
> My third maxim was to try always to master myself rather than fortune, and to change my desires rather than the order of the world. In general I would become accustomed to believing that nothing lies entirely within our power except our thoughts, so that after doing our best in dealing with matters external to us, whatever we fail to achieve is absolutely impossible so far as we are concerned ...[32]

This kind of approach is the psychological foundation of Hobbes's political thought. The wise man sees his own beliefs, like everyone else's, as wholly subjective and without external validity,

---

[32] *Philosophical Writings,* I, pp. 122–3.

but he is not thereby left rudderless. He can proceed to construct for himself a provisional morality, or a set of rules of thumb, which will procure the best consequences for him: moral (and indeed many other) beliefs are not to be chosen on the basis of *truth*, but on the basis of *convenience*. What Hobbes noticed, unlike both Montaigne and Descartes, was that this could be a collective programme and, indeed, that if the evil consequences of false convictions were properly to be overcome there had to be collective action of this kind.

So the laws of nature in Hobbes are simply the principles which will ensure collective agreement about the opinions which are to be adopted by wise men in association with each other. Since the essence of Hobbes's theory is that ideological conflict has to be eliminated, it follows that the wise men will have to construct a society in which there is only one source of judgement about all potentially disputed issues, and this source of judgement is, by definition, Hobbes's sovereign. The scope of the sovereign's judgement was in principle all inclusive, and particularly on all moral issues it decided the matter – 'what is to count as a *theft* on the part of a citizen or as *murder*, or *adultery* or a *wrongful act* is to be determined by the *civil*, not the *natural*, law' (VI.16). This could go to remarkable lengths:

> suppose a woman gives birth to a deformed figure, and the law forbids killing a human being, the question arises whether the new-born is a human being. The question then is, what is a human being? No one doubts that the commonwealth will decide – and without taking account of the Aristotelian definition, that a Man is a rational Animal. (*De Cive*, XVII.12)

Although the sovereign had no greater access to the truth than any of his citizens, it was vital for the elimination of contention that its judgements were absolute, and no one was tempted to revert to the private calculation of self-interest (V.4). This was the point of the power of the sword, the capacity the sovereign possessed to force citizens into alignment with one another.

There were, however, some important limitations to the sovereign's power in practice. We have already seen that the sovereign can break the law of nature if he acts insincerely; moreover, Hobbes explained to critical readers of the first edition that although '*There is virtually no dogma either in religion or the human sciences, from which disagreements may not arise and from them conflicts, quarrelling and eventually, war*', it should be possible for such arguments to be prevented from spilling over into civil conflict without intellectual disagreement being suppressed (VI.11n). Furthermore, on some issues there could scarcely be disagreement: for example, even the sovereign would have to agree that a citizen would preserve himself best by using his own power to resist *in extremis*, against an obvious and uncontentious threat. It was in this sense that Hobbes always insisted that men always retain the right of defending themselves against violence (V.7, VI.13). But the most important exception to the power of the sovereign to determine opinion was in the area of religion.

As we saw above, Hobbes was very hostile to Descartes's attempt to provide an *a priori* proof of the existence of a conventional God, who could then be used as a guarantor of the validity of our senses. Like the sceptics whom he so often resembled, Hobbes disliked all rational or natural theology, at least in so far as it tried to base an orthodox religion on rational principles: in his view, the only valid proposition of a natural religion was that the world must have been created by something, but we could not properly say what. However, it is a general human trait to respect and admire anything more powerful than oneself, and our admiration and wonder at the power of the universe and its creator finds expression in a language of honour, in which (for example) we describe the creator as all-powerful (XV.14). Hobbes was emphatic that this language does not carry any truth values, and in a work written shortly after the first edition of *De Cive* he went so far as to explain away the problem of evil by arguing that all descriptions of God are 'oblations' rather than 'propositions', and that there was therefore no inconsistency between describing God as all powerful (in order to honour him), and not describing him as the author of evil (which would dishonour him).[33] But like all language, terms of honour and worship

---

[33] *Critique du 'De Mundo' de Thomas White*, p. 434, slightly emended. See Richard Tuck, 'The civil religion of Thomas Hobbes', in *Political Discourse in Early Modern Britain*, ed. Nicholas Phillipson and Quentin Skinner (Cambridge University Press, 1993), pp. 122–3. This argument of Hobbes's puts his remarks about our need to submit to God's power even in evil matters (XV.6) in a rather different light.

had to be under the control of the sovereign, and natural religion therefore became civil religion, of the kind (he believed) the Greeks and Romans had practised.[34]

At this stage in his life, however, Hobbes was not prepared to say the same thing about the Christian religion. Chapter XVII of *De Cive* contains a subtle argument about the relationship between the sovereign and a Christian church, in which Hobbes managed to stay loyal to the principles of his Anglican friends. The argument turns on a distinction (made in articles 12–15) between spiritual and temporal matters. The determination of all controversies involving temporal matters belongs to the sovereign, but those matters 'which cannot be known by natural reason but only by revelation' (XVII.13) are to be determined for Christians by Christ *or his successors*. Hobbes took this to be a defining characteristic of Christianity, insisting that it concerned itself exclusively with claims about God which were inaccessible to (though not incompatible with) natural reason. As Hobbes made abundantly clear in articles 24 and 28, the successors to Christ are the men who stand in apostolic succession to Christ, that is, who have been ordained by the imposition of hands. Ministers of the Church are to be appointed by the sovereign (XVII.24), but they are to be anointed by existing ministers. The sovereign is to promulgate interpretation of spiritual matters to the citizens, but he is not to make the interpretations himself:

> to decide questions of faith, i.e. questions *about God*, which are beyond human understanding, one needs God's blessing (so that we may not err, at least on essential questions) and this comes from CHRIST himself by *laying on of hands*. For our eternal salvation we are obliged to accept a supernatural doctrine, which because it is supernatural, is impossible to understand. It would go against equity if we were left alone to err by ourselves on essential matters. Our Saviour promised this Infallibility (in matters essential to salvation) to the *Apostles* until the day of judgement, i.e. to the *Apostles* and to the *Pastors* who were to be consecrated by the *Apostles* in succession by the *laying on of hands*. As a Christian, therefore, the holder of power in the commonwealth is obliged to interpret holy scripture, when it is a question about the mysteries of faith, by means of duly ordained Ecclesiastics. (XVII.28) [See also XVI.16

[34] See *The Elements of Law*, Tönnies, p. 145 (II.6.2).

for a comparable discussion of the relationship between Kings and Priests in Israel.]

A theory of this kind was more or less in line with the doctrine of the Church of England, which accepted the sovereign as its Supreme Governor and allowed the sovereign to appoint bishops and many other ministers, but which also believed in its own right to decide doctrine. It is true that it saw itself as part of a universal apostolic church, and was loath (as it still is) to decide matters unilaterally, but Hobbes was certainly not as far removed from Anglicanism as he later became. As I showed in the introduction to the Cambridge *Leviathan*, it was his break with the Anglicans in the late 1640s which spurred him on to write a new work of political theory, handing the power of interpretation in spiritual matters exclusively to the sovereign, and which left him unwilling to sanction an English translation of *De Cive*.

While Hobbes's sovereign might have these limitations upon his powers of interpretation, there was never any suggestion in Hobbes's work that the sovereign might be under conventional constitutional constraints. In the politics of England during the 1630s and 1640s, Hobbes was a committed royalist of an outspoken and extreme character, and in *De Cive* he systematically denied all the claims which had been made against the king's power during the constitutional struggles prior to the outbreak of the Civil War. It should be noted that battle was not actually joined in the war until shortly after the composition of *De Cive*, though by the second edition Hobbes had had four years to reflect on events and read the propaganda of both sides. However, though he was a committed royalist, he was not at all an orthodox one: in particular, he was completely unsympathetic to any defence of royal power which presupposed that kings *qua* kings have special rights. Many royalists who thought that they were fighting for the principle of monarchy deeply mistrusted Hobbes, a feeling voiced most clearly by Sir Robert Filmer.[35] What they spotted was that Hobbes's theory began from the same premise as that of some of the king's most radical opponents, that men are born free and equal; the gulf between Hobbes and patriarchalists like Filmer was further emphasized by

---

[35] See *Patriarcha and Other Writings*, ed. Johann P. Sommerville (Cambridge University Press, 1991), pp. 187–97.

Hobbes's striking claim that dominion over children belongs (if to anyone) to the *mother* (IX.2–6). So Hobbes was always faced by a strategic problem: how could he link his fundamental political ideas to the practical requirements of the royalist cause?

This was made particularly difficult in *De Cive* by his claim that the creation of civil sovereignty was a *democratic* act. 'When men have met to erect a commonwealth, they are, almost by the very fact that they have met, a *Democracy*' (VII.5). He envisaged the creation of the sovereign as requiring that each member of the prospective society 'obligates himself, by an Agreement with each of the rest, not to resist the *will* of the *man* or *Assembly* to which he has submitted himself; that is, not to withhold the use of his wealth and strength against any other men than himself (for he is understood to retain the right of defending himself against violence)' (V.7). He also assumed that this initial contract produced a democracy which could then vote to transfer its powers either to an aristocracy or to a monarchy. So far, he was dangerously close to the opponents of monarchy, for it might simply be concluded from his argument that the democracy which appointed the monarch could also dismiss him. To forestall this conclusion, Hobbes had to argue for a strong and (to his first readers) a puzzling distinction between a *people* and a *multitude* or *crowd*:

> A *people* is a *single* entity, with a *single will*; you can attribute *an act* to it. None of this can be said of a crowd. In every commonwealth the *People* Reigns; for even in *Monarchies* the *People* exercises power [*imperat*]; for the *people* wills through the will of *one man*. But the citizens, i.e. the subjects, are a *crowd*. In a *Democracy* and in an *Aristocracy* the citizens are a *crowd*, but the *council* is the *people*; in a *Monarchy* the subjects are a *crowd*, and (paradoxically) the *King* is the *people*. (XII.8)

In an annotation to VI.1, Hobbes explained to his baffled readers what he meant. A 'people' is a civil person, defined by its common and explicit allegiance to a sovereign, while a 'crowd' is the same body of individuals in their original and natural separation from one another. In *Leviathan*, the people in this sense becomes the Leviathan itself, and some of the adverse political implications of Hobbes's terminology were avoided; but in *De Cive* Hobbes could not fully disentangle himself from a political language associated with the king's enemies. To say that the people of England was sovereign was on the face of it to make an anti-royalist claim, and the king's cause would not be helped much by the gloss that the 'people' here meant the king! It was a particularly problematic claim for Hobbes to have made, since the English Parliament claimed to represent the people as distinct from the king: there was a third element in England which was neither the king nor (on the face of it) the crowd. Hobbes always insisted that because Parliament could only meet at the king's summons, it could not compete for the sovereignty; but the fact that it was elected (notionally) by the people of England to represent their wishes meant that its function resembled uncomfortably closely the function of Hobbes's sovereign. Indeed, the subsequent history of Europe suggests that a Hobbesian notion of the state as the construct of the citizens in order to govern themselves fits most easily on to government by representative assemblies.

As I have just observed, sorting out this element of his theory was one of the tasks Hobbes undertook in *Leviathan*. To do so, he employed much fuller and more precise notions of representation and authorship than he had done in his earlier work, an approach which seems to have begun with advice to Sorbière on his translation of *De Cive*.[36] The other, and more important, alteration which he undertook was, as we have also seen, of the side of his theory devoted to religion: the principal reason for the writing of *Leviathan* seems to have been Hobbes's desire to dissociate himself from the Anglicans and to argue for a new religious order introduced by the sovereign.[37] But after the Restoration, Hobbes realized that *De Cive* could still be an important statement of his views, and in his *Opera* of 1668 it sits alongside a greatly modified Latin translation of *Leviathan*. His sense of the matter was (as always) acute: if we are interested in Hobbes's *political* thought, we will still find it at least as clearly set out in *De Cive* as in *Leviathan*, with the additional advantage of compactness. This edition also offers another advantage: for the first time, we can read a major work on politics by Hobbes in a modern English translation, which may make accessible to the modern reader the ideas of the greatest English political philosopher.

---

[36] For a discussion of this point, see Tuck, *Leviathan*, p. xxxvi.
[37] *Ibid.*, pp. xliii–xliv, and Richard Tuck, 'The civil religion of Thomas Hobbes', pp. 120–38.

The translation

In May 1650 an old friend of Hobbes, Robert Payne, who had been purged from his Oxford fellowship by the victorious parliamentary army but continued to live near the town, heard that an English translation of *De Cive* was about to be published. He had kept in touch with Hobbes in Paris, and he apparently knew that Hobbes had not authorized any such translation:

> I sent notice to Mr. Hobbes that his book *De Cive* was translated into English, and desired him to prevent that translation by one of his own, but he sends me word he hath another trifle on hand, which is Politique in English, of which he hath finished thirty-seven chapters, (intending about fifty in the whole,) which are translated into French by a learned Frenchman of good quality, as fast as he finishes them, and that his book *De Cive* is translated into French and printed already. And now I am come hither [Oxford] I meet with the two first parts of that *De Cive* printed in English, but the last (viz. *Religio*) left out, a copy whereof I purpose to send him by the next opportunity, and this I do to urge him to hasten the edition of all his works entire, and not suffer himself to be thus mangled by strangers.[1]

In fact, what Payne had found in an Oxford bookshop was a pirated edition of the second part of *Elements of Law, Natural and Politic*,

---

[1] Payne to Gilbert Sheldon, 13 May [1650], printed in 'Illustrations of the State of the Church During the Great Rebellion', *The Theologian and Ecclesiastic*, 6 (1848), p. 172.

which had just been published under the title *De Corpore Politico; or, the Elements of Law, Moral and Politic*.[2] At a casual glance this book would indeed look very like the first two parts of *De Cive*. But the news he had heard about a translation of *De Cive* was quite accurate, and in March 1651 one duly appeared from the press of Richard Royston in London, with the title *Philosophicall Rudiments Concerning Government and Society*.[3]

Some copies of the translation contained a dedicatory letter by the translator, 'C.C.', in which he virtually acknowledged that he had not been authorized by Hobbes:

> except Master *Hobbes* (if he should chance to hear me nam'd) be a man as well practis'd in the Lawes of Nature, as he hath shewed himselfe eminent in their speculation, I see not how the injury my infirmity hath done his Book will be reconcileable with the respect I beare to his Person . . .[4]

He also admitted that he did not fully understand one passage of the book – something which would be surprising had he been in contact with the author.[5]

'C.C.' dedicated his translation to the widow of Sir George Fane, a member of a well-known royalist family; the publisher, Royston, specialized in royalist works during the Interregnum. Before each part of the translation, the printer added an engraving dealing with its subject matter, and the picture before 'Religion' unmistakably shows Charles I as a royal martyr. As we have seen in the introduction (above pp. xxiff.), *De Cive* was genuinely a royalist work, but by 1650 Hobbes had abandoned the kind of royalism associated with Richard Royston and the cult of Charles the Martyr. All of these considerations add weight to the supposition that 'C.C.' acted independently of Hobbes, and indeed that had Hobbes known what was going on he would (as Payne guessed) have been very opposed to it.

A translation had been projected a few years earlier, by Hobbes's

---

[2] Thomason, the London bookseller and book collector, received a copy on 4 May 1650.

[3] For the date, see *De Cive: the Latin Version*, p. 15. Royston originally registered his translation in November 1650 (*ibid.*).

[4] *De Cive: the English Version*, p. 269.

[5] *Ibid.*, p. 271.

friend the poet Edmund Waller. John Aubrey, in his life of Waller (compiled twenty or thirty years later) recorded that

> I have heard him [Waller] say that he so much admired Mr. Thomas Hobbes' book *De Cive*, when it came forth, that he was very desirous to have it donne into English, and Mr. Hobbes was most willing it should be done by Mr. Waller's hand, for that he was so great a master of our English language. Mr. Waller freely promised him to doe it, but first he would desire Mr. Hobbes to make an essaye; he (T.H.) did the first booke, and did it so extremely well, that Mr. Waller would not meddle with it, for that nobody els could doe it so well. Had he thought he could have better performed it, he would have himself been the translator.[6]

This may be true, but we do possess Hobbes's actual reply to Waller, written from Rouen on 8 August 1645:

> I was told you had an inclination to put a booke Called de Cive into English. I can not hope it should have that honor, and yet now I thinke of it, the honor will come all to the English booke, when it is of your doing, but so will the envy also. I will not presse you to it but I must thanke you for having once entertayned the thought . . .[7]

Either way, it is clear that the project lapsed, presumably being overtaken first by the prospect of a new and enlarged edition of the Latin text, and then by the change in Hobbes's political ideas manifested by *Leviathan*.

Not only did 'C.C.' work without Hobbes's approval, but he also worked in an extremely slapdash manner: there are many mistranslations or misunderstandings of Hobbes's text. For these reasons, Cambridge University Press decided not to follow the example of the late Professor Warrender, who chose to reprint the 'C.C.' translation as the companion volume to his major edition of the Latin

---

[6] *Brief Lives*, ed. A. Clark (Oxford, 1898), II, p. 277.
[7] Hobbes, *Correspondence*, ed. Noel Malcolm (Oxford University Press, 1994), p. 124.

De Cive for Oxford University Press.[8] Instead, it commissioned Professor Silverthorne to provide an accurate modern translation, so that a general audience can once again appreciate the power of Hobbes's first systematic work of political thought.

---

[8] Professor Warrender was somewhat equivocal about whether the translation was by C.C.: he discussed the evidence, but concluded (*The English Version*, pp. 6–8) that at the least Hobbes must have authorized the translation. Though aware of the Payne letters (see his discussion of them in *The Latin Version*, pp. 14–16), he did not cite them in this context, and most scholars agree that they strongly suggest that Hobbes did not approve the translation.

The present translation is made from Warrender's Latin text, with amendments where the text is clearly erroneous, as noted in the footnotes.

Key words

In *De Cive*, as elsewhere, Hobbes advocates 'the method of starting with definitions and avoiding equivocation' (II.1); accordingly, throughout the book he gives a definition of each new term of his account as it occurs. For example, in erecting the framework of his political doctrine, Hobbes first gives a general definition of right (*jus*, I.7), then proceeds to define the essential notions of the renunciation and transfer of a right (II.4), and follows this up with short definitions of kinds of transfer – gift (II.8) and contract (II.9) and, as a subdivision of the latter, agreement (II.9).

Hobbes aims to be consistent in the use of such terms throughout his exposition, and a translator must therefore attempt a similar consistency. It is of course true in general that no one Latin word is equivalent to any one English word in all the contexts of its use, and this may seem to be particularly true of the relatively sparse vocabulary available in classical Latin for philosophical concepts. But Hobbes was not writing the live and fluid language of antiquity, but the rather artificial imitation of that language which was the normal medium of international scholarship in the seventeenth century. He was also writing in a particular tradition of discourse, that of natural law, which had evolved its own characteristic vocabulary. And, finally, as Hobbes's native language was English, he may have been using some of the Latin terms simply as specifically chosen counters for English words, which may be recoverable from his other works, and particularly from the *Elements of Law*.

Despite, then, the immense difference between the English and the Latin languages, these three factors – the artificial nature of the medium in which Hobbes was writing, the natural-law tradition of discourse, and the existence of equivalent English works by Hobbes himself – encourage an attempt to respect the 'method of starting with definitions' by trying for a greater degree of consistency than is often possible in translation. In translating a few key terms we have attempted to be consistent in the simple sense of using the same English word for a particular Latin word whenever it occurs in its dominant sense; where a passage simply refuses the chosen equivalent, and we have been obliged to find another, we have normally indicated this by putting the Latin word in parentheses.

The choice of appropriate equivalents for the key terms of a text is clearly crucial, in that the terms chosen determine the implicit interpretative bias of the translation. Since some of the key terms used by Hobbes are open to dispute, this note is intended to alert the reader to the choices which we have made.

civitas

Hobbes gives his definition at v.9: 'CIVITAS ergo (ut eam definiamus) est *persona una*, cuius *voluntas*, ex pactis plurium hominum, pro *voluntate* habenda est ipsorum omnium; ut singulorum viribus et facultatibus uti possint, ad pacem & defensionem communem' (v.9).[1] In the same paragraph a *civitas* is paraphrased as a *societas civilis* and a *persona civilis*. This definition seems to bring *civitas* close to what is expressed in twentieth-century English by the word 'state'. Hobbes himself does not often use the word 'state' in this sense, and not at all in the *Elements of Law*, the work most closely related to *De Cive*. But he does use it occasionally, most famously in the introduction to *Leviathan*: 'For by Art is created that great LEVIATHAN called a COMMON-WEALTH or STATE (in Latine CIVITAS) which is but an Artificiall Man.'[2] So one might choose 'state' to translate *civitas*.

---

[1] This is translated as follows: 'A COMMONWEALTH, then, (to define it) is *one person*, whose *will*, by the agreement of several men, is to be taken as the *will* of them all; to make use of their strength and resources for the common peace and defence.'

[2] Cf. Q. Skinner, 'The state', *Political Innovation and Conceptual Change*, ed. T. Ball, J. Farr and R. L. Hanson (Cambridge, 1989), pp. 116–21.

However the word Hobbes himself most frequently uses is 'commonwealth', both in the *Elements of Law* and in *Leviathan*. This may seem to be a remarkable choice given that he himself felt that the word has a suggestion of republican government, or at least of government by agreement. At *Elements of Law* I.19.8–11 he calls the civil union formed by the amalgamation of wills 'a BODY POLITIC or civil society; and the Greeks call it πόλις, that is to say, a city', and then distinguishes two kinds of 'body politic'. The one is 'dominion paternal and domestic', which is formed naturally, by conquest; and the other is the kind that is formed by men submitting themselves to a leader 'by mutual agreement amongst many'. On the latter he comments that 'the body politic they make, is for the most part called a commonwealth, in distinction from the former, though the name be the general name for them both'. In adopting this equivocal word in its more general sense, perhaps Hobbes wished to capture both it and *civitas* for an absolutist position.[3]

In any case, in view of Hobbes's overwhelming preference for the word, we have opted for 'commonwealth'.

multitudo

No modern English word seems to be an adequate substitute for the archaic 'multitude' (which is Hobbes's own equivalent in both *Elements of Law* and *Leviathan*). *Multitudo* is the key word of plurality. But it is more than numerical. A *multitudo* becomes *unus* by effecting an *unio* (V.1–11, especially 9); and in this contrast with *unus* and *unio*, *multitudo* carries an implication of disorder (made explicit in some contexts by the phrase *dissoluta multitudo*, e.g. VII.5). We have felt therefore that merely to stress the plurality of *multitudo* by using some such phrase as 'a number of men' was inadequate,

---

[3] In 1656 James Harrington used the word in opposition to absolutism by entitling his defence of aristocratic government, *The Commonwealth of Oceana*. By contrast Pufendorf, who read Hobbes closely, also uses *civitas* as his key word and gives it a very similar definition to that of Hobbes (*On the Duty of Man and Citizen*, II.6.6). Further discussion in Michael Silverthorne, 'Civil society and state, law and rights: some Latin terms and their translation in the natural jurisprudence tradition', in *Acta Conventus Neo-Latini Torontonensis*, ed. A. Dalzell, C. Fantazzi and R. J. Schoek (Binghamton, 1990), pp. 680–3.

and we have attempted to convey the other connotations of the word by using 'crowd' (cf. VI.I and note).

ius and *lex*

We have attempted to maintain the characteristic[4] distinction which Hobbes draws between these two words at *Leviathan* 1.14: '. . . though they that speak of this subject, use to confound *Jus*, and *Lex*, *Right* and *Law*; yet they ought to be distinguished; because RIGHT, consisteth in liberty to do, or to forbeare; Whereas LAW, determineth, and bindeth to one of them: so that Law, and Right, differ as much, as Obligation, and Liberty; which in one and the same matter are inconsistent.' The same point is made in *De Cive* at I.7 where the definition of right is given as 'libertas quam quisque habet facultatibus naturalibus secundum rectam rationem utendi'.[5] One may also compare XIII.15, where liberty in one sense is to be understood 'as that part of natural right which is allowed and left to the citizens by the civil laws'.[6] No explicit definition of law seems to be given in *De Cive*, but at X.8 legislation is assumed to be the forbidding of actions, and at XIII.15 law is portrayed as the banks of the river which restrain and direct human actions, implying that within the parameters of the laws human beings have rights and that is the area of their liberty.

The contrast with rights as liberties is implicit in the definition of 'civil laws' as commands (*mandata*) at VI.9: '. . . CIVIL LAWS (to define them) are nothing other than commands about the citizens' future actions from the one who is endowed with *sovereign authority* [*summa potestas*]'.[7] Their scope extends to the definition of all morality and the determination of all individual property rights. The obligation to obey them arises from the transfer of the right to defend oneself which constitutes the union which is the commonwealth,

---

[4] Pufendorf, for example, does not follow Hobbes in this distinction (Silverthorne, 'Civil society and state', pp. 684–6).
[5] I.7 'Neque enim Iuris nomine aliud significatur, quam libertas quam quisque habet facultatibus naturalibus secundum rectam rationem utendi.'
[6] 'Pro iure naturali parte ea, quae civibus a legibus civilibus permissa, & relicta est.'
[7] 'Et LEGES CIVILES (ut eas definiamus,) nihil aliud sunt, quam eius qui in civitate summa potestate praeditus est, de civium futuris actionibus mandata.'

and creates the *jus imperandi* or *jus civitatis* which is held by the sovereign.

imperium and *potestas*

These two words seem to be used almost interchangeably. The key passage is V.11, where the power which holds together the union of all is defined as follows: 'In omni civitate, Homo ille, vel Concilium illud, cuius voluntati singuli voluntatem suam (ita ut dictum est) subiecerunt, SUMMAM POTESTATEM, sive SUMMUM IMPERIUM sive DOMINIUM habere dicitur.'[8] The right so described is essentially the *Ius imperandi* (*ibid.*), and consists essentially in the citizens' having given up their right to resist. Among the commands (*mandata*) of the sovereign are the civil laws. It thus seemed reasonable to translate *imperium* normally as 'power', a word in which the idea of superior capacity outweighs, but does not extinguish, the idea of legitimacy; in certain contexts also *imperium* has the more concrete sense of 'government'. The notion of legitimacy is strengthened by the synonymous use of *potestas* (e.g. VI.17); *potestas* is normally translated 'authority', since it seemed necessary to take account of the common distinction of *potestas* as 'authority' from *potentia* as sheer power or capacity to do.[9] The use of *potestas* for the authority of the parent over its child (IX.2; cf. the Roman law phrase *patria potestas*) is a nice illustration of the way the word conveys both a natural fact and a moral right.

The *potestas* or *imperium* of the recipient of the rights of all is described as *summum* or *summa*. This could be translated 'highest' or 'supreme', but we have followed Hobbes in using 'sovereign'. The whole phrase thus becomes 'sovereign power' or 'sovereign authority' or simply 'sovereignty'. The citizens (*cives*) of a *civitas* so conceived are therefore also properly called *subditi* ('subjects').

servus and *dominus*

The word *dominium* is not so frequently used as *imperium* and *potestas* to indicate the power of the sovereign. We normally translate

---

[8] 'In every commonwealth, the *Man* or *Assembly* to whose will individuals have subjected their will (in the manner explained) is said to hold SOVEREIGN AUTHORITY [*SUMMAM POTESTATEM*] or SOVEREIGN POWER [*SUMMUM IMPERIUM*] or DOMINION [*DOMINIUM*].'

[9] There is, however, a counter-example at XVI.15.

it as 'dominion'. Hobbes, however, is well aware that this word is used in Latin and especially in the language of Roman law to indicate 'ownership',[10] and this has particular consequences for his theory of power when it is applied to power over slaves. The *dominus* is both master (or lord) and owner of the *servus*. Hence we have chosen 'slave' (not 'servant') for *servus*, the word which Hobbes uses of both bound and unbound slaves in chapter VIII. In that the slave is like the subject of the sovereign in having surrendered his rights to him, Hobbes does not hesitate to make an analogy in certain respects between the *subditus* and the *servus* (e.g. VIII.7, 8). These passages read harshly, but consistency in the sense explained above seems to require this translation.

concilium, curia, senatus, coetus, ecclesia

Though Hobbes argues in chapter X that Monarchy has fewer disadvantages than either aristocracy or democracy, he is usually careful to allow that sovereignty may be vested in a group of men as well as in one man. He has a variety of language in *De Cive* for what in *Leviathan* is normally called the sovereign 'assembly'. In the definition of sovereignty at V.11 the word used is *concilium*. In the equivalent passage in *Elements of Law* (1.19.8) he gives 'council', but in *Leviathan* (II.17) 'assembly'. The classical usage (e.g. *concilium plebis* of the public meeting of the *plebs* of Rome) suggests a large gathering, and we have chosen 'assembly'. *Concilium* is perhaps the most frequent word, but *curia* is also quite common, and *senatus* is used occasionally. At VII.10, 14 (*curia optimatum*) Hobbes uses *curia* specifically of an aristocratic council, and both *curia* and *senatus* were used in classical Latin of the Roman senate; we have translated them both as 'council',[11] since they seem to imply a smaller group than *concilium*. Hobbes also occasionally uses *coetus*, particularly in

---

[10] Used in this technical sense at e.g. VII.16, where, in an analogy from Roman law, the power of the people is called *dominium* by contrast with the power of a time-limited monarch, who is described as a usufructuary.

[11] Hobbes makes the threefold distinction at VI.18, while characteristically setting the monarch off from the other two: 'manifestum est igitur, esse in omni civitate aliquem *hominem unum*, vel *concilium* sive *curiam* unam, quae potentiam in cives singulos iure habet tantam ...' ('It is evident therefore that in every commonwealth there is some *one man* or *one assembly* [*concilium*] or *council* [*curia*], which has by right as much power over individual citizens ...').

the later chapters. It often has the sense 'group', but is also frequently, though not exclusively, used of religious gatherings; in that
context it has been translated by 'assembly'.[12] He also uses the word
congregatio,[13] which seems to be a calque from the English 'congregation'.

The most interesting discussion is reserved for the word *ecclesia*.
At XVII.19 Hobbes insists that the word originally referred to the
sovereign assembly of the *polis*: 'Now for the word *Church* [*Ecclesia*]:
in origin it has the same meaning as the Latin word *Concio* or
assembly of citizens'[14] and he gives two examples from the Acts of
the Apostles (XIX.32, 40) of its use in this sense as the public political
assembly of the ancient Greek *polis*. He then traces how the word
is used of assembled Christians in the New Testament and by
extension in various other senses, and how it has subsequently been
illegitimately extended to refer on the one hand to a supra-national
church, and on the other to bodies of men meeting without authority. This example shows Hobbes training his linguistic expertise
on a venerable but to him deeply corrupted word, and attempting
to restore it to its proper sense of a group of people subject to a
legitimate head and therefore identical with a commonwealth.

---

[12] On *societas*, see I.4n.
[13] E.g. XVII.19.
[14] 'Quod ad nomen attinet *Ecclesiae*, ab origine idem sonat quod latinè Concio, sive
conventus civium.'

Principal events in Hobbes's life

1588   *5 April*: born Malmesbury (Wilts.).

1602   Admitted to Magdalen Hall, Oxford.

1608   *February*: BA Oxford. Appointed tutor to William, the son of William Lord Cavendish, and joined his pupil in July at St John's College, Cambridge, incorporating as a BA.[1] Later that year settled with his pupil at the Cavendishes' houses, Hardwick Hall and Chatsworth in Derbyshire and Devonshire House in London.

1614   *Summer*: left England with his pupil to tour France and Italy. Probably met Paolo Sarpi in Venice.[2]

1615   *Summer*: returned to England.

1618   Lord Cavendish created first earl of Devonshire.

---

[1] Hobbes, *Correspondence*, ed. Noel Malcolm (Oxford University Press, 1994), p. 856.

[2] This differs from the chronology in the first edition, and from that usually found in accounts of Hobbes's life. It is clear from the Hardwick account books that Hobbes was in England from 1611 to 1614; he was given William's quarterly allowance in February 1614. (I owe this fact to Quentin Skinner.) It is also clear that William (and therefore Hobbes) was in Italy by September 1614, and that he had returned by September 1615 (Noel Malcolm, 'Hobbes, Sandys and the Virginia Company', *Historical Journal*, 24 (1981), pp. 297–321; Richard Tuck, *Philosophy and Government 1572–1651* (Cambridge University Press, 1994), pp. 280–1). Traditionally, Hobbes is supposed to have left for the trip in 1610; this date is based on the life of Hobbes by John Aubrey and Richard Blackbourne (*Vitae Hobbianae Auctarium, Opera Latina*, I, ed. Molesworth, p. xxiv), but that life, though quite authoritative, may have been inaccurate on the details of Hobbes's early career. There is no suggestion either in that life or in Hobbes's own autobiographical sketches (*Opera Latina*, I, pp. xiii–xxi, lxxxi–xcix) that he made two visits to the Continent at this time.

1619   Hobbes in contact with Francis Bacon.[3] Between this year
        and 1623 he acted as amanuensis to Bacon, on loan from
        the Cavendishes.

1620   Probably published a *Discourse upon the Beginnings of Tac-
        itus* and a couple of other discourses, in a volume otherwise
        consisting of essays by William Cavendish, his former
        pupil, entitled *Horae Subsecivae*.[4]

1622   Became landowner in Virginia and associate of William
        Cavendish on the board of the Virginia Company, until its
        dissolution in 1624.

1626   *March*: first earl of Devonshire died.

1628   *June*: second earl of Devonshire died. Hobbes left service
        of Cavendishes.[5]

1629   Hobbes published translation of Thucydides, dedicated to
        third earl of Devonshire (aged 11). He joined the house-
        hold of Sir Gervase Clifton of Clifton (Notts.), and
        accompanied Clifton's son on a tour of France and Geneva.

1630   *Autumn*: returned to England and settled again with Cav-
        endishes.[6] Probably began to associate with the earl of
        Newcastle (cousin to the earl of Devonshire) at Welbeck
        (Notts.).

1634   *Autumn*: took the earl of Devonshire's son on a tour of
        France and Italy.

1635   Associated with Marin Mersenne, Gassendi and other
        French philosophers in Paris.

1636   *Spring*: visited Galileo in Florence.
        October: returned to England.

1637   Published *A brief of the art of rhetorick*.
        October: received Descartes's *Discourse on the Method* from
        Sir Kenelm Digby.

1640   *March*: suggestion that Hobbes should stand for Derby in
        the Short Parliament.
        May: finished manuscript of *Elements of Law* (published in
        two pirated parts in 1650, and completely in 1889).

[3] Hobbes, *Correspondence*, pp. 628–9.
[4] N. B. Reynolds and J. L. Hilton, 'Thomas Hobbes and authorship of the *Horae
    Subsecivae*', *History of Political Thought*, 14 (1993), pp. 361–80.
[5] Hobbes, *Correspondence*, p. 808.
[6] *Ibid.*, p. 17; this seems to imply that he was 'home' earlier than Malcolm suggests
    at p. 808.

	November: fled to Paris, anxious about being implicated in the Long Parliament's attack on Strafford.
1641	Contributed to the *Objections* to Descartes's *Meditations*.
1642	*March*: Civil War began in England. *April*: Hobbes published *De Cive* at Paris.
1643	Drafted manuscript reply to Thomas White's *De Mundo* (published 1973).
1644	Contributed an essay on ballistics to Mersenne's *Ballistica*.
1646	Appointed reader in mathematics to the prince of Wales in Paris. Controversy with John Bramhall over free will and determinism (published in 1654–5).
1647	*January*: published second edition of *De Cive*. *August*: fell seriously ill.
1649	*January*: Charles I executed in London.
1651	*April*: Hobbes published *Leviathan*. *December*: excluded from Charles's court.
1652	*February*: returned to England.
1655	Published *De Corpore*.
1658	Published *De Homine*.
1660	*May*: Charles II restored; Clarendon one of his chief ministers.
1666	*October*: Bill introduced into the House of Commons which would have rendered Hobbes liable to prosecution for atheism or heresy. Hobbes drafted manuscript *Dialogue . . . of the common laws* (published 1681).
1668	Drafted other manuscripts on heresy; published *Opera* at Amsterdam, including a Latin translation of *Leviathan*. Clarendon fell, to be replaced by the 'Cabal' Ministry, in which Hobbes found supporters.
1670	Composed manuscript of *Behemoth* (published in 1679).
1674	Cabal Ministry fell.
1675	Hobbes left London for the last time and settled finally at Hardwick and Chatsworth.
1679	Drafted a manuscript on the Exclusion Crisis for the third earl's son, supporting the moderate Whig position. *3 December*: died at Hardwick and was buried at Ault Hucknall.

Further reading

Other works by Hobbes

Oxford University Press is producing a modern edition of Hobbes's collected works, but so far only two works have appeared. The first was *De Cive* (1983) edited by Howard Warrender (*The Latin Version* and *The English Version* are in separate volumes; but the English version, as I show above, is not (despite Warrender) in fact a translation by Hobbes himself, and this Cambridge edition is intended to provide the first accurate translation of the work). The second was an exemplary edition of Hobbes's *Correspondence* edited by Noel Malcolm (1994). The standard collected edition is therefore still *The English Works of Thomas Hobbes*, edited by Sir William Molesworth (11 vols., London 1839–45), and *Thomas Hobbes . . . Opera Philosophica quae Latine scripsit Omnia*, also edited by Molesworth (5 vols., London 1839–45). There are useful editions of some other works: in particular, *The Elements of Law, Natural and Politic*, edited by Ferdinand Tönnies (London, 1889), reprinted with new introductions by M. M. Goldsmith (London, 1969) and J. C. A. Gaskin (Oxford, 1994); *Thomas White's 'De Mundo' Examined*, translated by H. W. Jones (Bradford, 1976) – this is a translation of the Latin text contained in *Critique du 'De Mundo'* edited by Jean Jacquot and H. W. Jones (Paris, 1973); *Behemoth*, edited by Ferdinand Tönnies (London, 1889), reprinted with new introductions by M. M. Goldsmith (London, 1969) and Stephen Holmes (Chicago, 1990); and *A Dialogue Between a Philosopher and a Student of the Common Law of England* edited by Joseph Cropsey (Chicago, 1971). Part of *De*

Homine is translated in *Man and Citizen*, ed. Bernard Gert (Humanities Press,1972).

Hobbes's biography

The most entertaining (and often the most perceptive) life of Hobbes is John Aubrey's in *Brief Lives*, of which there are many editions. Fuller accounts are in G. C. Robertson, *Hobbes* (London, 1886) and my own *Hobbes* (Oxford, 1989). A. Rogow, *Thomas Hobbes* (New York, 1986) has a lot of information, but it must be used with caution. The biographical notes about Hobbes's correspondents appended to Malcolm's edition of the *Correspondence* constitute in effect the scaffolding for a biography, and are full of new and interesting information. Useful articles about Hobbes's life include J. Jacquot, 'Sir Charles Cavendish and his learned friends', *Annals of Science*, 8 (1952); J. J. Hamilton, 'Hobbes's study and the Hardwick library', *Journal of the History of Philosophy*, 16 (1978); N. Malcolm, 'Hobbes, Sandys and the Virginia Company', *Historical Journal*, 24 (1981); Q. R. D. Skinner, 'Thomas Hobbes and his disciples in France and England', *Comparative Studies in Society and History*, 8 (1966) and Q. R. D. Skinner, 'Thomas Hobbes and the nature of the early Royal Society', *Historical Journal*, 12 (1969); and Richard Tuck, 'Hobbes and Descartes', in G. A. J. Rogers and Alan Ryan (eds.), *Perspectives on Thomas Hobbes* (Oxford, 1988), pp. 11–41. M. M. Goldsmith, 'Picturing Hobbes's politics?', *Journal of the Warburg and Courtauld Institutes*, 44 (1981) and Keith Brown, 'The artist of the *Leviathan* Title-Page', *British Library Journal*, 4 (1978), discuss the iconography of Hobbes's books. Important letters connected with Hobbes (of particular relevance to *Leviathan*) are to be found in [Anon], 'Illustrations of the state of the Church during the Great Rebellion', *The Theologian and Ecclesiastic*, 6 (1848), pp. 161–75.

Introductions to Hobbes's ideas

The best general introductions are probably Richard Peters, *Hobbes* (Harmondsworth, 1956), J. W. N. Watkins, *Hobbes's System of Ideas* (2nd edn, London, 1973), Tom Sorell, *Hobbes* (London, 1986) and my own *Hobbes* (Oxford, 1989). Four useful collections of essays on various aspects of Hobbes's thought are K. C. Brown (ed.), *Hobbes Studies* (Oxford, 1965); M. Cranston and R. Peters (eds.), *Hobbes and Rousseau: a Collection of Critical Essays* (New York, 1972); G. A. J. Rogers and Alan Ryan (eds.), *Perspectives on Thomas Hobbes* (Oxford, 1988); and Tom Sorell (ed.), *The Cambridge Companion to Hobbes* (Cambridge, 1995).

Hobbes's scientific ideas

The principal works on Hobbes's science are F. Brandt, *Thomas Hobbes's Mechanical Conception of Nature* (Copenhagen, 1928) and A. Pacchi, *Convenzione e ipotesi nella formazione della filosofia naturale di Thomas Hobbes* (Florence, 1965). S. Shapin and S. Schaffer have discussed Hobbes's disputes with Boyle and Wallis in *Leviathan and the Air-Pump* (Princeton, 1985), and A. E. Shapiro has given a careful account of Hobbes's optics in 'Kinematic optics: a study of the wave theory of light in the seventeenth century', *Archive for the History of the Exact Sciences*, 11 (1973). Terence Ball's 'Hobbes' linguistic turn', *Polity*, 17 (1985), is a perceptive discussion of Hobbes's ideas on language, and Noel Malcolm's 'Hobbes and the Royal Society', in Rogers and Ryan (above) is the latest account of a notoriously vexed issue.

Hobbes's ethical and political ideas

The most distinctive and contentious modern accounts of Hobbes's ideas are those of C. B. Macpherson, in his edition of *Leviathan*, his essay 'Hobbes's bourgeois man' reprinted in Brown, *Hobbes Studies*, and his *The Political Theory of Possessive Individualism: Hobbes to Locke* (Oxford, 1962); Leo Strauss, in his chapter on Hobbes in *Natural Right and History* (Chicago, 1953), also reprinted in *Hobbes Studies*, and his earlier book on Hobbes, *The Political Philosophy of Hobbes: its Basis and Genesis* (Oxford, 1936); Michael Oakeshott, in *Hobbes on Civil Association* (Oxford, 1975) – a collection of his earlier essays on Hobbes, including his famous introduction to *Leviathan*; and Howard Warrender in *The Political Philosophy of Hobbes: his Theory of Obligation* (Oxford, 1957). Warrender also published a useful summary of his views in Brown's *Hobbes Studies*. The controversy about Warrender is best studied in that collection, with the addition of Thomas Nagel, 'Hobbes's concept of obligation', *Philosophical Review*, 68 (1959) and Q. R. D. Skinner, 'Hobbes's *Leviathan*', *Historical Journal*, 7 (1964).

More recent general accounts of Hobbes's ideas include M. M. Goldsmith, *Hobbes's Science of Politics* (New York, 1966), D. D. Raphael, *Hobbes: Morals and Politics* (London, 1977), Miriam M. Reik, *The Golden Lands of Thomas Hobbes* (Detroit, 1977), Johann P. Sommerville, *Thomas Hobbes: Political Ideas in Historical Context* (London, 1992) and Richard E. Flathman, *Thomas Hobbes: Skepticism, Individuality and Chastened Politics* (Newbury Park/London, 1993).

Works which deal principally with Hobbes's ethical ideas include R. E. Ewin, *Virtues and Rights: the Moral Philosophy of Thomas Hobbes* (Boulder/Oxford, 1991); S. A. Lloyd, *Ideals as Interests in Hobbes's Leviathan: the Power of Mind over Matter* (Cambridge, 1992); and my own 'Hobbes's moral philosophy', in Sorell (ed.), *The Cambridge Companion to Hobbes* (Cambridge, 1996).

There are a few distinguished works which consider Hobbes's theory in the light of modern accounts of rational self-interest; they include David Gauthier, *The Logic of Leviathan* (Oxford, 1969), Jean Hampton, *Hobbes and the Social Contract Tradition* (Cambridge, 1986) and Gregory S. Kavka, *Hobbesian Moral and Political Theory* (Princeton, 1986).

Hobbes's account of the state and the concrete realities of government are dealt with in Deborah Baumgold, *Hobbes's Political Thought* (Cambridge, 1988), Lucien Jaume, *Hobbes et l'état représentatif moderne* (Paris, 1986) and Quentin Skinner, 'The state' in Terence Ball, James Farr and Russell L. Hanson (eds.), *Political Innovation and Conceptual Change* (Cambridge, 1989).

The connection between Hobbes's ethical and political ideas and his view of rhetoric has attracted much recent attention. Good accounts are to be found in David Johnston, *The Rhetoric of Leviathan: Thomas Hobbes and the Politics of Cultural Transformation* (Princeton, 1986); Tom Sorell, 'Hobbes's persuasive civil science', *The Philosophical Quarterly*, 40 (1990) and 'Hobbes's unAristotelian political rhetoric', *Philosophy and Rhetoric*, 23 (1990); Raia Prokhovnik, *Rhetoric and Philosophy in Hobbes's 'Leviathan'* (New York,

1991); and Quentin Skinner, '*Scientia civilis* in classical rhetoric and in the early Hobbes', in Nicholas Phillipson and Quentin Skinner (eds.), *Political Discourse in Early Modern Britain* (Cambridge, 1993).

Other useful articles on aspects of Hobbes's thought include R. Ashcraft, 'Hobbes's natural man', *Journal of Politics*, 33 (1971); two related articles by Quentin Skinner, 'The ideological context of Hobbes's political thought', *Historical Journal*, 9 (1966) and 'Conquest and consent: Thomas Hobbes and the engagement controversy', in G. E. Aylmer (ed.), *The Interregnum* (London, 1972); the same author's 'Thomas Hobbes on the proper signification of liberty', *Transactions of the Royal Historical Society*, 5th Series, 40 (1990); and Glenn Burgess, 'Contexts for the writing and publication of Hobbes's *Leviathan*', *History of Political Thought*, 11 (1990).

Hobbes's religious ideas

There has been much interesting work recently in this area. The pioneer was J. G. A. Pocock, in 'Time, history and eschatology in the thought of Thomas Hobbes', in his *Politics, Language and Time* (London, 1972); see also his 'Thomas Hobbes: atheist or enthusiast? His place in a Restoration debate', *History of Political Thought*, 11 (1990). Subsequent contributions include R. J. Halliday, T. Kenyon and A. Reeve, 'Hobbes's belief in god', *Political Studies*, 1983; Alan Ryan, 'Hobbes, toleration, and the inner life', in D. Miller (ed.), *The Nature of Political Theory* (Oxford, 1983) and 'A more tolerant Hobbes?' in Susan Mendus (ed.), *Justifying Toleration* (Cambridge, 1986); Edwin Curley, '"I Durst Not Write So Boldly": how to read Hobbes's theological-political treatise', in E. Giancotti (ed.), *Proceedings of the Conference on Hobbes and Spinoza* (Urbino, 1988); David Johnston, 'Hobbes and mortalism', *History of Political Thought*, 10 (1989); A. P. Martinich, *The Two Gods of 'Leviathan': Thomas Hobbes on Religion and Politics* (Cambridge, 1992); and a couple of connected articles by myself, 'The Christian atheism of Thomas Hobbes', in M. Hunter and D. Wootton (eds.), *Atheism from the Reformation to the Enlightenment* (Oxford, 1992) and 'The civil religion of Thomas Hobbes', in Nicholas Phillipson and Quentin Skinner (eds.), *Political Discourse in Early Modern Britain* (Cambridge, 1993).

Philosophical Elements
On the Citizen

To the Right Honourable
William
Earl of Devonshire
My Most Honoured Lord

[1] *The Roman People had a saying* (Most Honoured Lord) *which came from the mouth of* Marcus Cato, the Censor, *and expressed the prejudice against Kings which they had conceived from their memory of the Tarquins and the principles of their commonwealth; the saying was that Kings should be classed as predatory animals.*[1] *But what sort of animal was the Roman People? By the agency of citizens who took the names* Africanus, Asiaticus, Macedonicus, Achaicus *and so on from the nations they had robbed, that people plundered nearly all the world. So the words of* Pontius Telesinus *are no less wise than* Cato's. *As he reviewed the ranks of his army in the battle against* Sulla *at the Colline Gate, he cried that Rome itself must be demolished and destroyed, remarking that there would never be an end to* Wolves *preying upon the liberty of Italy, unless the forest in which they took refuge was cut down.*[2] *There are two maxims which are surely both true:* Man is a God to man, *and* Man is a wolf to Man.[3] *[2] The former is true of*

The paragraph numbers in the dedication were added by Warrender (1983).

[1] Marcus Porcius Cato, the 'Censor' (234–149 BC). The saying is reported at Plutarch, *Parallel Lives*, 'Life of Cato', 8.13.

[2] Pontius Telesinus, leader of the Samnites during the Social War against Rome's domination of Italy. His advance on Rome was stopped by Sulla at the battle of the Colline Gate (82 BC). Hobbes's account is taken almost verbatim from the account given at Velleius Paterculus, *Compendium of the History of Rome*, II.27.2.

[3] Cf. Plautus, *Asinaria*, 495.

3

the relations of citizens with each other, the latter of relations between commonwealths. In justice and charity, the virtues of peace, citizens show some likeness to God. But between commonwealths, the wickedness of bad men compels the good too to have recourse, for their own protection, to the virtues of war, which are violence and fraud, i.e. to the predatory nature of beasts. Though men have a natural tendency to use rapacity as a term of abuse against each other, seeing their own actions reflected in others as in a mirror where left becomes right and right becomes left, natural right does not accept that anything that arises from the need for self-preservation is a vice. [3] It may seem surprising that prejudice should so impose upon the mind of Cato, *a man renowned for wisdom, and partiality should so overcome his reason, that he censured in Kings what he thought reasonable in his own people. But I have long been of the opinion that there was never an exceptional notion that found favour with the people nor a wisdom above the common level that could be appreciated by the average man; for either they do not understand it, or in understanding it, they bring it down to their own level. The famous deeds and sayings of the Greeks and Romans have been commended to History not by Reason but by their grandeur and often by that very wolf-like element which men deplore in each other; for the stream of History carries down through the centuries the memory of men's varied characters as well as of their public actions. [4] True Wisdom is simply the knowledge* [scientia] *of truth in every subject. Since it derives from the remembrance of things, which is prompted by their fixed and definite names, it is not a matter of momentary flashes of penetrating insight, but of right Reason, i.e. of Philosophy. For Philosophy opens the way from the observation of individual things to universal precepts. [5] Philosophy is divided into as many branches as there are areas where human reason has a place, and takes the different names which the difference of subject matter requires. In treating of figures it is called* Geometry, *of motion* Physics, *of natural law,* Morals, *but it is all* Philosophy; *just as the sea is here called British, there Atlantic, elsewhere Indian, so called from its particular shores, but it is all Ocean. The Geometers have managed their province outstandingly. For whatever benefit comes to human life from observation of the stars, from mapping of lands, from reckoning of time and from long-distance navigation; whatever is beautiful in buildings, strong in defence-works and marvellous in machines, whatever in short distinguishes the modern world from the barbarity of the past, is almost wholly the gift of* Geometry;

for what we owe to Physics, Physics *owes to* Geometry. *[6] If the moral Philosophers had done their job with equal success, I do not know what greater contribution human industry could have made to human happiness. For if the patterns of human action were known with the same certainty as the relations of magnitude in figures, ambition and greed, whose power rests on the false opinions of the common people about right and wrong* [jus et iniuria], *would be disarmed, and the human race would enjoy such secure peace that (apart from conflicts over space as the population grew) it seems unlikely that it would ever have to fight again. [7] But as things are, the war of the sword and the war of the pens is perpetual; there is no greater knowledge* [scientia] *of natural right and natural laws today than in the past; both parties to a dispute defend their right with the opinions of Philosophers; one and the same action is praised by some and criticized by others; a man now approves what at another time he condemns, and gives a different judgement of an action when he does it than when someone else does the very same thing. All these things are obvious signs that what moral Philosophers have written up to now has contributed nothing to the knowledge of truth; its appeal has not lain in enlightening the mind but in lending the influence of attractive and emotive language to hasty and superficial opinions. This part of Philosophy is in the same situation as the public roads, on which all men travel, and go to and fro, and some are enjoying a pleasant stroll and others are quarrelling, but they make no progress. [8] The single reason for this situation seems to be that none of those who have dealt with this subject have employed a suitable starting point from which to teach it. For the starting point of a science* [scientia] *cannot be set at any point we choose as in a circle. In the very shadows of doubt a thread of reason (so to speak) begins, by whose guidance we shall escape to the clearest light; that is where the starting point for teaching is; that is where we must find our illumination as we direct our course to clear away doubts. Hence whenever an author loses the thread through ignorance or breaks it through passion he is no longer delineating the tracks of science but his own erratic path. [9] And so when I turned my thoughts to the inquiry about natural justice I was alerted by the very name of justice (by which is meant a constant will to give every man* his right) *to ask first how it is that anyone ever spoke of something as* his own *rather than* another's; *and when it was clear that it did not originate in nature but in human agreement (for human beings have distributed what nature had placed in common), I was led from there to another question, namely, for whose benefit and under what necessity, when all things belonged to all men, they preferred that each man should have things that belonged to himself alone. And I saw that war and every kind of calamity must necessarily follow from community in things, as men came into violent conflict over their use; a thing all seek by nature to avoid. [10] Thus I obtained two absolutely certain postulates of human nature, one, the postulate of human greed by which each man insists upon his own private use of common property; the other, the postulate of natural reason, by which each man strives to avoid violent death as the supreme evil in nature. From these starting points I believe I have demonstrated by the most evident inference in this little work the necessity of agreements and of keeping faith, and thence the Elements of moral virtue and civil duties. [11] The section on the Kingdom of God has been added so that no conflict should be thought to exist between the dictates of God through nature and the law of God given in the scriptures. I have paid careful attention through the whole length of my discourse not to say anything of the civil laws of any nation, i.e. not to approach shores which are sometimes dangerous because of rocks, sometimes because of current storms. [12] I know how much hard work and painstaking care has gone into my investigation of the truth. What I have achieved I do not know; for we are all poor judges of our own discoveries because we love them. Hence I offer this little book more for your criticism than for your praise, since I have come to know by sure experience that opinions gain favour with you not by the fame of the authors or the novelty of the views or the attractive way they are presented, but by the strength of their reasoning. If it pleases, if it proves to be vigorous, useful and above the common level, then I most humbly give and dedicate it to you* (Most Honoured Lord, my patron and my glory)*; but if I am mistaken, you have still a testimony of my gratitude,*[4] *in that I have attempted to use the leisure you gave me to deserve your favour. May the Great and Good God protect you, best of citizens, in this mortal life, and when your time is over, – and may that be many years from now – may he Crown you with the glory of the heavenly city.*

Paris November 1st., 1641.

Your Excellency's
most humble servant
T. H.

---

[4] Reading *meae* for Warrender's *mea*.

Preface to the Readers

[1] I promise you, Readers, all that is usually thought to encourage attentive Reading: an important and useful Subject, a correct Method in the treatment of it, a good reason and an honest purpose in the writing and good sense in the writer; and in this Preface I offer you a brief view of it all. This book sets out men's duties, first as men, then as citizens and lastly as Christians. These duties constitute the elements of the law of nature and of nations, the origin and force of justice, and the essence of the Christian Religion (so far as the limits of my design allow).

[2] The wise men of remotest antiquity believed that this kind of teaching (with the exception of anything relating to the Christian Religion) should be given to posterity only in the pretty forms of poetry or in the shadowy outlines of Allegory, as if to prevent what one might call the high and holy mystery of government from being contaminated by the debates of private men. Philosophers meanwhile were active, some in observing the motions and shapes of things to mankind's great benefit, others in contemplating the natures and causes of things, which did man no harm. In the following period Socrates is said to have been the first to fall in love with this civil science; it had not yet been conceived as a whole at the time but was, so to speak, showing a bit of itself through the clouds in the matter of civil government. He is said to have valued this science so much that he spurned and rejected every other part of Philosophy,

---

The 'Preface to the Readers' is absent from the first edition (1642). The paragraph numbers were added by Warrender (1983).

judging only this part to be worthy of his intellect. [3] After him, Plato, Aristotle, Cicero and all the other Greek and Roman Philosophers, and finally all the Philosophers of all nations, and not only philosophers, but gentlemen also in their leisure hours, have attempted it, and continue to do so, as if it were easy and accessible without effort, open and available to anyone naturally inclined to it. What most contributes to its dignity is that those who think they possess it or are in a position where they ought to possess it, are so very pleased with themselves for the semblance of it which they do possess, that they will gladly allow specialists in the other sciences to be considered intelligent, learned and erudite, and to be called so, but they never want them to be called Statesmen [*Prudentes*]. Because of the preeminence of this political expertise they believe the term should be reserved to themselves. In any case, whether the dignity of a science is to be judged by the dignity of those to whom it belongs, or from the number who have written about it, or by the judgement of the wisest men, certainly this science has the highest dignity of them all. It belongs to Princes and to those whose business it is to govern mankind; almost everyone is delighted to have even a false semblance of it; and the greatest Philosophical intellects have occupied themselves with it. [4] Its Usefulness, when rightly taught, i.e. when it is derived by self-evident inference from true principles, we shall see best, if we consider what damage to mankind follows from a false and rhetorical semblance of it. For if an error creeps into speculation on subjects which we take up as intellectual exercises, no harm is done, all that's lost is time. But in subjects which each man should reflect on for the conduct of life, error and even ignorance must necessarily give rise to offences, quarrels and killing. [5] It is because the damage is so great that a properly expounded doctrine of duties is so Useful. How many Kings, themselves good men, have been killed because of the one error that a Tyrant King may be rightfully put to death by his subject? How many men have been slaughtered by the error that a sovereign Prince may be deprived of his kingdom for certain reasons by certain men? How many men have been killed by the erroneous doctrine that sovereign Kings are not masters but servants of society? Finally, how many Rebellions have been caused by the doctrine that it is up to private men to determine whether the commands of Kings are just or unjust, and that his commands may rightly be discussed before they are carried out, and in fact ought to be discussed? In the prevailing moral Philosophy there are many other points, no less dangerous than these, which do not need to be enumerated. [6] I think that those ancients foresaw this who preferred that the knowledge of Justice be wrapped up in fables rather than exposed to discussion. Before questions of that kind began to be debated, Princes did not lay claim to sovereign power, they simply exercised it. They did not defend their power by arguments but by punishing the wicked and defending the good. In return the citizens did not measure Justice by the comments of private men but by the laws of the commonwealth; and were kept at Peace not by discussions but by the power of Government. In fact, they revered sovereign power, whether it resided in a man or in an Assembly, as a kind of visible divinity. And thus they did not, as they do now, side with ambitious or desperate men to overturn the order of the commonwealth. For they could not be persuaded to oppose the security of the thing which gave them their own security. The simplicity of those times evidently could not understand such sophisticated stupidity. It was peace therefore and a golden age, which did not end until Saturn was expelled and the doctrine started up that one could take up arms against kings.[1] [7] This, I say, the ancients not only seem to have seen, but to have very aptly symbolized in one of their fables. They say that when Ixion was invited by Jupiter to a banquet, he fell in love with Juno herself and harassed her. In place of the Goddess, a cloud was offered to him in the form of Juno. From the cloud were born the Centaurs, partly human in nature, partly horses, a belligerent and restless race.[2] Change the names, and it is as if they had said that private men, summoned to Councils on the highest questions of state, attempted to subject Justice, the sister and wife of sovereign Power, to their own understanding, but, embracing a false and empty semblance of her like a cloud, have generated the ambivalent dogmas of the moral philosophers, partly correct and attractive, partly brutal and irrational, the causes of all quarrels and killings. [8] Since such opinions arise every day, anyone who dispels those clouds and shows by the soundest reasoning that there are no authentic doctrines of just and

---

[1] Compare the Ages of Man described at Ovid, *Metamorphoses*, I.89ff.
[2] Cf. Pindar, *Pythian Odes*, II.21ff.

unjust, good and evil, except the laws established in each common-wealth, and that questions as to whether an action will be just or unjust, good or evil, should be addressed only to those mandated by the commonwealth to interpret its laws, he will certainly reveal not only the royal road to peace but also the dark and shadowy ways of sedition; and nothing can be imagined more useful than that.

[9] As far as my Method is concerned, I decided that the conventional structure of a rhetorical discourse, though clear, would not suffice by itself. Rather I should begin with the matter of which a commonwealth is made and go on to how it comes into being and the form it takes, and to the first origin of justice. For a thing is best known from its constituents. As in an automatic Clock or other fairly complex device, one cannot get to know the function of each part and wheel unless one takes it apart, and examines separately the material, shape and motion of the parts, so in investigating the right of a commonwealth and the duties of its citizens, there is a need, not indeed to take the commonwealth apart, but to view it as taken apart, i.e. to understand correctly what human nature is like, and in what features it is suitable and in what unsuitable to construct a commonwealth, and how men who want to grow together must be connected. [10] Following such a Method I put in first place, as a Principle well known to all men by experience and which everyone admits, that men's natural Disposition is such that if they are not restrained by fear of a common power, they will distrust and fear each other, and each man rightly may, and necessarily will, look out for himself from his own resources. [11] You will object perhaps that some deny this. That is so; many do deny it. Surely then I am contradicting myself, saying both that they admit it and that they deny it? No, I am not contradicting myself. They are, however, because they admit by their actions what they deny in their words. We see that all commonwealths, even if they are at peace with their neighbours, still defend their borders with garrisons of soldiers, their cities with walls, gates and guards. What would be the point of this if they had nothing to fear from their neighbours? Even within commonwealths, where there are laws and penalties set against wrongdoers, individual citizens do not travel without a weapon to defend themselves or go to bed without barring their doors against their fellow citizens and even locking their chests and boxes against their servants in the house. Can men express their

universal distrust of one another more openly? All commonwealths and individuals behave in this way, and thus admit their fear and distrust of each other. But in argument they deny it, i.e. in their eagerness to contradict others, they contradict themselves. [12] Some object that if we admit this principle, it follows directly not only that all Men are evil (which perhaps, though harsh, should be conceded, since it is clearly said in holy Scripture), but also (and this cannot be conceded without impiety) that they are evil by nature. However, it does not follow from this Principle that men are evil by nature. For we cannot tell the good and the bad apart, hence even if there were fewer evil men than good men, good, decent people would still be saddled with the constant need to watch, distrust, anticipate and get the better of others, and to protect themselves by all possible means. Still less does it follow that those who are evil were made so by nature. For although they have from nature, i.e. from their birth itself, from the fact that they are born animals, this characteristic, that they immediately want what pleases them and do whatever they can, in fear or anger, either to flee or to ward off the evils that threaten them, they are not normally thought to be evil on that account. For the passions [*affectus animi*] which arise from animal nature are not themselves evil, though the actions that proceed from them sometimes are, namely, when they are harmful and contrary to duty. [13] Unless you give infants everything they want, they cry and get angry, they even beat their own parents, and nature prompts them to do so. But they are not to blame, and are not evil, first, because they cannot do any harm, and then because, not having the use of reason, they are totally exempt from duties. If they continue to do the same things when they are grown up and have acquired the strength to do harm, then they begin to be evil and to be called so. Thus an evil man is rather like a sturdy boy, or a man of childish mind, and evil is simply want of reason at an age when it normally accrues to men by nature governed by discipline and experience of harm. Unless then we say that men were made evil by nature simply because they do not have discipline and the use of reason from nature, it must be admitted that they can have greed, fear, anger and all the other animal passions from nature, but still not be made evil by nature. [14] On the basis therefore of the foundation I have laid, I show first that the condition of men outside civil society (the condition one may call the state of nature) is no other than a war of all men against all men; and in that war all men have right to all things. Secondly, all men, by necessity of their nature, want to get out of that miserable and hateful state, as soon as they recognize its misery. But they can only do so by entering into agreements to give up their right to all things. I then proceed to explain and confirm what the nature of agreements is, how rights must be transferred from one to another for valid agreements to take place; likewise what rights must necessarily be ceded to establish peace and to whom, i.e. what are the dictates of reason which may properly be called natural laws. These things are in the section of the book entitled Liberty [*Libertas*].

[15] On this basis I show what a commonwealth is, how many forms it takes, and how it comes into being, and similarly for the sovereign power of a commonwealth; and I show what rights must be transferred by individual men intent on establishing a common-wealth to the sovereign ruler, whether he be one man or an assembly of men; and I show that this transfer is so indispensable, that if it does not occur, no commonwealth comes into being, and the right of all men to all things persists, which is the right of War. Next I distinguish the different kinds of commonwealth, Monarchy, Aris-tocracy, Democracy, the Dominion of a father and the Dominion of a Master, show how they are formed, and compare the advantages and disadvantages of each form. I then survey the factors that destroy a commonwealth and the duties of anyone who exercises sovereign power. Lastly, I explain the nature of law and the nature of offence, and I distinguish law from advice, agreement and right. All this comes under the title of Government [*Imperium*].

[16] In the final part entitled Religion [*Religio*] I aim to show that the right of Sovereigns over citizens, which I had previously proved by reason, is not in conflict with the holy Scriptures. I show first that it is not in conflict with Divine right in that God gives com-mands to sovereigns through nature, i.e. through the dictates of natural reason. Secondly, that it is not in conflict with Divine right in that God had a particular government over the Jews by the old agreement of circumcision. Thirdly, that it is not in conflict with Divine right in that God gives commands to Christians by the agreement of baptism, and thus the right of Sovereigns or the right of the commonwealth is not in conflict with Religion at all. [17]

Finally, I show what duties are indispensably requisite to entrance into the kingdom of heaven; and from these I very clearly demonstrate and prove from the testimonies of holy Scripture, in accordance with universally accepted interpretation, that the Obedience which I had affirmed to be due from individual Christian citizens to their Christian Prince cannot conflict with the Christian Religion. [18] You have seen the Method, now hear the reason and purpose of my writing. I took up Philosophy for intellectual enjoyment, and in every branch of it I was assembling the first Elements. I arranged them into three Sections, and was gradually writing them up, so that the first Section would discuss body and its general properties; the second, Man and his particular faculties and passions; the third, the Commonwealth and the duties of citizens. And so the first Section contains first Philosophy and some elements of Physics. In it the concepts of Time, Place, Cause, Power, Relation, Proportion, Quantity, Figure and Motion are worked through. The second Section is concerned with imagination, memory, understanding, reasoning, appetite, will, Good, Evil, Moral and Immoral, and other such topics. As for this third part I have already said what it deals with. [19] While I was filling it out, and putting it in order, writing slowly and painfully (for I was thinking it through not composing a rhetorical exercise), it happened that my country, some years before the civil war broke out, was already seething with questions of the right of Government and of the due obedience of citizens, forerunners of the approaching war. That was the reason why I put the rest aside and hurried on the completion of this third part. And so it has come about that the part which was last in order has come out first; especially as I saw that it did not need the preceding parts, since it rests upon its own principles known by reason.

[20] I did not do this to win praise (though if I had done so I could use the defence that few except those who love praise do anything to deserve it), but for your sake, Readers. My hope is that when you have got to know the doctrine I present and looked well into it, you will patiently put up with some inconveniences in your private affairs (since human affairs can never be without some inconvenience) rather than disturb the state of the country. My hope is that you will measure the Justice of what you are thinking of doing by the laws of the commonwealth, not by the talk or counsel of private citizens, and no longer allow ambitious men to get

power for themselves by shedding your blood. My hope is that you will think it better to enjoy your present state (though it may not be the best) rather than go to war, and after you have been killed or died of old age, leave other men in other times to have a better life. [21] As for those who refuse to be subject to the civil Magistrate and want exemption from public burdens and yet demand to be in a commonwealth and to be protected by it from violence and wrongs, I hope that you will regard them as enemies and saboteurs and not gullibly accept all that they put before you openly or secretly as the Word of God. I will speak more plainly. If any preacher or confessor or casuist says that this doctrine is consistent[3] with the Word of God: that a sovereign may rightly be killed, or any man without the sovereign's orders, or that citizens may rightly take part in any rebellion, conspiracy or covenant prejudicial to their commonwealth, do not believe him, but report his name. Anyone who approves of this will also approve my design in writing.

[22] Finally throughout my discourse it has been my aim, first, not to give decisions on the Justice of particular actions, but to leave them to be settled by the laws. Secondly, not to say anything about the laws of any particular commonwealth, i.e. to say what law is rather than what the laws are. Thirdly, not to give the impression that citizens owe less obedience to an Aristocratic commonwealth or a Democratic commonwealth than they owe to a Monarchical commonwealth. For though I have deployed some arguments in the tenth chapter to press the point that Monarchy has more advantages than other forms of commonwealth (the only thing in this book which I admit is not demonstrated but put with probability), I say everywhere explicitly that every commonwealth must be allowed supreme and equal power. Fourthly, not to argue in any direction about the doctrines of the Theologians, except about those which undermine citizens' obedience and weaken the state of the commonwealth. Finally, so as not to rashly publish anything that ought not to be published, I refused to allow what I had written to be made public immediately, and took the trouble to distribute to friends a few privately printed copies, so that after testing other people's reactions, I might correct, soften and explain anything that seemed erroneous, harsh or obscure.

---

[3] Reading *consentaneam* for Warrender's *consentaneum.*

[23] I found my book very sharply criticized: on the ground that I have immoderately enhanced the civil power, but by Churchmen; on the ground that I have taken away liberty of conscience, but by Sectarians; on the ground that I have exempted Sovereigns from the civil laws, but by lawyers. I was not moved by their criticisms to do more than tie those knots more tightly, as each one was simply defending his own position. [24] But for the sake of those who have been perplexed by the principles, namely the nature of man, the right of nature, the nature of agreements and the generation of a commonwealth, as they have not followed their passions but their own real understanding in making their comments, I have added notes in some places, which I thought might satisfy my critics. Finally I have everywhere taken very great care not to offend anyone except those whose projects this book opposes, and those whose sensibilities are invariably offended by any difference of opinion whatsoever.

For these reasons I beg and beseech you, Readers, to be good enough to have patience if you find some things either less certain or more sharply expressed than was necessary, since they are not the words of a partisan but of one who has a passion for peace, whose justified grief at his country's present calamity reasonably merits some indulgence.

Index of chapters

Liberty

Government

Religion

Liberty

Chapter I
On the state of man without civil society

1. Introduction. 2. The beginning of civil society *is from mutual fear. 3. Men are by nature equal with each other. 4. Where the will to do each other harm arises. 5. Discord from comparison of talents. 6. And from more than one man's wanting the same thing. 7. Definition of* right. *8. A right to an end gives a right to the necessary means. 9.* By natural right *each man is judge of the means to his self-preservation. 10.* By natural right *all things belong to all men. 11. A right of all men to all things is useless. 12. The state of men outside Society is* war. *The definitions of* War *&* Peace. *13. War is incompatible with men's preservation. 14. By natural right, one may Compel anyone who is in one's power to give a guarantee of future obedience. 15.* Nature *dictates that peace is to be sought.*

1. The faculties of human nature may be reduced to four kinds: Physical force, Experience, Reason, Passion.[1] They are the starting point of the doctrine which follows. We shall first describe the attitude men have towards each other, being endowed with these faculties; and ask whether they are born fit [*apti nati*] for society and for preserving themselves from each other's violence, and which faculty makes them so. We shall go on from there to explain the policy which they had inevitably to adopt for that purpose, and to lay out the conditions of society and Peace among men, which are simply the fundamental *laws of nature* under another name.

2. The majority of previous writers on public Affairs either assume or seek to prove or simply assert that Man

---

The title in the first edition is 'The Elements of Philosophy, Section Three, On the Citizen'. A complete account of variant readings between the first (1642) and second (1647) editions may be found in the critical apparatus in Warrender (1983).

[1] The 1642 edition begins: 'In the previous section the whole of human nature has been described, comprising the faculties of both body and mind; they may all be reduced to four *kinds*; which are, Physical force, Experience, Reason and Passion. We shall begin the present section with a consideration of the human condition, namely, what attitude men have towards each other, being gifted with these natural endowments. And whether . . .'. See the introduction, pp. xiii–xiv.

is an animal (*) born fit for Society, – in the Greek phrase, Ζῷον πολιτικὸν.[2] On this foundation they erect a structure of civil doctrine, as if no more were necessary for the preservation of peace and the governance of the whole human race than for men to give their consent to certain agreements and conditions which, without further thought, these writers call laws. This Axiom, though very widely accepted, is nevertheless false; the error proceeds from a superficial view of human nature. Closer observation of the causes why men seek each other's company and enjoy associating with each other, will easily reach the conclusion that it does not happen because by nature it could not be otherwise, but by chance. For if man naturally loved his fellow man, loved him, I mean, as his fellow man, there is no reason why everyone would not love everyone equally as equally men; or why every man would rather seek the company of men whose society is more prestigious and useful to him than to others. By nature, then, we are not looking for friends but for honour or advantage [*commodum*] from them. This is what we are primarily after; friends are secondary. Men's purpose in seeking each other's company may be inferred from what they do once they meet. If they meet to do business, everyone is looking for profit not for friendship. If the reason is public affairs, a kind of political relationship develops, which holds more mutual fear than love; it is sometimes the occasion of faction, but never of goodwill. If they meet for entertainment and fun, everyone usually takes most pleasure in the kind of amusing incident from which (such is the nature of the ridiculous) he may come away with a better idea of himself in comparison with someone else's embarrassment or weakness. Even if this is sometimes harmless and inoffensive, it is still evident that what they primarily enjoy is their own glory [*gloria*] and not society. But the more usual thing in this social kind of gathering is that people who are not there are attacked, their words and actions, their whole

---

[2] Aristotle, *Politics*, I.2, 1253a3.

manner of life, is scrutinized, judged, condemned and
exposed to witty scorn; people who are there and talking
with the others are not spared the same treatment as soon
as they leave, so that it was a good policy that someone
had to be always the last to make his exit. These are the
true delights of society; we are drawn to them by nature,
that is, by the passions innate in every animal, until as a
result of bad experience or good advice one finally finds
(though some people never do) that one's appetite for
present pleasures is spoiled by memories of the past; and
without these delights the most eloquent talkers on these
topics are dull and dry. And if people happen to be sitting
around swapping stories, and someone produces one
about himself, every one of the others also talks very eag-
erly about himself; if one of them says something sen-
sational, the others bring out sensations too, if they have
any; if not, they make them up. To speak finally of those
who profess to have more wisdom than other men, the
Philosophers: at their gatherings everyone lectures everyone else, in fact everyone wants to be thought a Master;
otherwise not only do they fail, like other men, to love
their companions, they actively pursue their resentments
against them. So clear is it from experience to anyone
who gives any serious attention to human behaviour, that
every voluntary encounter is a product either of mutual
need or of the pursuit of glory; hence when people meet,
what they are anxious to get is either an advantage for
themselves or what is called εὐδοκιμεῖν, which is reputation and honour among their companions. Reason
reaches the same conclusions from the actual definitions
of *Will*, *Good*, *Honour* and *Interest* [*Utilis*]. For since a
society is a voluntary arrangement, what is sought in
every society is an Object of will, i.e. something which
seems to each one of the members to be Good for himself.
Whatever seems Good is pleasant, and affects either the
organs (of the body) or the mind. Every pleasure of the
mind is either glory (or a good opinion of oneself), or
ultimately relates to glory; the others are sensual or lead
to something sensual, and can all be comprised under the

name of advantages. All society, therefore, exists for the sake either of advantage or of glory, i.e. it is a product of love of self, not of love of friends. However, no large or lasting society can be based upon the passion for glory. The reason is that glorying, like honour, is nothing if everybody has it, since it consists in comparison and pre-eminence; nor does association [*societas*][3] with others increase one's reason for glorying in oneself, since a man is worth as much as he can do without relying on anyone else. It is true that the advantages of this life can be increased with other people's help. But this is much more effectively achieved by Dominion over others than by their help. Hence no one should doubt that, in the absence of fear, men would be more avidly attracted to domination than to society. One must therefore lay it down that the origin of large and lasting societies lay not in mutual human benevolence but in men's mutual fear (*).

Born fit] *Since we see that men have in fact formed societies, that no one lives outside society, and that all men seek to meet and talk with each other, it may seem a piece of weird foolishness to set a stumbling block in front of the reader on the very threshold of civil doctrine, by insisting that* man is not born fit for society. *Something must be said in expla-nation. It is indeed true that perpetual solitude is hard for a man to bear by nature or as a man, i.e. as soon as he is born. For infants need the help of others to live, and adults to live well. I am not therefore denying that we seek each other's company at the prompting of nature. But civil Societies are not mere gatherings; they are Alliances* [Foedera], *which essentially require good faith and agreement for their making. Infants and the uninstructed are ignorant of their Force, and those who do not know what would be lost by the absence of Society are unaware of their usefulness. Hence the former cannot enter Society because they do not know what it is,*

---

[3] *Societas* is normally translated 'society'. Where 'association' seems more appropri-ate, the Latin word is given in parentheses.

and the latter do not care to because they do not know the good it does. It is evident therefore that all men (since all men are born as infants) are born unfit for society; and very many (perhaps the majority) remain so throughout their lives, because of mental illness or lack of training [disciplina]. *Yet as infants and as adults they do have a human nature. Therefore man is made fit for Society not by nature, but by training. Furthermore, even if man were born in a condition to desire society, it does not follow that he was born suitably equipped to enter society. Wanting is one thing, ability another. For even those who arrogantly reject the equal conditions without which society is not possible, still want it.*

In men's mutual fear] *The following objection is made: it is not true that men could combine into society through mutual fear; to the contrary, if they had been so afraid of each other, they could not even have borne the sight of each other. The objectors believe, I think, that fearing is nothing but being actually frightened. But I mean by that word any anticipation of future evil. In my view, not only flight, but also distrust, suspicion, precaution and provision against fear are all characteristic of men who are afraid. On going to bed, men lock their doors; when going on a journey, they arm themselves because they are afraid of robbers. Countries guard their frontiers with fortresses, their cities with walls, through fear of neighbouring countries. Even the strongest armies, fully ready for battle, open negotiations from time to time about peace, because they fear each other's forces and the risk of being beaten. Men take precautions because they are afraid – by running away and hiding if they see no alternative but most often by using arms and instruments of defence; the result is that when they do risk an advance, each tries to probe the other's mind. And then if they do fight, a commonwealth comes into being as the result of victory; and if they make an agreement, a commonwealth comes into being through an accord.*

3. The cause of men's fear of each other lies partly in their natural equality, partly in their willingness to hurt

each other. Hence we cannot expect security from others or assure it to ourselves. Look at a full-grown man and see how fragile is the structure of his human body (and if it fails, all his force, strength and Wisdom fail with it); see how easy it is for even the weakest individual to kill someone stronger than himself. Whatever confidence you have in your own strength, you simply cannot believe that you have been made superior to others by nature. Those who have equal power against each other, are equal; and those who have the greatest power, the power to kill, in fact have equal power. Therefore all men are equal to each other by nature. Our actual inequality has been introduced by civil law.

4. In the state of nature there is in all men a will to do harm, but not for the same reason or with equal culpability. One man practises the equality of nature, and allows others everything which he allows himself; this is the mark of a modest man, one who has a true estimate of his own capacities. Another, supposing himself superior to others, wants to be allowed everything, and demands more honour for himself than others have; that is the sign of an aggressive character. In his case, the will to do harm derives from vainglory [*inanis gloria*] and over-valuation of his own strength. For the first man, it derives from the need to defend his property and liberty against the other.

5. Intellectual dissension too is extremely serious; that kind of strife inevitably causes the worst conflicts. For even apart from open contention, the mere act of disagreement is offensive. Not to agree with someone on an issue is tacitly to accuse him of error on the issue, just as to dissent from him in a large number of points is tantamount to calling him a fool; and this is apparent in the fact that the bitterest wars are those between different sects of the same religion and different factions in the same country [*respublica*], when they clash over doctrines or public policy. And since all the heart's joy and pleasure lies in being able to compare oneself favourably with others and form a high opinion of oneself, men cannot

avoid sometimes showing hatred and contempt for each other, by laughter or words or a gesture or other sign. There is nothing more offensive than this, nothing that triggers a stronger impulse to hurt someone.

6. But the most frequent cause why men want to hurt each other arises when many want the same thing at the same time, without being able to enjoy it in common or to divide it. The consequence is that it must go to the stronger. But who is the stronger? Fighting must decide.

7. Amid so many dangers therefore from men's natural cupidity, that threaten every man every day, we cannot be blamed for looking out for ourselves; we cannot will to do otherwise. For each man is drawn to desire that which is Good for him and to Avoid what is bad for him, and most of all the greatest of natural evils, which is death; this happens by a real necessity of nature as powerful as that by which a stone falls downward. It is not therefore absurd, nor reprehensible, nor contrary to right reason, if one makes every effort to defend his body and limbs from death and to preserve them. And what is not contrary to right reason, all agree is done justly and *of Right*. For precisely what is meant by the term *Right* is the liberty each man has of using his natural faculties in accordance with right reason. Therefore the first foundation of natural *Right* is that *each man protect his life and limbs as much as he can.*

8. But a *right* to an end is meaningless, if the *right* to the means necessary to that end is denied; it follows that since each man has the *right* of self-preservation, he has also the *right to use any means and to do any action by which he can preserve himself.*

9. By natural law *one is oneself the judge* whether the means he is to use and the action he intends to take are necessary to the preservation of his life and limbs or not. For if it were contrary to right reason that I should be my own judge of my danger, someone else would judge it; since someone else is judging a matter that concerns me, then on the same grounds that we are equal by nature, I will be judge of what concerns him. Therefore

it is a requirement of right reason, i.e. of natural right, that I make a judgement whether his view of the matter is helpful to my preservation or not.

10. Nature has given *each man a right to all things*. That is, in the pure natural state (*), or before men bound themselves by any agreements with each other, every man was permitted to do anything to anybody, and to possess, use and enjoy whatever he wanted and could get. The argument is as follows: whatever anyone wants seems good to him precisely because he wants it, and it may either contribute to his preservation or at least seem to do so (and in the last article we made him the judge of whether it really does so or not, so that whatever he judges necessary is to be deemed to be so). By article 7 also, things are done *by right of nature*, and are held to be so done, if they necessarily contribute to the protection of life and limb. It follows that all men are permitted to have and to do all things in the state of nature. And this is what is meant by the common saying, *Nature has given all things to all men*. This is also the basis of the conclusion that in the state of nature the Measure of *right* [*ius*] is Interest [*Utilitas*].

In the pure natural state, etc.] *This must be understood as meaning that nothing that one does in a purely natural state is a wrong against anyone, at least against any man. Not that it is impossible in such a state to sin against God or to violate the Natural Laws. For injustice against men presupposes Human Laws, and there are none in the natural state. The attentive reader will notice that the truth of the proposition so understood has been demonstrated in the last few articles. But because in certain cases the harshness of the conclusion expels the memory of the premises, I will compress the argument and enable it to be taken in at a glance. Each man has a right of self-preservation (by article 7), therefore he also has the right to use every means necessary to that end (by article 8). The necessary means are those that he shall judge to be so himself (by article 9). He therefore has the right to do and to possess everything that he shall judge to be necessary to his self-preservation. In the judgement of the person actually doing it, what is done is rightly done, even if it is a wrong, and so is rightly done. It is therefore true that in the natural state, etc. A person may sin against the Natural Laws, as has been explained in chapter* III,[4] *if he claims that something contributes to his self-preservation, but does not believe that it does so. In objection the question has been raised whether if a son kills his father, he has not done a wrong* [injuria] *to his father. I have replied:* son *in the natural state cannot be understood to mean one who as soon as he is born is in the power and under the authority of the person to whom he owes his preservation: i.e. his mother or father, or the person who provides his sustenance, as was demonstrated in chapter* IX.

11. But it was of no use to men to have a common *right* of this kind. For the effect of this *right* is almost the same as if there were no *right* at all. For although one could say of anything, *this is mine*, still he could not enjoy it because of his neighbour, who claimed the same thing to be his by equal *right* and with equal force.

12. If to the natural tendency of men to exasperate each other, the source of which is the passions and especially an empty self-esteem, you now add the right of all men to all things, by which one man *rightly* attacks and the other *rightly* resists (an unfailing spring of suspicion and mutual resentment); if you add also how difficult it is, with few men and little equipment, to take precautions against enemies who attack with the intention to overwhelm and subdue, it cannot be denied that men's natural state, before they came together into society, was War; and not simply war, but a war of every man against every man. For what else is WAR but that time in which the will

---

[4] 'Has been explained in chapter III': Hobbes's use of the past tense here, rather than the future, which would seem more natural in referring to a subsequent chapter of the text, seems to reflect the fact that he added the notes for the second edition of 1647, and is thinking of the chapter as already written and published. This locution occurs a number of times (e.g. in the reference to ch. IX in this note). See the introduction, pp. xii–xiv and preface, 24.

to contend by force is made sufficiently known by words or actions? All other Time is called PEACE.

13. One may easily see how incompatible perpetual *War* is with the preservation of the human race or of individual men. Yet a war which cannot be brought to an end by victory because of the equality of the contestants is by its nature perpetual; for the victors themselves are so constantly threatened by danger that it must be regarded as a miracle if even the strongest survives to die of years and old age. The present century presents an example of this in the Americans. Past centuries show us nations, now civilized and flourishing, whose inhabitants then were few, savage, short lived, poor and mean, and lacked all the comforts and amenities of life which *peace* and society afford. Anyone who believes that one should remain in that state, in which all is allowed to all, is contradicting himself; for by natural necessity every man seeks his own good, but no one believes that the *war* of all against all which naturally belongs to such a state, is good for him. And so it comes about that we are driven by mutual fear to believe that we must emerge from such a state and seek allies [*socii*]; so that if we must have *war*, it will not be a war against all men nor without aid.

14. Allies are acquired either by force or by consent: by force when the victor in a conflict compels the vanquished to serve him by fear of death, or by taking him prisoner; by consent, when an association [*societas*] for mutual assistance is made with the consent of both parties, without violence. And the victor may *rightly* compel the vanquished (as a strong and healthy person may compel the sick or an adult an infant) to give a guarantee of future obedience, unless he prefers to die. For since the *right* of protecting ourselves at our own discretion proceeds from our danger, and the danger arises from equality, it is more rational and gives more assurance of our preservation if we make use of our present advantage to build the security we seek for ourselves by taking a guarantee, than to attempt to recover it later with all the risks of conflict when the enemy has grown in numbers

and strength and escaped from our power. And from the other side it is the height of absurdity, when you have him in your power in feeble condition, to make him strong again as well as hostile by letting him go. From this another corollary follows, that in the natural state of men, *sure and irresistible power gives the right of ruling and commanding those who cannot resist*; so that the right to do anything whatsoever is an essential and direct attribute of omnipotence.

15. However, because of their natural equality of strength and of the other human faculties, men in the state of nature, i.e. men who live in a state of war, cannot expect long preservation. *Therefore, to seek peace when some hope of having peace exists, and to seek aid for war when peace cannot be had, is a dictate of right reason*, i.e. *a law of Nature*, as will be shown next.

Chapter II
On the natural law of contracts

1. The natural law *is not an agreement between men, but a* dictate of reason. *2. The fundamental law of nature is* to seek Peace, if it can be had; if it cannot be had, to seek to defend oneself. *3. The first particular* law of nature *is that* the right to all things must not be held on to. *4. What it is to give up a right, and to transfer it. 5. The will of the recipient is necessary to the transfer of a right. 6. Only words which have reference to the present transfer a* right. *7. Words which have reference to the future avail to* transfer *a right, if other signs of will are present. 8. In a free Donation, the right is not passed by Words which refer to the future. 9. Definition of* Contract *& of* Agreement. *10. In Agreements the right is* passed *by words referring to the future. 11.* Agreements *of mutual trust are vain and invalid in the state of nature; but not in a commonwealth. 12. One cannot* make agreements *with animals; nor with God, without revelation. 13. Nor can one make a Vow to God. 14.* Agreements *do not obligate beyond one's best effort. 15. The ways by which we are released from* Agreements. *16.* Promises *extracted by fear of death are valid in a state of nature. 17. A later* Agreement *which contradicts a prior* Agreement *is invalid. 18. An* Agreement *not to resist an attempt at bodily harm is invalid. 19. An* Agreement *to accuse oneself is invalid. 20. Definition of an* Oath. *21. An* Oath *should be couched in a formula used by the party taking it. 22.* Swearing an oath *adds nothing to the obligation; that arises from the* Agreement. *23. An* Oath *is to be required only when violation of the agreement can be concealed or is punishable only by God.*

1. Authors have frequently made use of the term *Natural law* in their writings without however agreeing on its definition. The method of starting with definitions and avoiding equivocation is of course the proper method for those who leave no opportunity for counter-argument. Others go about it differently. Some of them argue that a particular act is against natural law because it runs counter to the united opinion of all the wisest or most civilized nations. However, they do not tell us who is to pass judgement on the wisdom, learning and morals of all the nations. Others argue from the position that an act is contrary to the agreed opinion of

the whole human race. This definition we must certainly not accept; for it would be impossible on this account for anyone except infants and the retarded to offend against such a law. For in the term *human race* they certainly include all who actively have the use of reason. Offenders therefore are either not acting against the law of nature or are acting against it without their own consent, and are therefore to be excused. But to take the laws of nature from those who more often violate them than observe them is surely unreasonable. Moreover, men condemn in others what they approve in themselves, publicly praise what they secretly reject, and form their opinions from a habit of listening to what they are told, not from their own observation. They give their consent out of hatred, fear, hope, love, or any other passion or emotion rather than from reason. That is why it quite often happens that whole peoples do with uniform agreement and complete confidence what those authors freely admit is against *natural law*. However, all men allow that any act not contrary to right reason is *right*, and therefore we have to hold that any act in conflict with right reason (i.e. in contradiction with some truth reached by correct reasoning from true principles) is *wrong*. But we speak of an act as *wrong* because it is contrary to some *law*. Thus law is a certain *right reason*, which (since it is no less part of human nature than any other faculty or passion of the mind) is also said to be natural. The *Natural law* therefore (to define it) is the Dictate of right reason (*) about what should be done or not done for the longest possible preservation of life and limb.

Of right reason] *By right reason in men's natural state, I mean, not, as many do, an infallible Faculty, but the act of reasoning, that is, a man's own true Reasoning about actions of his which may conduce to his advantage or other men's loss. I say his own reasoning, because, although in a Commonwealth the reason of the Commonwealth itself (which is the civil Law) must be regarded as right by individual citizens, outside of a Commonwealth, where no one can distinguish right reason from false except by making comparison with his own, each man's own reason must be regarded not only as the measure of his own actions, which are taken at his own risk, but also as the measure by which to judge the reasoning of others in his affairs. By true reasoning I mean reasoning that draws conclusions from true principles correctly stated. For every violation of Natural Laws consists in false reasoning or in*

stupidity, when men fail to see what duties towards other men are necessary to their own preservation. The Principles of right Reasoning about
such duties are those laid out in Chapter I, articles 2–7.

2. The first *law of nature* (the foundation) is: *to seek peace when it
can be had; when it cannot, to look for aid in war* [*auxilia belli*]. In
the final article of the last chapter we showed that this precept is a
dictate of right reason; and we have just defined natural laws as
dictates of right reason. It is the first law, because the rest are
derived from it; they are instructions on the means of securing
either peace or self-defence.

3. The first of *the Natural Laws* derived from this fundamental
natural law is that *the right of all men to all things must not be held
on to; certain rights must be transferred or abandoned*. For if each man
held on to his *right to all things*, it necessarily follows that some men
would be attacking and others defending themselves, and both by
right (for each man strives by necessity of nature to defend his Body
and whatever is necessary for its protection). *War* would ensue.
Anyone, therefore, who does not give up his *right to all things* is
acting contrary to the ways of peace, that is, contrary to the *law of
nature*.

4. One is said to *give up a right* either when he simply renounces
it or when he transfers it to someone else. He *simply renounces* it
when he declares by an appropriate sign or signs that he no longer
wants it to be licit for him to do some specific thing which previously he might *rightly do*. He *transfers* a right when he declares
by an appropriate sign or signs to the party which wants to acquire
that particular right from him that he no longer wants it to be licit
for him to offer resistance to his doing some specific thing in which
he could *rightly* resist him before. The argument that *transfer of
right* consists solely in non-resistance is that the recipient already
had a right to all things *before the transfer of the right*; hence the
transferor could not give him a new *right*. Justified resistance, however, on the part of the transferor, which previously prevented the
recipient from enjoying his *right*, is now extinguished. Whoever
therefore acquires a *right* in men's natural state, does so simply in
order to enjoy his *original right* in security and without justified
interference. For example, if a person passes his estate to another

by sale or gift, he deprives himself (though not others) of his *right* to that estate.

5. The *transfer of a right* requires the will of the recipient as well as of the transferor. If either is missing, the *right* does not pass. For if I have attempted to give something of mine to someone who refuses to take it, I have by that move not renounced my right simply, or transferred it to anyone who wants it; for the reason why I wished to give it to one particular person lies in him alone and not in others.

6. If the only signs of abandonment or transfer of a right are words, the words must have reference to *the present* or to *the past*. For if they refer to *the future*, they effect no transfer. If, for example, one refers to the future in the words *I will give tomorrow*, this clearly implies that he has not yet given; for the whole of today therefore the right is unchanged, and remains so on the next day too, unless in the meantime he actually gives; for what is mine remains mine, unless I subsequently give it. But if I speak of *the present*, as by saying *I give* or *I have given* to be held tomorrow, I signify by those words that *I have given* and have transferred *today* the *right* of holding *tomorrow*.

7. However, since words alone are not adequate signs to declare one's will, other signs of one's will may give words which refer to the future the same force as if they referred to the present. For if other signs make it quite certain that in speaking of the future he wished his words to effect a full *transfer of his right*, they ought to do so. For the *transfer of a right* depends not on words but, as has been said in article 4 of this chapter, on a declaration of will.

8. The transfer of a right to another person not for a good received in return nor on the basis of an agreement, is called a GIFT or *free Donation*. In a free donation only words which refer to *the present* or to *the past* give rise to obligation. Words which refer to *the future* do not oblige *as words* for the reason given in the last article but one. In that case the obligation must arise from other indications of one's will. And since whatever is done *voluntarily* is done for some *good thing* for the man willing, the only sign that justifies ascription of a will to give is that he has got or will get some *good* by giving the gift. But the assumption is that no such *good* has been acquired and that no agreement exists, because in those cases it would not be a *free donation*. The only possibility

remaining therefore is that *a return of good* is expected without agreement. No sign can be given that in using words referring to the future, he wanted them to be understood as putting him under an obligation to someone who was not bound to return the benefit. And it is not reasonable that people who are full of goodwill to others should be put under an obligation by every promise reflecting their momentary feelings; and for that reason such a promisor is to be taken to be deliberating and to be as free to change his mind as the recipient of the promise is capable of renouncing what is owed him. When a person is deliberating, he does have that degree of freedom, and is not said to have yet given; however, if he often promises and rarely gives, he ought to be criticized for fickleness, and not called a Giver but an About-to-give [*Doson*].[1]

9. The action of two or more persons reciprocally *transferring* their *rights* is called CONTRACT [*CONTRACTUS*]. In every contract either both parties immediately perform what they contracted to do, so that neither trusts anything to the other; or one performs and the other is trusted; or neither party performs. When both parties perform immediately, the *contract* ends with the performance. But when either or both are trusted, the trusted party promises to make performance later; and a promise of this kind is called an AGREEMENT [*PACTUM*].

10. An *agreement* made by a party who is trusted with a party who has already performed, even if the promise is made in words referring to the future, is no less a transfer of a *right* at the future time than if it had been made in words referring to the present or the past. For performance is the most evident sign that the one who has performed his part understood the words of the other party (the trusted party) as expressing an intention to perform at a specified time. By that sign also the trusted party knew that he was so understood; and because he did not correct it, he intended it to be so taken. *Promises* therefore which are made in return for *good* received (such promises too are *agreements*) are signs of will, that is (as has been shown in the previous article), signs of the last act of deliberation by which the liberty not to perform is lost; consequently they are obligatory; for obligation begins where liberty ends.

---

[1] This is a reference to Antigonus Doson, king of Macedonia, who was noted for not fulfilling his promises (e.g. Plutarch, *Parallel Lives*, 'Life of Coriolanus', 11). At *Elements of Law* I.15.7, Hobbes has written Antiochus, apparently in error for Antigonus.

11. In the state of nature agreements made by a contract of mutual trust (by which both parties trust the other and neither makes any performance immediately) are invalid if a just cause for fear arises (*) on either side. For most men are of evil character, bent on securing their own interest by fair means or foul; and so the man who performs his part first is laying himself open to the greed of the other party to the contract. For it is not reasonable for anyone to make performance first if it is not likely that the other will perform his part later. And it is for the fearful party to decide whether that is likely or not, as has been shown in article 9 of the last chapter. This is the situation, I say, in the state of nature. But in the civil state where there is someone to coerce both parties, whichever party is called upon by the contract to perform first should do so; since the reason why he was afraid that the other party might not perform no longer exists, as the other can be compelled.

Arises, etc.] *The reason is that a justifiable fear can only be planted in someone's mind if there is a new cause for fear arising from some action or other sign from the other party that he does not intend to make performance. For a cause which was unable to impede the making of an agreement ought not to impede its performance.*

12. From the fact that acceptance of the transferred right is a requirement of all *gifts* and *agreements*, it follows that no one can *make an agreement* with someone who gives no sign of acceptance. That is why we cannot make agreements with animals or credit them with rights or take their rights away, because they lack language and understanding. Nor can one enter into *agreements* with the majesty of God nor be bound by a *vow* to him, except in so far as it has pleased him, through the holy scriptures, to make certain men his substitutes, with authority to review and accept such vows and agreements and to accept them as his representatives.

13. Thus men who live in a state of nature, where they are not bound by any civil law, make vows in vain (unless they know by certain revelation that the will of God accepts their *vow* or *agreement*). For if what they vow is contrary to the law of nature, they are not bound by it, because no one is bound to perform anything illicit; if what they vow is prescribed by the law of nature,

37

then they are bound by the *law* itself, not by the *vow*. If they were free to do or not to do before they made their *vow*, that liberty remains; the reason is that if we are to be obligated by a *vow*, we need the will of the obligating party to be openly expressed, and that is assumed not to be the case in the given situation. By the *obligating* party I mean the one to whom someone is bound or obligated; the *obligated* party is the one who is bound.

14. Agreements are made only about actions which are susceptible of deliberation; for an agreement requires the will of its maker, and will is the final act of deliberation. *Agreements are therefore only about possible, future things.* Hence no one obligates himself by his *agreement* to the impossible. But whereas we very often agree to things which seem possible at the time that we promise them but which later are incontestably impossible, we are not therefore free of all obligation. The reason is that in promising something uncertain in the future, one receives a present benefit on condition of making a return; for the intention of the party who offers the immediate benefit has for object simply a *good for himself* of the value of the thing promised; the thing itself is not his object simply, but only if it can be done. And if it turns out that even this is not possible, as much must be performed as can be. The obligation of *agreements*, then, is not to the actual thing which is the subject of the agreement, but to the highest possible effort; for this alone, not the things themselves, is in our power.

15. We are released from *agreements* by two things, by performance and by condonation. By performance, because that is the extent of our obligation. By condonation, because the party to whom we are obligated is understood by condoning to effect the return to us of the *right* which we transferred to him; for condonation is a *donation*, i.e. (by article 4 of this chapter) the transfer of a right to the recipient of the donation.

16. The question is often asked whether *agreements* extorted by fear are obligatory or not. For example, am I obligated if, to save my life, I make an *agreement* with a highway robber to pay him a thousand gold pieces tomorrow, and to do nothing that might result in his arrest and arraignment? There are times when an *agreement* like that should be held to be invalid; but it will not be invalid simply because it was motivated by fear. For this would imply that the *agreements* by which men unite in civil life and make laws are

invalid (for one's submission to government by another person is motivated by fear of mutual slaughter); and that one is not acting rationally in putting one's trust in an agreement with a captive on the price of his ransom. The truth is that agreements are universally valid once the benefit has been accepted, and if the act and the content of the promise are licit. And it is licit to make a promise to ransom my life and to give anything I like of my own to anyone, even to a robber. Thus we are obligated by agreements motivated by fear, unless a civil law forbids it by making what is promised illicit.

17. Anyone who makes an agreement to do or not to do something, and afterwards makes a contrary agreement with someone else, renders the second *agreement* illegal, not the first; for when one has already transferred his *right* to someone else by making the first *agreement*, he no longer has the *right* to do or not to do. Hence he transfers no right by the second agreement, and what he promises he promises without the right to do so. He is therefore bound only by the first *agreement*, and it is illicit to break it.

18. No one is obligated by any *agreement* he may have made not to resist someone who is threatening him with death, wounds or other bodily harm. For there is in every man a kind of supreme stage of fearfulness, by which he sees the harm threatening him as the worst possible, and by natural necessity does his best to avoid it; and is understood not to be able to do otherwise. When one has reached this level of fear, he must be expected to look out for himself either by flight or by fighting. Since no one is bound to do the impossible, no one is obliged to accept the *death* with which he is threatened (the greatest harm of nature) or wounds or other bodily harm which he is not strong enough to endure. Moreover, a person bound by an agreement is normally trusted to perform (for trust is the only bond of agreements), but when people are being led out to punishment (whether capital or not), they are held in chains or escorted by guards; that is the clearest indication that they are not seen as sufficiently obligated by an agreement not to resist. It is one thing to agree: *If I do not do such-and-such by a certain date, kill me.* It is another thing to agree: *If I do not do such-and-such, I will not resist your killing me.*[2] Everyone makes use of the first mode of agree-

---

[2] Italics supplied by the translator.

ment if there is need to do so, and sometimes there is; no one uses the second mode, and there never is a need to do so. For in the purely natural state, if you wish to kill, you have the right to do so on the basis of the natural state itself; so that there is no need to trust first and kill later when he lets you down. But in the civil state, where the right of life and death and of all corporal punishment are the responsibility of the commonwealth, this very right of killing cannot be allowed to a private person. Nor need the commonwealth itself require of anyone, as a condition of punishment, an agreement not to resist, but only that no one protect others. If in a state of nature – for instance in relations between commonwealths – an agreement were made to kill if a certain condition is not fulfilled, the implication is that this agreement was preceded by another agreement, not to kill before a certain date. Hence if the condition is not fulfilled by that date, the right of war returns, i.e. a state of enmity, in which all things are allowed, including therefore resistance. Finally an obligation not to resist is an obligation to choose what will seem the greater of two present evils. For certain death is a greater evil than fighting. But it is impossible not to choose the lesser of two evils. Hence by such an agreement we would be obligated to the impossible, and that is contrary to the nature of agreements.

19. Similarly, one is not bound by any agreement to accuse oneself or anyone whose loss would embitter one's own life. Hence a father is not obliged to give evidence against his son, nor spouse against spouse, nor son against father; nor anyone against the person on whom he depends for survival; for evidence which is presumed to be tainted by nature is useless. But although one is not obliged by any agreement to accuse oneself, one may be compelled by torture to reply in a public trial. Such replies are not evidence of fact, but a means of investigating the truth. So whether he gives a true or a false answer under torture or says nothing at all, he is acting rightly.

20. *An Oath* is an utterance attached to a promise; by it the promisor gives up his claim to God's mercy if he does not do as he promises. This definition follows from the actual words in which the essence of *swearing* is contained, namely, *So help me God*, or the equivalent, as, among the Romans, *O Jupiter, kill the oath-breaker*

as I kill this Sow. It is no objection that sometimes an *Oath* may be said to be not promissory but declarative. For in strengthening an affirmation by means of an *oath*, he declares that he is giving a true reply. It is true that there was a custom in certain countries for subjects to swear by their kings, but this arose from the fact that the kings there wished to have divine honours paid to them. For *Swearing oaths* was introduced precisely in order to strike men with a greater fear of breaking faith than the fear we have of men (from whom our actions may be hidden) by consideration of the power of God and by religious scruple.

21. It follows that *the Oath* should be couched in a formula which is used by the person taking it; it is pointless to force someone to *swear* by a God he does not believe in and therefore does not fear. For although God's existence may be known by natural light, no one believes he is swearing by Him if a different formula or a different name is used from the one current in the teachings of his own religion, i.e. (in the swearer's belief) the true religion.

22. One may see from the given definition of *swearing an oath* that a mere *agreement* carries as much obligation by itself as a sworn agreement. For it is the *agreement* that binds us; the *oath* relates to God's punishment, which it would be inappropriate to invoke if violation of an agreement were not illicit in itself; and it would not be illicit, if the *agreement* did not create an obligation. Besides, in giving up his claim to God's mercy, he does not obligate himself to be punished, because one may always attempt to get off a penalty, however much he may have brought it on himself, and take advantage of God's forgiveness, if it is offered. The only effect then of an *oath* (men being prone by nature to break the faith they have pledged) is to give those who have taken an oath more reason to be afraid to do so.

23. It is going beyond the requirements of self-defence to exact an *oath* when violation of an agreement, should it occur, could not be concealed and when the person to whom the promise is made has enough power to exact a penalty. It indicates an attitude not so much of concern for oneself as of ill-will towards the other. For by the formula of swearing, the *oath* relates to provoking the wrath of God; i.e. the wrath of one who is *omnipotent* against those who

break faith in the belief that their power will save them from human punishment; and of one who is *omniscient* against those who are accustomed to break faith, because they expect to be able to escape human detection.

Chapter III
On the other laws of nature

1. The second of the derivative laws of nature is: *Stand by your agreements*, or keep faith. In the last chapter it was shown, that the

law of nature instructs each and every man, as the necessary means of securing peace, to make a reciprocal transfer of certain of their own *rights*; it was also shown that when the transfer is to take place in the future, it is called an *agreement*. This is instrumental to securing peace, since by the very fact of agreement, we are doing (or not doing) what we agree should be done (or not done); and agreements would be pointless if we did not stand by them. Since *standing by Agreements* or *keeping faith* is necessary for securing peace, it will take its place, by chapter II, article 2, as a precept of *natural law*.

2. In this matter, we may not make any exception among the persons with whom we make agreements, for instance, if they do not themselves keep faith with others and do not believe in doing so, or have any other fault. For in making an agreement, one denies by the very act of agreeing that the act is meaningless. And it is against reason knowingly to take away the meaning of anything. If he does not believe the agreement should be fulfilled, by the very fact that he so believes he affirms that the agreement is meaningless. Anyone therefore who makes agreement with someone, but does not believe he is obliged to keep faith with him, believes that *making agreements* is meaningless and at the same time meaningful, and that is absurd. Therefore either one should keep faith with every one or one should not make agreements, that is, one must either declare war or maintain a firm and faithful Peace.

3. The breaking of an *Agreement*, like asking for the return of a gift, (which always occurs by some action or failure to act) is called a WRONG [*INIURIA*]. Such an action or failure to act is said to be *unjust* (*iniusta*); so that *wrong* and *unjust* action or failure to act have the same meaning, and both are the same as breaking an agreement or *breaking faith*. It seems that the name *wrong* [*iniuria*] is applied to an action or a failure to act, because it is *without right* [*sine iure*], inasmuch as the party which acted or failed to act had already transferred the right to someone else. And there is an analogy between what in ordinary life is called wrong and what in the schools is usually called *absurdity*. He who is compelled by arguments to deny an assertion he had previously upheld, is said to be reduced to *absurdity*; in the same way he who, through weakness of will, does or fails to do what he had previously promised by *agreement* not to do or not to fail to do, does a *wrong*, and falls into a contradiction no less than someone in the schools who is reduced to absurdity.

For by agreeing to a future action he wills that it be done; by not doing it, he wills that it not be done; which is to will that the same thing be done and not done at the same time, and that is a contradiction. A *wrong* therefore is a kind of *absurdity* in behaviour, just as an *absurdity* is a kind of *wrong* in disputation.

4. It follows that a wrong (*) can only be done to someone with whom an *agreement* has been made, or to whom something has been given as a gift, or promised by *agreement*. And hence, a distinction is very often made between *loss* [*damnum*] and *wrong*. For if a master orders a servant who has agreed to obey him, to pay money to a third party or do a service for him, the servant, if he fails to do so, causes loss to the third party but wrongs only the master. So too in a commonwealth, if one harms anyone with whom he has no agreement, he causes *loss* to the person he maltreats, but does a *wrong* only to the holder of authority over the whole commonwealth. For if the victim of the harm should claim to have been wronged, the person who did the action would say, *What are you to me? Why should I act at your pleasure rather than my own, since I am not preventing you from acting at your discretion, not mine?*[1] I do not see how one could fault that response, since there has been no agreement.

A wrong can only be done to someone, etc.] *The word Injustice has meaning in relation to law; Wrong in relation to law and a specific Person. For what is Unjust, is unjust to all; but there can be a Wrong which is not a wrong against me or against him, but against someone else, and sometimes not against any private person at all but against the commonwealth only, and even a wrong which is against neither man nor commonwealth, but against God alone. For the result of agreement and transfer of right is that wrong is said to be done against particular persons. Hence – as we see happens in every commonwealth – what private men contract between themselves in word or writing may be required or remitted at the discretion of the obligating party. But harm inflicted contrary to the commonwealth's laws, e.g. theft, murder, and so on, is not punished at the discretion of the man who suffers loss, but at the will of the commonwealth, that is, in accordance with the laws in effect. There can therefore be no wrong against a particular man except after transfer of a right to him.*

---

[1] Italics supplied by the translator.

5. These words *Just* and *Unjust*, like *Justice* and *Injustice* are equivocal; they mean one thing when applied to Persons, another when
applied to Actions. When applied to actions, *Just* means the same
as rightly done [*jure factum*], and *Unjust*, *Wrongly* done [*injuriâ
factum*]. And he who has done something *Just* is not called *Just* but
Innocent; and we speak of one who has done something *Unjust* not
as *unjust* but as *guilty*. When used of persons, *to be just* means the
same as to delight in doing justice [*iuste faciendo*], to strive for justice, or to attempt in everything to do what is just. And *to be Unjust*
is to disregard justice or to suppose that the measure of it is present
advantage, not a man's agreement. Consequently, the *justice* and
injustice of a disposition, practice or man are one thing; of a single
action or failure to act another; and a great many of a *just* man's
actions may be *unjust*, and of an *unjust* man, *just*. But a man is to
be called *just*, who does just things because the law so instructs, and
unjust things only because of weakness; he is to be called *unjust*,
who does just things because of the penalty attached to the law, and
unjust things from the wickedness of his heart.

6. Justice of actions is commonly divided into two kinds: *commutative* and *distributive*; the former, it is said, lies in an Arithmeti-
cal proportion, the latter in a Geometrical. The sphere of the former
is barter, sale, purchase, borrowing, payment of loan, letting, hiring,
and all other actions of mutually contracting parties; in these transactions they say that commutative justice occurs when equal is given
for equal. The latter [distributive] is concerned with men's dignity
and deserts, so that if awards are made κατὰ τὴν ἀξίαν,[2] – more
to the more worthy, less to the less worthy, and it is done proportionately – *distributive justice* occurs. I recognize here a distinction between two kinds of equality. The first is equality simply, as
when two things of equal value are compared, e.g. a pound of silver
with twelve ounces of the same silver. The second is proportionate
equality [*secundum quid*], as when a thousand pounds is to be distributed among a hundred men, and six hundred is given to sixty men,
and four hundred to forty. Here there is no equality between 600
and 400, but since there is the same inequality in the number of
the recipients, each one of them will take away an equal share; hence

---

[2] 'By merit'. Cf. e.g. Aristotle, *Politics* III.5, 1278a20.

it is said to be an equal distribution. Such an equality is the same thing as Geometrical proportion. But what does this have to do with justice? For we do not do a wrong [*iniuria*] to a buyer if we sell our property at the best price we can get for it, since he wanted it, and sought to get it. And if I give a larger share of something of mine to someone who is less deserving [than someone else], I am not doing a wrong to either of them, provided I have given what I agreed to give. Our Divine saviour, Christ himself, witnesses to this in the Gospel. It is not therefore a division of justice but a division of equality. It cannot however be denied, perhaps, that justice is some kind of equality; a kind namely which rests simply on the fact that since we are all equal by nature, one may not take for himself more *right* than he allows to another, unless he got this *right* by agreement. Let this be all we say in criticism of this division of *justice*, though it is almost universally accepted, so that no one may think that a *wrong* is anything but a breach of faith or agreements, as defined above.

7. *No wrong is done to a consenting party*,[3] is an old saying. But we may derive the truth of it from our principles. Suppose that something is done with a man's consent which he thinks is a wrong to him. This means that something which is not allowed by the agreement is being done with his consent. But since he consents to the doing of what was not allowed by the *agreement*, the *agreement* itself (by article 15 of the last chapter) becomes void; and thus the right to act returns. Hence the thing is done *rightly*, and is therefore not a *wrong*.

8. The third precept of natural law is: *if someone has conferred a benefit on you, relying on your good faith [fiducia tui], do not let him lose on it*; or: *no one should accept a benefit without the intention to try to ensure that the giver not have reason to be sorry he gave it*. Without this precept it is against reason to confer a benefit which one sees will perish without effect; all kindness and trust between men will thus be lost, and all benevolence too; and there would be no mutual assistance nor any initiative to win gratitude. As a result, the state of war will inevitably persist, contrary to *the fundamental law of nature*. Since violation of this law is not a violation of faith or of

---

[3] *Volenti non fit iniuria*, a Roman law maxim.

agreement (for it is assumed that no agreements have taken place between them), it is not called a *wrong*; but because *benefit* and *gratitude* go together, it is called INGRATITUDE.

9. The fourth precept of nature is that *everyone should be considerate* [*commodus*] *of others*. To understand this properly, one has to realize that when men enter into society there are differences of opinion among them which spring from the diversity of their passions. It is rather like the differences among stones collected for construction, which arise from their differences of material and shape. A stone of rough and irregular shape takes more space from the others than it fills itself; it cannot be compressed or cut because it is so hard, but it prevents the structure from being fitted together, so it is thrown away as unsuitable [*incommodus*]. Just so a man who keeps more than he needs for himself and, in the hardness of his heart, takes the necessities of life from other people, and is too temperamentally stubborn to be corrected, is normally said to be *inconsiderate* of others and difficult. Now since our basic principle is that every man is not only *right*, but *naturally compelled*, to make every effort to win what he needs for his own preservation, anyone who tries to thwart him for the sake of luxuries will be to blame for the war which breaks out, because he was the only one who had no need to fight; and is therefore acting against the *fundamental law of nature*. Hence it follows (and this is what I was aiming to show) that it is a precept of nature to be considerate of others. Anyone who violates this *law* may be said to be *inconsiderate* and difficult. Cicero regards *inhuman* as the opposite of *considerate*, as if he had this law in mind.[4]

10. The fifth precept of natural law is, that *one should pardon another for the past, if he is sorry and asks for pardon, provided one gets a guarantee for the future*. Pardon (for the past) or remission of an offence, is simply the granting of *peace* to one who after provoking *war*, repents of his action and asks for *peace*. But the *granting of peace* to one who does not repent (i.e. one who persists in a hostile frame of mind), or who does not give a guarantee for the future (i.e. is not looking for peace but a chance to recover), is not *peace* but *fear*, and is not therefore prescribed by nature. But he is no friend of peace itself who refuses to forgive one who repents and gives a guarantee for the future, and that is contrary to *natural law*.

---

[4] E.g. Cicero, *Orations against Verres*, 3.23.

11. The sixth precept of *natural law*: *In revenge* [*ultio*] *or Punishment* [*Poenae*] *consider future good, not past evil.* That is, it is only permitted to inflict a penalty in order to correct the wrongdoer or so that others may be reformed by taking warning from his punishment. The first argument for this is that everyone is obliged by *natural law* to forgive others, provided assurance is taken for the future, as shown in the previous article. Besides, because *revenge* considers only the past, it is simply triumphing and glorying to no purpose (for it looks only to the past and a purpose is a future thing). Anything that has no purpose is Vain. Revenge, which does not look to the future, is motivated by vainglory, and therefore is without reason. But to hurt another without reason initiates war, and is contrary to the *fundamental law of nature*. It is therefore a precept of *natural law*, that in revenge one must not look back, but forward. And the violation of this law is usually called CRUELTY.

12. Any sign of hatred and contempt is more provocative of quarrels and fighting than anything else, so that most men prefer to lose their peace and even their lives rather than suffer insult. Hence follows the seventh precept of *natural law*: *no one should show hatred or contempt of another by deeds, words, facial expression or laughter.* Violation of this law is called INSULT. Nothing is commoner than taunting and offensive remarks by the powerful against the less powerful and especially by judges against defendants, which have nothing to do with the charge and are not part of the judge's duty; such men are acting against the *natural law* and should be considered *insolent*.

13. Which of two men has higher worth [*dignior*] is a question for the civil state, not the state of nature. It has been shown before (1.3) that by nature all men are equal with each other; and hence that existing inequalities, for instance in wealth, power, and nobility of birth, arose *from civil law*. I know that in the first book of the Politics *Aristotle* asserts as a foundation of all political knowledge that some men have been made by nature worthy to rule, others to serve, as if Master and slave were distinguished not by agreement among men, but by natural aptitude, i.e. by their knowledge or ignorance. This basic postulate is not only against reason, but contrary to experience. For hardly anyone is so naturally stupid that he does not think it better to rule himself than to let others rule him. Nor in a conflict between the wise and the strong are the wise

always or often superior to the strong. If then men are equal by nature, we must recognize their equality; if they are unequal, since they will struggle for power, *the pursuit of peace* requires *that they be regarded as equal*. And therefore the eighth precept of natural law is: *everyone should be considered equal to everyone*. Contrary to this law is PRIDE.

14. Just as it was necessary for each man's preservation that he should relinquish certain of his *rights*, so it is no less necessary to his preservation that he retain certain *rights*, namely the *Right* of protecting his person, the right of enjoying the open air, water, and all other things necessary for life. Since therefore men entering into *peace* retain many common *rights* and acquire many personal *rights*, the ninth dictate of *natural law* arises, namely: *whatever rights each claims for himself, he must also allow to everyone else*. Otherwise he makes nonsense of the equality recognized in the previous article. For what else is the recognition of equality of rights in entering into society but to allow equal rights to those who otherwise have no reason to enter into society? To allow *equal* rights to *equals* is the same as the principle of proportionality. Observance of this law is called *Modesty*, its violation πλεονεξία [arrogance]; the Latin for such violators is *immoderate* and immodest.

15. In the tenth place, *natural law* commands: *in awarding rights to others, you should be fair [aequalis] to both sides*. The previous law forbade us to claim on the basis of nature more right for ourselves than we allow to others. We may claim less, if we want to; as *modesty* sometimes requires. But if ever we have to distribute *Right* to others, this law forbids us from giving more or less to one person than to another as a favour. For if you do not keep to natural equality but give more or less to one than to the other, you are *insulting* the person who is not favoured. And it has been shown above that *insult* is contrary to the *natural laws*. The observation of this precept is FAIRNESS [*AEQUITAS*], violation of it is discrimination; the Greek word for it is προσωποληψία.[5]

16. The eleventh *law* follows from the last one. *Things that cannot be divided should be used in common, if possible, and (if there is enough of a thing) each should have as much as he wants. But if there is not*

---

[5] Cf. Acts 10.34–5: 'Of a truth I perceive that god is no respecter of persons [προσωπολήπτης]: But in every nation he that feareth him, and worketh righteousness, is accepted with him' (King James translation).

enough of the thing, then it should be used in fixed shares and proportionately to the number of users; for there is no other way to preserve the equality which we demonstrated in the previous section is commanded by natural law.

17. Likewise, if it cannot be divided or held in common, it is laid down by *natural law* (and this is the twelfth precept) that: *it should either be used in turn or be allotted to one person alone; in the case of alternate use, an adjudication must also be made by lot as to who should be the first to use it.* For here too regard should be had to equality, and in this case lottery is the only form equality can take.

18. There are two kinds of lottery, *discretionary* and *natural*. A discretionary lottery takes place if the contending parties agree to it. It depends upon pure chance, and perhaps on what they call luck. Natural forms are *primogeniture* (in Greek κληρονομία, as if awarded by lot) and *first occupation*. Thus things which cannot be divided or held in common, go to the first occupier; likewise a father's possessions go to the first-born, unless the father himself has transferred that *right* beforehand. Let this be then the thirteenth *law of nature*.

19. The fourteenth precept of natural law is that *Mediators of Peace should have immunity*. The reason which enjoins the end, enjoins also the necessary means. Now the first dictate of reason is *Peace*, the rest are the necessary means to *Peace*. But *Peace* cannot be had without mediation, nor mediation without immunity. It is therefore a dictate of reason, i.e. a *law of nature*, that immunity should be given to mediators of *Peace*.

20. Men may agree to all these *laws of nature* and whatever others there may be, and try hard to observe them, yet doubtful points and disputes will arise every day about their application to actions, namely whether something that has been *done* is contrary to *law* or not (this is called a question of right). It is a source of conflict, as both parties to a dispute believe themselves to be the injured party. It is therefore necessary to the preservation of *Peace* (since no other fair remedy can be devised in this case) that both parties agree on some third party, whose verdict on the matter in dispute they oblige themselves by *mutual agreement* to respect. The person on whom they agree is called an *Arbitrator*. The fifteenth precept therefore of *natural law* is: *parties who have a dispute of right among them should both submit to the arbitration of a third party.*

21. It follows from the fact that the *Arbitrator* or *Judge* was chosen by both disputants to settle the controversy, that the arbitrator should not be one of the parties to the dispute. For every man is assumed to be naturally after his own good; he seeks *Justice* only incidentally, for the sake of *peace*; thus he cannot respect the equality prescribed by *natural law* so carefully as a third party would. The natural law therefore contains a sixteenth precept: *no one should be judge or Arbitrator in his own case.*

22. The seventeenth precept follows: *No one should be an arbitrator, who has a greater expectation of profit or glory from the victory of one party than of the other.* The same reasoning applies here as in the previous law.

23. When a dispute arises about a matter of fact, namely whether what is said to have happened actually occurred or not, the *natural law* (by article 15) requires an Arbitrator to give equal weight to the testimony of both parties, that is, (since they contradict each other) no weight at all. To arrive therefore at a judgement of a matter of fact which cannot be known by other evidence, he ought to accept the testimony of a third person or of a third and a fourth or more. The eighteenth natural *law* then instructs *arbitrators* or *judges* of a matter of fact *to govern their verdict, where sure evidence of the fact is lacking, by witnesses who seem fair to both parties.*

24. It may further be understood from the definition of an *arbitrator* given above that *there exists no agreement or promise between himself and the parties to the arbitration, which would oblige him to pronounce in favour of one or the other, or by which he would be obliged not to pronounce a fair verdict or what he believes to be a fair verdict.* An *arbitrator* is obliged to give the judgement which he believes to be fair, by the *law of nature* reviewed in article 15. Nothing can be added to the obligation of that law as the result of an agreement. Such an agreement would therefore be pointless. Moreover, if such an agreement were not invalid, he could bring in an unfair verdict and claim that it was fair, and the dispute would continue after the verdict, and that destroys *the point of an Arbitrator*, who is appointed by the parties precisely in order to oblige each other to accept the sentence he pronounces as binding. The *law of nature* therefore insists on the *independence* of the Arbitrator; and that may stand as the nineteenth precept.

25. The *laws of nature* being simply the dictates of right reason, one is not able to observe them unless he makes an effort to maintain his ability to reason properly. Hence, clearly, anyone who willingly and knowingly does things which will have the effect of weakening or destroying his rational faculty is willingly and knowingly violating the law of nature. For there is no difference between acting contrary to duty and doing something which prevents one from doing one's duty. Reasoning ability is destroyed or impaired by activities which subvert the mind's natural state, as is obviously the case when people are Drunk or *crapulous*. Hence, in the twentieth place, *Drunkenness* is an offence against natural law.

26. All these *natural precepts* are derived from just one dictate of reason, that presses on us our own preservation and security [*incolumitas*]. Someone will perhaps say, on seeing this, that the deduction of these laws is so difficult that they cannot be expected to become widely known, and hence are not obligatory. For laws do not oblige unless they are known, are not in fact laws. I give him this reply. It is true that *hope, fear, anger, ambition, greed, vainglory* and the other emotions do impede one's ability to grasp the laws of nature, while they prevail. But no one is without his calmer moments, and at those times, nothing is easier to grasp, even for the ignorant and uneducated. The only rule he needs is that when he is in doubt whether what he proposes to do to someone is in accordance with *natural right* [*jus*] or not, he should think himself into the other person's place. Immediately the passions which were prompting him to act will now discourage him from action, as if transferred to the other pan of the scales. This rule is not only easy; it has long been famous in the words: *Do not do to another what you would not have done to you.*

27. In the face of an inordinate desire for an immediate good, most men are disinclined to observe the laws given above, however well they recognize them. If a few men, more modest than everybody else, practised the fairness and consideration which reason dictates, and the rest did not do so, they would certainly not be acting rationally. For they would not be securing peace for themselves but early and certain ruin; the law-abiding would fall prey to the lawbreakers. One should not therefore suppose that men are obliged by nature, i.e. by reason, to keep all the laws (*) in a state

of mankind in which they are not practised by others. At such times we are obliged to try to keep them, whenever keeping them seems likely to achieve the end for which they were made. Hence the conclusion must be that a law of nature gives rise to an obligation in *the internal Court* [*in Foro interno*] or *in conscience* always and everywhere; but *in the external court* [*in foro externo*] it gives rise to obligation only when it can be kept with safety.

To keep all the laws]: *In fact there are some things in these laws whose omission (provided it is done for the sake of Peace and self-preservation) seems rather to be a fulfilment than a violation of natural law. To take every measure against those who will stop at nothing – to steal from thieves – is to act reasonably. Conversely, it is cowardice and self-betrayal* [sui proditio] *to behave in war as one normally should in peace and as a modest man would. However, there are some natural laws whose observance does not cease even in war. For I cannot see what drunkenness or cruelty (which is vengeance without regard to future good) contribute to any man's peace or preservation. Briefly, in a state of nature, Just and Unjust should be judged not from actions but from the intention and conscience of the agents. What is done of necessity, or in pursuit of peace, or for self-preservation is done rightly. Apart from this, all infliction of harm on men is a violation of natural Law and a wrong against God.*

28. Laws which bind the conscience may be violated not only by an action contrary to them but also by an action consonant with them, if the agent believes it to be contrary. For although the act itself is in accordance with the laws, his conscience is against them.

29. The *laws of nature* are *immutable and eternal*; what they forbid can never be lawful; what they command, never unlawful. Never will *pride, ingratitude, violation of Agreements (or wrong), unkindness, or insult* be lawful, nor the contrary virtues ever unlawful, considered simply as dispositions of mind, i.e. viewed *in the court of conscience*, where alone they obligate and are laws. Actions however may be so varied by circumstances and the civil law, that what is fair at one time may be unfair at another time, and what at one time was rational may at another be against reason. Reason itself however changes neither its end, which is *peace and self-defence*, nor its means, namely those virtues of character which we have laid out

above, and which can never be repealed by either custom or civil laws.

30. It is clear from what we have said so far how easy the *laws of nature* are to observe, since they require only an effort (but a real, sustained effort), and we are entitled to call any man JUST who has made such an effort. For anyone who makes every effort to conform all his actions to the *precepts of nature*, is clearly evincing his intention to fulfil all these laws; and that is all that we are obligated to by our rational nature. And anyone who has fulfilled the whole of his obligation is *just*.

31. All authors agree that the *natural law* is the same as the *moral law*. Let us see why this is true. One must recognize that *good* and *evil* are names imposed on things to signify desire for or aversion from the things so named. Men's desires differ, as their temperaments, habits and opinions differ; one may see this in the case of things perceived by the senses, by the taste, for instance, or by touch or smell, but it is much more so in everything to do with the ordinary actions of life, where what one man *praises*, i.e. calls *good*, the other *abuses* as *bad*; indeed the same man at different times *praises* or *blames* the same thing. This behaviour necessarily gives rise to discord and conflicts. Men are therefore in a state of war so long as they judge *good* and *evil* by the different measures which their changing desires from time to time dictate. All men easily recognize that this state is evil when they are in it; and consequently that peace is good. Thus though they cannot agree on a present good, they do agree on a future good. And that is the work of reason; for *things present* are perceived by the senses, *things future* only by reason. Reason teaches that *peace* is *good*; it follows by the same reason that all necessary means to peace are good, and hence that *modesty, fairness, good faith, kindness* and *mercy* (which we have proved above are necessary for peace) are *good manners* [*mores*] or habits, i.e. *virtues*.[6] Hence by the very fact that *law* teaches the means to peace, it teaches *good manners* or virtues. And is therefore called *moral*.

32. Men cannot divest themselves of the irrational desire to reject future goods for the sake of present goods (which inevitably entail

---

[6] *Mores*: the translation 'manners' is based on a comparison with *Elements of Law* I.18.1, '. . . and also [called] moral laws, because they concern men's manners and conversation one towards another'.

unexpected evils). The result has been that, though all agree in praise of the said virtues, they still disagree on their nature, that is, on what each one of them consists in. For whenever someone dislikes another person's good action, he applies the name of some related vice to it; likewise wickedness that pleases is given the name of a virtue. The result is that the same action is approved by one party and called a virtue, and criticized by others and construed as a vice. Philosophers have heretofore found no remedy for this situation. For as they have not observed that the goodness of actions lies in their tendency to peace,[7] their evil in their tendency to discord, they have constructed a *moral Philosophy* which is alien to the *moral law*, and inconsistent with itself. For they have they have taken the view that the nature of the *virtues* lies in a certain *mean* between two *extremes*, and vices in the *extremes* themselves, and this is patently false. For even extreme daring is approved and taken as a virtue and given the name of *courage*, if the cause is approved. Likewise, it is not the quantity of the thing given as a gift, whether large, small or in-between, that makes *generosity*, but the reason for giving. Nor is it *injustice* if I give someone more of my own than is due. The *natural laws* therefore are the summa of *moral* Philosophy, and I have given its precepts here only so far as they are relevant to our preservation against the dangers which arise from discord. There are other precepts of rational nature, from which other virtues derive. For *Self-control* [*Temperantia*] is a precept of reason, because lack of self-control leads to disease and death. And so is courage, i.e. the capacity to put up a strong resistance in a pressing danger which it is riskier to avoid than to face and overcome; and that is because it is a means to the preservation of the resister.

33. Now what we call the *laws of nature* are nothing other than certain conclusions, understood by reason, on what is to be done and not to be done; and a law, properly and precisely speaking, is an utterance by one who by right commands others to do or not to do. Hence, properly speaking, the natural laws are not laws, in so far as they proceed from nature. But in so far as the same laws have been legislated by God in the holy scriptures, as we shall see in the next chapter, they are very properly called by the name of laws; for

---

[7] Reading *in eo* for Warrender's *in ea*.

holy scripture is the utterance of God, who issues commands in all things with the highest right.

Chapter IV
That the natural law is the divine law

[1. The natural and moral law is the divine law. 2. This general point confirmed from scripture. 3. In particular, with regard to the fundamental law of nature, on seeking peace. 4. And to the first natural law, on the abolition of the common ownership of all things. 5. And to the second natural law, on keeping faith. 6. And to the third natural law, on gratitude. 7. And to the fourth natural law, on being considerate. 8. And to the fifth natural law, on pity. 9. And to the sixth natural law, that punishment regards only the future. 10. And to the seventh law of nature, against insult. 11. And to the eighth natural law, against Pride. 12. And to the ninth natural law, on modesty. 13. And to the tenth natural law, against discrimination. 14. And to the eleventh natural law, on having things in common which cannot be divided. 15. And to the twelfth natural law, on dividing things by lot. 16. And to the fifteenth natural law, on appointing an arbitrator. 17. And to the seventeenth natural law, that Arbitrators should not accept a reward for their verdict. 18. And to the eighteenth natural law, on Witnesses. 19. And to the twentieth natural law, against Drunkenness. 20. And with respect to our statement, that the law of nature is eternal. 21. And that the Laws of nature are a matter of conscience. 22. And that the laws of nature are easy to observe. 23. And with respect to the rule by which it can be instantly ascertained whether something is against the law of nature or not. 24. The law of Christ is the law of nature.][1]

1. The *Moral* and *Natural* law is normally also called the *Divine law*. And that is right, for two reasons: because *reason*, which is the *law of nature* itself, has been given to each and every man directly by God as a Rule for his actions; and because the precepts for living derived from it are the same as the precepts which have been promulgated by God's own Majesty as the *laws of the Kingdom of heaven* through our Lord *Jesus Christ* and the holy *Prophets* and *Apostles*. So we shall attempt in this chapter to confirm from holy

---

[1] The table of subtitles for this chapter is absent from all early editions. It was compiled by Warrender (1983), p. 121, from the marginal subtitles in the second (1647) edition.

scripture the understanding of *natural law* which we arrived at above by process of reasoning.

2. In the first place we shall point to the passages which declare that the divine law lies in right reason. Psalm. 36.30–1: *The mouth of the just shall meditate wisdom, and his tongue shall speak justice, the law of God shall be in his heart.* Jerem. 31.33: *I will give my law in their entrails, and will write it in their heart.* Psal. 18.8: *The law of the Lord is immaculate converting the soul,* v. 9. *The Lord's precept is lucid, enlightening the eyes.* Deut. 30.11: *This command which I give you this day is not above you nor is it set far away, etc.,* v. 14: *But the word is very close to you, in your mouth and in your heart.* Psalm. 118.34: *Give me understanding and I will explore your law,*[2] v. 105: *Your word is a lamp to my feet, and a light to my paths.* Prov. 9.10: *The knowledge of the holy is prudence.* At John 1.1 the legislator himself, who is *Christ*, is called λόγος. At verse 9 *Christ* is called *the true light that illuminates every man that comes into this world.* All these are descriptions of *right reason,* and it has been shown before that *the natural laws* are its dictates.

3. Next it will be clear from the following passages that the law which we have laid down as *the fundamental law of nature,* namely, *the pursuit of peace,* is also the sum of the divine law. Rom. 3.17: *Justice* (which is the sum of the law) is called *the way of peace.* Psalm. 84.11: *Justice and Peace have kissed.* Math. 5.9: *Blessed are the peacemakers, for they shall be called the children of God.* And after St Paul has said in the last verse of chapter 6 of the Letter to the Hebrews that *Christ* (the legislator of the law under discussion) is *a Priest for ever after the order of Melchisedech,* he adds in the first verse of the following chapter, *This Melchisedech was the King of Salem a Priest of the most high God,* etc., and in verse 2: *He is interpreted first as the King of justice, and then as King of Salem, which is King of peace.* From which it is settled that *Christ the King* couples *justice* with *peace* in his kingdom. Psal. 33.15: *Turn away from evil and do good, seek peace and pursue it.* Isaiah 9.6-7: *For a child has been born to us, and a child has been given to us; and a princedom has been set upon his shoulder, and his name shall be called, Wonderful, Counsellor; the mighty God; the Father of the age to come; the Prince*

---

[2] Throughout this chapter, and normally elsewhere, Hobbes gives scriptural references and text from the Vulgate rather than the King James version.

of Peace. Isaiah 52.7: *How beautiful over the mountains are the feet of the one who preaches, who brings a message of peace, who brings a message of good, who preaches security [salus], saying to Zion, Your God shall reign*. At Luke 2.14, at the birth of *Christ* a voice of those praising God and saying, *glory to God in the highest, and on earth Peace to men of good will*.[3] And at Isaiah 53.6 the Gospel is called, *the discipline of peace*.[4] At Isaiah 59.8 *justice* is called the way of peace. *They have not known the way of peace and there is no justice in their steps*. Micah 5.5, speaking of the *Messiah*, says thus: *He shall stand and feed in the strength of the Lord etc., because he shall be magnified even to the ends of the earth, and he shall be peace*. Prov. 3.1: *My son, do not forget my law; and let your heart keep my precepts; for they will bring you length of days, and years of life, and peace*.

4. As for the first law on the *abolition of common ownership of all things*, or the introduction of *Mine* and *Thine*, we have first the words of *Abraham* to *Lot* how inimical such common ownership is to peace, Gen. 13.8: *Let there not be, I beg you, a quarrel between me and thee and between my shepherds and your shepherds. Look, the whole world is before you, leave me, I beg you*. And the law on the distinction between *what is Ours* and *what is Another's* is confirmed by all the passages of holy Scripture which forbid encroachment on what is another's, e.g. *thou shalt not kill, thou shalt not steal, thou shalt not commit adultery*. For they all presuppose that *the right of all men to all things has been abolished*.

5. The same precept confirms the second natural law, on keeping faith. For what else is, *You shall not encroach on another's* but *You shall not encroach on that which has ceased to be yours by your own agreement*. And explicitly at Psalm. 14, v 5, to the question, *Lord who shall live in your tabernacle?* the response is *he who swears to his neighbour and does not deceive him*. And Proverb. 6.1: *My son, if you have made a promise on behalf of a friend, you are hung by the words of your own mouth*.

6. The following passages give expression to the third *law*, on gratitude. Deut. 25.4: *You shall not muzzle a threshing ox*. St. Paul

---

[3] The insertion of a comma between *hominibus* and *bonae voluntatis* seems to be an error.

[4] Warrender notes that Hobbes does not here give the Vulgate reference (which is 53.5).

at 1 Cor. 9.9 interprets this as spoken of men and not merely of cattle. Prov. 17.13: *Evil will not leave the house of the man who returns evil for good.* And Deut. 20.10-11: *when you approach a city to storm it, first offer it peace: if it accepts it, and opens its gates to you, the whole people which is in it shall be saved, and shall serve you as tribute.* Prov. 3.29: *Do not work evil against your friend since he has confidence in you.*

7. The following passages are consistent with the fourth law, *on being considerate*: Exod. 23.4–5: *If you meet your enemy's ox or ass straying, take it back to him. If you see the ass of someone who hates you collapsed under its load, you shall not pass by but shall help him to get it up;* v. 9: *You shall not harass a foreigner.* Prov. 3.30: *Do not fight a man for no reason, when he has done you no harm.* Prov. 12.26: *He who overlooks a loss for a friend, is just.* Prov. 15.18: *the irritable man provokes quarrels, the patient man moderates them.* Prov. 18.24: *a man who loves society will be more of a friend than a brother is.* This is confirmed by the parable in Luke 10 of the Samaritan who took pity on the Jew wounded by robbers. And by the precept of *Christ* at Matth. 5.39: *But I say to you, Do not resist evil, but if someone strikes you on the right cheek, offer him the other one also.*

8. The following are among the innumerable passages which support the fifth law: Matth. 6.15: *For if you forgive men their sins, your heavenly father will forgive your sins also; but if you do not forgive men, neither will your heavenly father forgive you your sins,* etc. Matth. 18.21: *Lord, how many times shall my brother sin against me and I shall forgive him? as much as seven times?* Jesus says to him, *I do not say to you as much as seven times but as much as seventy times seven,* i.e. every time.

9. Relevant to the confirmation of the sixth law are all the passages which enjoin mercy, such as Matth. 5.7: *Blessed are the merciful, for they shall obtain mercy themselves.* Levitic. 19.18: *Do not seek vengeance, nor be mindful of a wrong done by a fellow citizen.* Some believe that this law is invalidated, not confirmed by scripture, because there is eternal punishment for the wicked after death, when there is no room either for reform or for deterrence. Some answer this objection by arguing that God is not bound by any law to make all things redound to his glory, but that man does not have the same licence. As if God sought glory, i.e. his own pleasure, in

the death of a sinner! A better response would be that eternal punishment was introduced before sin, and its only purpose was that men should fear to sin in the future.

10. Law 7 is confirmed by Christ's words at Matth. 5.22: *But I say to you, that everyone who is angry with his brother will be liable to judgement; he who says, Fool! will be liable to the fire of Gehenna.* Prov. 10.18: *He who utters an insult is a fool.* Prov. 14.21: *He who despises his neighbour sins,* 15.1: *Harsh words arouse anger,* 12.10: *Throw out the mocker, and conflict will go out with him, quarrels and insults will cease.*[5]

11. Law 8, on acknowledging natural equality, i.e. on *humility*, is confirmed by these passages: Math. 5.3: *Blessed are the poor in spirit, since the kingdom of heaven is theirs.* Prov. 6.16-19: *There are six things which the Lord hates and a seventh his soul detests, haughty eyes,* etc. Prov. 16.5: *Every arrogant man is an abomination to the Lord: even if hand shall be joined to hand, he is not innocent.* Prov. 11.2: *Where there is pride, there will also be insult; but where there is humility, there will also be wisdom.* Likewise Isai. 40.3 (*where the coming of* the Messiah is announced, in preparation for his kingdom) the voice of one crying thus in the wilderness: *Prepare the way of the Lord, make straight the paths of our Lord in the desert. Every valley shall be raised, and every mountain and hill made low,* – where assuredly the reference is to men, not mountains.

12. *Fairness* which we have given as the ninth *law of nature*, instructs every man to allow the same rights to others as he wishes to be allowed himself; it encompasses all the other laws within itself. It is the same law as is laid down by Moses at Lev. 19.18: *You shall love your friend as yourself.* Our *Saviour* too says that it is the sum of the *moral law* at Math. 22.36: *Master, what is the great command in the law? Jesus says to him: You shall love the Lord your God, etc. this is the first and greatest command, and the second is similar to it, You shall love your neighbour as yourself; the whole of the law depends upon these two commands, and so do the Prophets.* To love one's neighbour as oneself is nothing but granting him everything which we claim for ourselves.

13. Law 10 forbids *personal discrimination*, and so do the following passages. Math. 5.45: *That you may be sons of your father, who makes*

---

[5] The correct reference is 22.10.

his sun rise on the just and on the unjust. Coloss. 3.11: *There is not Gentile and Jew, Barbarian and Scyth, slave and free, but Christ is all things and in all.* Act. 10.34: *Truly I have seen that God does not discriminate against people.* 2. Par.[6] 19.7: *There is no iniquity in our God, nor discrimination against people.* Ecclesiastic. 35.16: *The Lord is the judge, there is no discrimination in him.* Rom. 2.11: *There is no discrimination of persons with God.*

14. I am not sure whether law 11 (which enjoins *the holding in common of what cannot be divided*) occurs in scripture in so many words. The practice however turns up everywhere in the common use of wells, ways, rivers, sacred objects, etc.; without it life would be impossible.

15. The *law of nature* which we have placed twelfth is that what cannot be divided or held in common must be awarded by lot. This finds support in the example of *Moses*, when on the instruction of God (Num. 34), he allotted the tribes portions of the promised land for their possession (*by lot*). Also in the example of the *Apostles* in Acts 1, when they made *Matthias* one of their number in preference to *Justus* by use of the *lot*: their introductory words were, *Show, Lord, whom you have chosen,* etc. The same follows from Prov. 16.33: *The lots are cast into the lap, but are controlled by the Lord.* And (law no.13) the succession would have gone to *Esau,* evidently as the first-born of *Isaac,* if he had not sold it (Gen. 25.30);[7] or unless his father decided otherwise.

16. St. Paul writing to the Corinthians (I Cor. 6) criticizes the Christians of that city because they were in dispute with each other in the law courts before unbelieving judges (their enemies). He says that it is a sin not rather to suffer wrong and be defrauded, for it is contrary to the law by which we are bidden to be helpful to each other. But what should one do if a dispute arises about essential matters? That is why the Apostle says at v.5, *I say it to your shame. Is there no one wise among you who can judge between his brothers?*[8] In these words he confirms the natural law which we have called no. 15, namely, where disputes cannot be avoided, an arbiter must be appointed by agreement of the parties, and he must be a third

---

[6] Paralipomena, the Vulgate title of the book called Chronicles in the King James Version.
[7] The correct reference is 25.33.
[8] Not printed as a question in Warrender's text.

person so that (law no. 16) neither of the litigants may be judge in his own case.

17. Exodus 23.8 agrees that a *judge* or *arbiter* should not accept a reward for his verdict (which is law 17), *You shall not accept gifts, which blind even the prudent, and subvert the words of the just*: and Ecclesiastic. 20.31: *Presents and gifts blind the eyes of judges.* It follows from this that he has no more obligation to one party than to the other; that is law no. 19, and is also confirmed by Deut. 1.17: *There shall be no distinction between persons, you shall hear the small and the great alike*; and by all the passages cited against discrimination.

18. Scripture not only confirms that one must bring witnesses to question of Fact (law no. 18), but requires several witnesses. Deut. 17.6: *he who is to be put to death shall die on the evidence of two or three witnesses* (repeated at Deut. 19.15).

19. We included drunkenness as the last of the violations of *natural Law* because it impedes the use of reason; holy scripture forbids it for the same reason. Prov. ch. 20. vers.1. *Wine is a wanton thing and Drunkenness a brawler; anyone who delights in them will not be wise*, and ch. 31. v. 4, 5. *Do not give wine to kings, in case they drink and forget judgements and pervert the cause of the children of the poor.* The wrongfulness of this vice consists formally not in the amount of wine drunk but in the fact that it weakens judgement and reason, as we may see from the next verse: *Give strong drink to the sorrowful, and wine to those who are bitter of heart. Let them drink and forget their need, and let them not remember their grief any more.* Christ gives the same reason in forbidding *Drunkenness* at Luke ch. 21. v.34. *But watch yourselves lest by chance your hearts be heavy with intoxication and Drunkenness.*

20. Our assertion in the last chapter that the law of nature is eternal is confirmed by Matth. 5.18: *Amen I say to you that until heaven and earth pass away, not one iota, not one dot, shall perish from the law*, and by Psal. 118. vers.160: *All the judgements of your justice are for ever.*

21. We also said that *the laws of nature* are a matter of *conscience*, i.e. *the just man* is the man who makes every effort to fulfil them. If one does all the actions that the law commands (showing external obedience), but does not do them for the sake of the law but of the penalty attached or for glory, one is still *unjust*. Both points are confirmed by holy scripture. First, Isaiah 55.7: *Let the impious man*

leave his way and the wicked man his thoughts, and let him return to the Lord, and he will have pity on him. Ezech. 18.31: *Cast from you all your prevarications in which you have prevaricated, and make your heart new, and why shall you die, house of Israel?* From these and similar passages one may see clearly that God will not punish the actions of men whose heart is right. Second, from Isaiah ch. 29, verse 13: *And the Lord said, because this people approaches me with their mouth and glorifies me with their lips, but their heart is far from me, therefore, behold, I will add*, etc. Math. 5.20: *For I say to you, unless your justice flows more abundantly than that of the Scribes and the Pharisees, you will not enter into the kingdom of heaven.* And in the following verses our Saviour explains that the commands of God are violated not only by acting but also by willing. For the Scribes and Pharisees practised the closest possible observance of the law in their external acts, but only for the sake of glory, but for which they would have broken it. There are also innumerable passages elsewhere in holy scripture which assert with absolute clarity that God accepts willing for doing in good and bad actions alike.

22. *Christ* declares at Matth. 11.28–30 that the law of nature is easy to observe. *Come to me all you who labour, etc. take my yoke upon you and learn from me because I am gentle and humble in heart, and you shall find rest for your souls. For my yoke is easy and my burden is light.*

23. The rule which I said enables every man to see whether what he is about to do is contrary to the law of nature or not, namely, *Do not do to another what you do not want done to you*, is uttered in practically the same words by our saviour, Matth. 6.12: *All things therefore that you wish that men should do to you, do you also to them.*

24. The whole of *the law of nature* is *divine*, and *conversely*, the whole of *the law of Christ* (fully laid out in chapters 5–7 of Matthew) is nature's teaching. (The one exception is the command not to marry a woman divorced for adultery, which Christ used in explication of the divine positive law against the Jews who were interpreting *the law of Moses* incorrectly.) The whole of Christ's law, I said, is laid out in the chapters I have mentioned, not the whole of Christ's teaching. For *Faith* is a part of Christian teaching, and that is not encompassed in the term *law*. For laws are made about *actions* that follow our will, not about *beliefs* nor about *faith*, which being beyond our power, do not follow our will.

Government

Chapter V
On the causes and generation of a commonwealth

1. The natural laws *are not enough to preserve Peace. 2. The* laws
of nature *are silent in the* state of nature. *3. Security in living by
the laws of nature consists in concord between many men. 4.* Concord *between many men is not stable enough to ensure lasting Peace.
5. Why the government of some dumb animals consists in concord
alone, but not human government. 6. What is required for Peace
between men is not simply* accord *but also* union. *7. What* union
is. 8. In a union *the Right of all is transferred to* one. *9. What a*
commonwealth *is. 10. What a* civil person *is. 11. What it is to*
have sovereign power, *and what a* subject *is. 12. Two kinds of
commonwealth,* natural *and* by design.

1. It is self-evident that men's actions proceed from their wills and
their wills from their hopes and fears; hence they willingly break
the law, whenever it seems that *greater good* or *lesser evil* will come
to themselves from breaking it. Each man's hope therefore of security and preservation, lies in using his strength and skill to stay one
step ahead of his neighbour either openly or by stratagems. One
sees from this that *the natural laws* do not guarantee their own
observance as soon as they are known; consequently, as long as a
person has no guarantee of security from attack, his primeval *Right*
remains in force to look out for himself in whatever ways he will
and can, i.e. a *Right to all things*, or a *Right of war*; he will satisfy
the requirements of *natural law* if he is ready to welcome peace
when it can be had.

2. It is a commonplace that *laws are silent among arms.*[1] This is
true not only of the *civil laws* but also of *natural law*, if it is applied
(by ch. III, art. 27) to actions rather than to state of mind, and if the
war in question is understood to be the war of every man against
every man. Such is *the state of pure nature*, though in wars between
nations a degree of restraint has normally been observed. Thus in
early times there was a way of life, which was also a kind of trade,
which they called λησтρικὴν, *living by Plunder*; in those conditions
it was not against the law of nature, nor without glory if practised

---

[1] E.g. Cicero, *On Behalf of Milo*, 11.

with courage and without cruelty.[2] Though they would take anything else, their way was to spare life and not touch plough-oxen
and agricultural equipment. This should not be thought to imply
that they were restrained by the law of nature; their motive was to
win glory but not to get a reputation for terrorism by being too
cruel.

3. Thus the practice of *natural law* is necessary for the preservation of peace, and *security* is necessary for the practice of *natural
law*. We must therefore consider what it is that can afford such
security. The only conceivable recourse is that each man get for
himself sufficient aid to render any attack so mutually dangerous
that both parties will think it better to stay their hand than to start
fighting. And it is obvious in the first place that such security is not
furnished by an accord [*consensio*] between two or three persons; for
the accession of one or two of them to the enemy is enough to
assure him of a clear and certain victory, and gives him an incentive
to aggression. To obtain the security that we seek therefore, the
number who act together for mutual aid must be sufficiently large
that if a few of them go over to the enemy, that would not give him
an overwhelming advantage for victory.

4. Again, however many come together in a coalition for defence,
nothing will be gained if they fail to agree on the best way of doing
it, and each one uses his resources in his own fashion. The reason
is that, having conflicting ideas, they will obstruct each other, or if
in the expectation of victory or booty or revenge, they do achieve
sufficient agreement for an action, they will still be so divided afterwards by differences of purpose and policy or by envy and rivalry
(natural causes of conflict), that they will refuse to help each other
or to keep peace among themselves, unless compelled to do so by a
common fear. It follows from this that an *accord* [*consensio*] between
several parties, i.e. an association [*societas*] formed only for mutual
aid, does not afford to the parties to the accord or association the
security which we are looking for, to practise, in their relations with
each other, the *laws of nature* given above. (An *accord* of several
persons, as defined in the previous section,[3] consists only in their

---

[2] Cf. for example, Thucydides 1.5 that piracy was 'a matter at that time nowhere
in disgrace but rather carrying with it something of glory' (Hobbes's translation).
[3] A reference, surviving from the 1642 edition, to the previous 'section' of the
projected three-part work. See the introduction, pp. xii–xiv. Cf. IX.8.

all directing their actions to the same end and to a *common good*.) But something more is needed, an element of fear, to prevent an accord on peace and mutual assistance for a *common good* from collapsing in discord when a *private good* subsequently comes into conflict with the *common good*.

5. Among the animals which Aristotle calls political he counts not only *Man* but many others too, including the *Ant*, the *Bee*, etc.[4] For although they are devoid of reason, which would enable them to make agreements and submit to government [*regimen*], still by their consenting, i.e. by desiring and avoiding the same objects, they so direct their actions to a common end that their swarms are not disturbed by sedition. Yet their swarms are still not *commonwealths* [*civitates*], and so the animals themselves should not be called *political*; for their government is only an accord, or many wills with one object, not (as a commonwealth needs) one will. It is true that among creatures who live by sense and appetite alone, *accord* of feelings is so lasting that nothing but their natural appetite is needed to maintain it and thus to keep peace among them. But it is otherwise with men. In the first place, men compete for honour and dignity, animals do not; hence men experience *resentment* and *envy*, which are sources of sedition and war, but animals do not. Secondly, the natural appetites of bees and similar creatures are uniform, and make for the common good, which among them does not differ from private good; but for man virtually nothing is thought to be good which does not give its possessor some superiority and eminence above that enjoyed by other men. Thirdly, animals without reason neither see, nor believe they see, any defects in the conduct of their common affairs; but any group of men includes a large number who suppose themselves cleverer than the rest, and make attempts to change things, and they differ among themselves and try different things, and that is dissension and civil war. Fourthly, however well the animals may be able to use their voices to indicate their feelings to each other, they still do not have the art of words that is needed to arouse the passions, notably, to make the Good appear Better, and the Bad Worse than they really are. But man's tongue is a trumpet to war and sedition; and it is said that *Pericles* once made thunder and lightning in his speeches and threw all

---

[4] Aristotle, *Politics*, I, 2, 1253a7ff.

Greece into confusion.[5] Fifthly, animals do not distinguish *wrong* from *harm*. This is why they do not criticize their companions when they are doing well themselves. But the men who are the greatest nuisance to their country are those who are allowed the greatest leisure; for men do not usually compete for public office, until they have won the battle against hunger and cold. Finally, the accord of those brute creatures is natural; but accord between men is based merely on agreement, i.e. is artificial; it is not therefore surprising that something more is needed if men are to live in peace. No *accord*, therefore, or *association* [*societas*] based on agreement can give the security required for the practice of *natural justice*, without some common power to control individuals by instilling a fear of punishment.

6. Since therefore a *combination* of several wills in the same end is not adequate to the preservation of peace and stable defence, it is required that there be a *single will* [*una voluntas*] among all of them in matters essential to peace and defence. This can only happen if each man subjects his *will* to the *will* of a *single* other [*alterius unius*], to the *will*, that is, of one *Man* [*Hominis*] or of one *Assembly* [*Concilium*], in such a way that whatever one *wills* on matters essential to the common peace may be taken as the *will* of all and each [*omnes et singuli*]. By ASSEMBLY I mean a group [*coetus*] of several men deliberating about what is to be done or not to be done, for the common good of all.

7. This *submission* of all their wills to *the will of one man* or of *one Assembly* comes about, when each of them obligates himself, by an Agreement with each of the rest, not to resist the *will* of the *man* or *Assembly* to which he has submitted himself; that is, not to withhold the use of his wealth and strength against any other men than himself (for he is understood to retain the right of defending himself against violence). This is called UNION. The *will of an Assembly* is understood as the *will of the greater part* of the men who make up the assembly.

---

[5] Aristophanes, *Acharnians* 530–1 is the source of this characterization of the oratory of Pericles, which became traditional (e.g. Plutarch, *Parallel Lives*, 'Life of Pericles', 8). Pericles was the leading politician at Athens in the years leading up to the Peloponnesian War. In 1629 Hobbes published a translation of Thucydides' account of this war.

8. The *will* itself, it is true, is not voluntary, but only the starting point of voluntary actions (for we do not will to will but to *act*); hence it is not capable of deliberation and agreements. Nevertheless a man who subjects his *will* to the *will* of another transfers to that other the *Right to his strength and resources*, so that when others have done the same, the recipient of their submissions may be able to use the fear they inspire to bring the wills of individuals to unity and concord.

9. A Union so made is called a *commonwealth* [*civitas*] or *civil society* [*societas civilis*] and also a *civil person* [*persona civilis*]; for since there is *one will* of all of them, it is to be taken as *one person*; and is to be distinguished and differentiated by *a unique* name from all particular men, having its own rights and its own property [*res sibi proprias*]. Consequently, no single citizen nor all together (except him whose will stands for the will of all) are to be *regarded as the commonwealth*. A COMMONWEALTH, then, (to define it) is *one person*, whose *will*, by the agreement of several men, is to be taken as the *will* of them all; to make use of their strength and resources for the common peace and defence.

10. Although every *commonwealth* is a *civil person*, not every *civil person* (by converse) is a *commonwealth*. For it may happen that several persons will, with the permission of their commonwealth, unite as one person for the purpose of transacting certain business. These will now be *civil persons*, as companies of merchants are, and any number of other groups, but they are not *commonwealths*, because they have not subjected themselves to the will of the group simply and in all things, but only in certain matters defined by the commonwealth; and on terms which allow any one of them to sue *the Corporation itself* before outsiders; which a citizen may not do against a commonwealth. Associations [*societas*] of this kind then are *civil persons* subordinate to the *commonwealth*.

11. In every commonwealth, the *Man* or *Assembly* to whose will individuals have subjected their will (in the manner explained) is said to hold SOVEREIGN AUTHORITY [*SUMMAM POTESTATEM*] or SOV-EREIGN POWER [*SUMMUM IMPERIUM*] or DOMINION [*DOMINIUM*]. This *Authority* [*Potestas*], this *Right to give Commands* [*Jus imperandi*], consists in the fact that each of the citizens has transferred all his own force and power [*potentia*] to that *man* or *Assembly*. To

have done this simply means (since no one can literally transfer his force to another) that he has given up his right to resist. Each of the *citizens*, and every *subordinate civil person*, is called a SUBJECT of him who holds the *sovereign power*.

12. What has been said is an adequate demonstration how and by what stages, in the passion for self-preservation, *a number of natural persons* from fear of each other have coalesced into *one civil person* to which we have given the name of *commonwealth*. But those who subject themselves to another through fear either submit to the person they fear or submit to some other whom they trust for protection. Men defeated in war do the first to avoid being killed; the latter is the way the undefeated avoid defeat. The first mode has its beginning in *natural power*, and may be said to be the *natural origin* of the commonwealth; the latter originates in the *determination and decision* [*a consilio & constitutione*] of the uniting parties, and that is the *origin by design* [*origo ex instituto*]. Hence there are two kinds of *commonwealths*: one kind is *natural*, like the *Paternal* and *Despotic*; the other is the kind of commonwealth which is *by design* [*institutivum*], and which may also be called *political*. In the first case a *Lord* [*Dominus*] acquires *citizens* for himself by his own will; in the second, the *citizens* impose a *Lord* upon themselves by their own decision, whether that be *one man* or *one group* of men with *sovereign power* [*summum imperium*]. We shall speak first of the *commonwealth by design*, and then of the *natural commonwealth*.

Chapter VI

On the right of the Assembly or Man, who holds sovereign authority in the commonwealth

1. No Right can be attributed to a Crowd outside of a commonwealth, nor any action to which they have not individually consented. 2. The beginning of a commonwealth is the Right of a majority in agreement. 3. Each man retains the Right to defend himself at his own discretion, as long as his security is not provided for. 4. Coercive Authority *is necessary to security. 5. What the Sword of justice* is. 6. The *sword of justice* is in the hands of the holder of sovereign power. *7. The* sword of war *is in the same hands. 8.* Judgements *are in the same hands. 9.* Legislation *is in the same hands. 10. The appointment of the* Magistrates and Ministers *of the commonwealth is in the same hands. 11.* Examination of doctrines *is in the same hands. 12. He has* immunity *in whatever he does. 13. The citizens* have granted him absolute power; the extent of obedience due to him. *14. He is* not bound by the laws *of the commonwealth. 15. No one has a right to property against the holder of* sovereign power. *16. One ascertains from the civil laws what* theft, murder, adultery & wrong *are. 17. The opinion of those who would establish a commonwealth in which there would be no one with* absolute power. *18. Marks of* sovereign Power. *19. If a comparison is made between a* commonwealth and a *man, the holder of* sovereign Power *is to the commonwealth as the human soul is to the man himself. 20. A* Sovereign Power *cannot rightly be dissolved by the agreement of those whose agreement established it.*

1. The first and crucial question is this: what actually is a *Crowd* (*Multitudo*)[1] (*) of men (who unite by their own decision in a single commonwealth)? For they are not a *single entity* but a number of men, each of whom has his own will and his own judgement about every proposal. Although each man has his own *right* and *property* by particular contracts, so that one man may say of *one thing* and another of *another thing* that it is his own, there will be nothing about which the whole crowd, as a *person* distinct from every individual, can rightly say, this is *mine* more than *another's*. Nor is there

---

[1] Normally translated 'multitude'.

any action which should be attributed to the crowd as *their action*; but (if all or several of them reach an agreement) it will not be one action but as many actions as there are men. For despite the fact that it is commonly said of some great rebellion that the *people* of the commonwealth has taken up arms, it is only true of those who have actually taken up arms or are in league with them. For a *commonwealth* which is *one person* cannot take up arms against itself. So whatever is done by a crowd must be understood as being done by each of those who make up that crowd. And someone who is in that crowd but has not approved or supported what has been done must be regarded as not having done it. Moreover, in a crowd which has not yet coalesced into one person in the way we have described, the *state of nature* persists, in which *all things belong to all men*. *Mine* and *Yours* (whose names are *dominion* and *property*) have no place there, because there is as yet none of that security which we showed above was a prerequisite of the practice of the *natural laws*.

Crowd [*Multitudo*], etc.] *The doctrine of the authority of the Commonwealth over the citizens depends almost wholly on a recognition of the difference between a crowd of men ruling and a crowd being ruled. For the nature of a commonwealth is that a crowd of citizens both exercises power and is subject to power, but in different senses. I thought I had given a good account of the difference in this first section. But I see from the objections many have brought against the sections which follow, that this is not so. So I have decided to add a few words to give a fuller explanation.*

Because crowd is a collective word, it is understood to signify more than one object, so that a crowd of men is the same as many men. Because the word is grammatically singular, it also signifies one thing, namely a crowd. Neither way of taking it implies that a crowd has one will given by nature, but that each man has his own will. And therefore one must not attribute to it a single action [una actio] of any kind. Hence a crowd cannot make a promise or an agreement, acquire or transfer a right, do, have, possess, and so on, except separately or as individuals, so that there are as many promises, agreements, rights, and actions, as there are men. For this reason a crowd is not a natural person. But if the same crowd individually agree that the will of some one man or the consenting wills of a majority of themselves is to be taken as the will of [them] all, that number then becomes one person; for it is endowed with a will, and can therefore perform voluntary actions, such as command, make laws, acquire and transfer a right, etc., and is more often called a people than a number. A distinction must therefore be made. Whenever we say that a People or a number [of men] is willing, commanding or doing something, we mean a commonwealth which is commanding, willing and acting through the will of one man or through the wills of several men who are in agreement; and this can only happen in a meeting [conventus]. *But whenever something is said to be done by a number of men, great or small, without the will of that man or meeting, it means that it was done by a people as subjects, that is, by many individual citizens at the same time, and that it does not spring from one will but from the several wills of several men, who are citizens and subjects but not a commonwealth.*

2. The next point to consider is this: if the move towards formation of a commonwealth is to get started, each member of a crowd must agree with the others that on any issue anyone brings forward in the group, the wish of the majority shall be taken as the will of all; for otherwise, a crowd will never have any will at all, since their attitudes and aspirations differ so markedly from one another. If anyone refuses consent, the rest will notwithstanding form a commonwealth without him. That is why the commonwealth retains its original Right against the dissenter, i.e. the *right of war*, as against an enemy.

3. We said in article 6 of the previous chapter that men's security requires not only accord [*consensio*] but also subjection of wills in matters essential to peace and defence; and that the nature of a *commonwealth* consists in that *union* or *subjection*. We must now see which of the many things proposed, discussed and decided in a group of men (all of whose wills are contained in the will of the majority) are necessary to peace and the common defence. First of all it is essential to peace that each man be adequately protected from the violence of other men, so that he may live in security, i.e. so that he may not have reasonable cause to fear other men as long as he refrains from wronging them. It is in fact impossible to secure people from harm from each other, so that they cannot be wrongly hurt or killed; and so this is not for discussion. But one can provide that there will be no reasonable ground for fear. Security is the End for which men subject themselves to others, and if it is not

forthcoming, the implication is that no one has subjected himself to others, or lost the right to defend himself as he thinks best. People are assumed not to have bound themselves to anything or to have given up their right to all things until arrangements have been made for their security.

4. This security cannot be achieved merely by each of those who are uniting in a commonwealth making an agreement with others, verbally or in writing, *not to kill, not to steal*, etc., and to observe other laws of this kind. The wickedness of human character is evident to all, and experience shows only too well how poorly the mere awareness of a promise made without threat of a penalty holds a man to his duty. Hence security is to be assured not by *agreements* but by *penalties*; and the assurance is adequate only when the penalties for particular wrongs have been set so high that the consequences of doing them are manifestly worse than of not doing them. For by necessity of nature all men choose what is apparently good for themselves.

5. The right of punishment is recognized to have been given to someone, when each one agrees that he will not go to the help of anyone who is to be punished. I will call this *Right the Sword of justice*. Men generally keep this kind of agreement well enough, except when they or those close to them are to be punished.

6. Thus the security of individuals, and consequently the common peace, *necessarily* require that the *right* of using the *sword* to punish be transferred to some man or some assembly; that man or that assembly therefore is necessarily understood to hold *sovereign power* [*summum imperium*] in the commonwealth by right. For whoever has the right [*jure*] to inflict penalties at his discretion, has the right to compel anyone to do anything he wants. No greater power can be imagined.

7. It is useless for men to keep peace amongst themselves, if they cannot protect themselves against outsiders; and it is impossible to defend themselves if their strength is not united. It is therefore *necessary* to the preservation of individuals that there be some *one Assembly* or *one man* who has the right to arm, muster and unite, on each occasion of danger or opportunity, as many citizens as the common defence shall require, taking into account uncertainty[2]

---

[2] *Pro incerto numero*. The English translation of 1651 appears to be reading *certo* for *incerto*.

about the number and strength of the enemy; as well as the right to make peace with the enemy when advantageous. It must therefore be recognized that the individual citizens have transferred the whole of this *Right of war and peace* to one *man* or *assembly*. And this right (which we may call the *Sword of war*) belongs to the same *man* or *assembly* as the *Sword of justice*. For the only one who can rightly compel the citizens to arms and the expenses of war is the one who has the right to punish anyone who disobeys. Both swords, therefore, the *Sword of war* and the *Sword of justice* are inherent in sovereign power, essentially and from the very nature of a commonwealth.

8. Since the *right of the sword* is simply the right of its holder to use the sword at his own discretion, it follows that he must also have the right to *decide* or make a *judgement* on its proper use. For if *power to judge* were in one man's hands and power of execution in another's, nothing would be done; his judgements would have no effect, because he would not be able to have his commands carried out; or if he has them carried out by the other man's right [*ius*], then the other is said to have the *right of the sword*, not himself; he becomes the other's minister. All *judgement*, therefore, in a commonwealth belongs to the possessor of the swords, i.e. to the holder of sovereign power.

9. Further, it is no less, in fact much more, conducive to peace to prevent quarrels arising than to settle them afterwards; and all disputes arise from the fact that men's opinions differ about *mine* and *yours*, *just* and *unjust*, *useful* and *useless*, *good* and *bad*, *honourable* and *dishonourable*, and so on, and everyone decides them by his own judgement. Consequently, it is the responsibility of the same *Sovereign power* to come up with rules or measures that will be common to all, and to publish them openly, so that each man may know by them what he should call *his own* and what *another's*, what he should call *just* and *unjust*, *honourable* and *dishonourable*, *good* and *bad*; in summary, what he should *do* and what he should *avoid doing* in social life. These rules or measures are normally called the *civil laws* or *laws of the commonwealth* because they are the *commands* of the holder of *sovereign power* in the commonwealth. And CIVIL LAWS (to define them) are nothing other than commands about the citizens' future actions from the one who is endowed with *sovereign authority* [*summa potestas*].

10. Now it is impossible for all the business of *war* and *peace*, to be handled by *one man or one assembly* without *ministers* and *subordinate officials* [*magistratus*]. And it is important for peace and defence that those who have the responsibility to give just judgements of disputes, to detect the Designs of neighbouring states, to conduct wars prudently and to look out for the commonwealth's interests all around, should perform their duties properly. It is therefore compatible with reason that they should owe their offices and appointments to the holder of *sovereign power* in *war* and in *Peace*.

11. It is also evident that all voluntary actions have a beginning and necessarily depend on the will, and the will to do or not to do depends on the opinion [*opinio*] each man has formed of the *good* or *evil*, *reward* or *penalty* to follow from doing or not doing the thing; so that every man's actions are governed by his opinions. The conclusion therefore follows, by necessary and evident inference, that it is utterly essential to the common peace that certain opinions or doctrines not be put before the citizens. These are opinions or doctrines which would encourage them to believe: that they cannot rightly obey the *laws* of the commonwealth, i.e. the commands of the *man* or *assembly* to whom the *sovereign power* of the commonwealth has been committed; or that it is licit to resist the sovereign; or that they must expect a greater penalty for refusing than for giving obedience.[3] For if one sovereign commands him to do something under penalty of natural death, and another forbids it under pain of eternal death, and both have right on their sides, it follows not only that innocent citizens may rightly be punished, but that the commonwealth is radically undermined. For no one can serve two masters, and the one to whom we believe that obedience is due, under fear of damnation, is no less a Master than the one to whom obedience is due through fear of temporal death, but rather more. It follows therefore that the one man or *council* [*curia*] to whom *sovereign power* has been committed by the commonwealth, also has the right (*) both to decide which opinions and doctrines are inimical to peace and to forbid their being taught.

Also has the right both to, etc.] *There is virtually no dogma either in religion or the human sciences, from which disagreements may not arise*

---

[3] The last clause seems to say the opposite of what the logic of the passage requires. Perhaps *minorem poenam* should be read for *maiorem poenam*.

and from them conflicts, quarrelling and eventually, war. This is not because the dogma is false, but because of human nature: men want to believe themselves wise and appear so to others. One cannot prevent such disagreements from occurring. However, by the use of sovereign power they can be kept from interfering with the public peace. That is why I have not spoken of opinions of that kind in this passage. There are certain doctrines which lead citizens imbued with them to the belief that they have the right and the duty to refuse obedience to the common-wealth, and to struggle against sovereign Princes and sovereign authorit-ies. Such for instance are the doctrines which, directly and openly or more covertly and by implication, require obedience to other men than those who have been given sovereign power. I do not conceal that this applies to the authority in foreign countries which many attribute to the Head of the Roman Church, and also to the power which bishops else-where, outside the Roman Church, demand for themselves in their own commonwealth, and finally to the liberty which even the lowest citizens claim for themselves on the pretext of religion. What war ever broke out in the Christian world that did not spring from this root or was fed by it? I therefore assign to the civil power the judgement of doctrines as to whether they are in conflict with civil obedience or not, and if they are in conflict, the authority to prevent them being taught. For since no one would refuse to grant the commonwealth the judgement of things perti-nent to the peace and defence of the commonwealth, and since it is obvious that the sort of opinions I have listed, are pertinent to the peace of the commonwealth, it necessarily follows that the examination of opi-nions as to whether they are in this category or not, should be referred to the commonwealth, i.e. to the holder of sovereign power in the Com-monwealth.

12. Finally, from the fact that each one of the citizens has subjected his will to the will of the holder of *sovereign power* in the common-wealth in such a way that he cannot use his own strength against him, it clearly follows that no action on the part of the sovereign is liable to punishment. For as by nature no one can punish him if he does not have enough strength to do it, so by right no one can punish him, if he does not have the strength by right to do so.

13. From what has been said it is perfectly clear that in every complete commonwealth (i.e. a commonwealth in which no citizen has the *Right* to use his strength at his own discretion to protect

himself, or in which the *right of the private sword* is excluded), there is somewhere a sovereign power, the greatest power that men can confer, greater than any power that an individual can have over himself. The greatest power that men can transfer to a man we call (*) ABSOLUTE power. For anyone who has subjected his will to the will of the commonwealth on the terms that it may *do with impunity* whatever it chooses – *make laws, judge disputes, inflict penalties*, and make use of everyone's *strength and wealth* at its own discretion – and may do all this by right, has surely given him the greatest power that he could give. The same conclusion can be reached from experience of all commonwealths that exist or ever have existed. For although there may sometimes be a doubt as to *which man* or *which assembly* holds *sovereign power* in a commonwealth, such a power always exists and is exercised, except in times of sedition and civil war; at those times the one *sovereign power* becomes two. But the efforts of seditious men who like to argue against absolute power are directed not so much to abolish it as to transfer it to others. For if this power is abolished, the commonwealth is abolished with it, and universal confusion returns. To absolute right on the part of the sovereign ruler corresponds so much obedience on the part of the citizens as is essential to the government of the commonwealth, that is, so much as not to frustrate the grant of that right. Though such obedience may sometimes rightly be refused for various reasons, we shall call it SIMPLE obedience, because it is the greatest obedience that can be given. The obligation to offer it does not arise directly from the agreement by which we transferred every right to the commonwealth, but indirectly, i.e. from the fact that the right of Government [*Imperium*] would be meaningless without obedience, and consequently no commonwealth would have been formed at all. For it is one thing to say, *I give you the right to command whatever you wish*, another to say, *I will do whatever you command.*[4] There are commands that I would rather be killed than perform. Since no one can be obliged to want to be killed, much less is he obliged to do something worse than death. Hence if I am told to kill myself, I have no obligation to do so. For if I refuse, the right of government is not frustrated, since others may be found who will not refuse to carry out the order, and I am not refusing to do any-

---

[4] Italics supplied by the translator.

thing I have agreed to do. Likewise if someone is given order by the sovereign to kill him (i.e. to kill the sovereign), he is not obliged to do so, because he cannot be taken to have agreed to this. Nor is he obliged to kill a parent, whether innocent or guilty and rightly condemned; since there are others who will do it, if ordered to do so, and a son may prefer to die rather than live in infamy and loathing. There are many other cases in which commands are dishonourable for some people to carry out but not for others; the former are right to refuse to do them but not the latter; and this will be without prejudice to the absolute right given to the ruler. For in no case is his right of killing those who refuse obedience excluded. But those who do kill in such circumstances are offending against the natural laws, i.e. against God, because although the right to do so has been given them by one who has that right, nevertheless they are using it contrary to the requirements of right reason.

ABSOLUTE] *A popular state* [status popularis] *obviously requires absolute power, and the citizens do not object. For even the politically unaware see the face of the commonwealth in the popular assembly and recognize that affairs are being managed by its deliberations. A Monarchy is no less a commonwealth than a Democracy, and absolute Kings have their Counsellors, by whom they wish to be advised and to have their commands in all important matters reviewed, though not revoked. But to most people it is less obvious that the commonwealth is contained in the person of the King. Their first objection, therefore, to absolute power is that if anyone had such a right, the citizens' condition would be miserable. For – they think – he will seize, rob and kill, and everyone believes that it will be his turn next. But why would he do it? Not because he can; for he will only do it if he wants to. Does he then want to rob all the others to favour one or a few? First, although he may do so rightly, i.e. without inflicting a wrong on himself, he will not do so justly, that is, without violating natural laws and wronging God. Hence a Prince's oath offers a certain security to his subjects. Then again, if he could do it justly, or if he ignored his oath, there is no reason why he would want to spoil his citizens, since that is not to his advantage. One cannot deny that a prince sometimes may have a mind to act wickedly. But suppose you had not given him absolute power but enough power to defend you from injury by others, which you must do if you wish for your own security, do you not still have all the same things to fear? For he who has enough strength to protect everybody, has enough to oppress everybody. There is no hardship here, beyond the fact that human affairs can never be without some inconvenience. And this inconvenience itself arises from the citizens, not from the power of government. For if men could rule themselves by individual self-government, that is, if they could live according to the natural laws, there would be absolutely no need of a commonwealth nor to be kept in check by a common power.*

Their second objection is that there is no absolute Power in the Christian world. This is certainly not true. All Monarchies and all other kinds [status] of commonwealth are absolute. For although holders of sovereign power do not do everything they wish to do and which they know is useful to the commonwealth, the reason for this is not lack of right but cognizance of the citizens, who can sometimes not be made to do their duty without danger to the commonwealth, because they are intent on their private concerns and ignorant of public affairs. Hence Princes sometimes refrain from exercising a right, and prudently give up something de facto, *while yielding nothing of their right.*

14. No one can give anything to himself, because he is already assumed to have what he can give to himself. Nor can one be obligated to oneself; for since *the obligated and the obligating party* would be the same, and the obligating party may release the obligated, obligation to oneself would be meaningless, because he can release himself at his own discretion, and anyone who can do this is in fact free. Hence the conclusion that the commonwealth itself is not obligated by the *civil laws*; for the civil laws are the laws of a commonwealth, and if it were obligated by them, it would be obligated to itself. Nor can a commonwealth be obligated to a citizen; for since he can release it from its obligation, if he so wishes, and does so wish whenever the commonwealth so wishes (since the will of each citizen is comprehended in the will of the commonwealth in all matters), the commonwealth is free whenever it so wishes: it is, in fact, free. The will of the *assembly* or the *man* to whom *sovereign power* has been committed is the will of the commonwealth; hence it comprehends the wills of individual citizens; and therefore one to whom *sovereign power* has been committed is not bound by the *civil laws* (which is an obligation to himself) nor obligated to any of the citizens.

15. We have shown above that until a commonwealth is instituted, *all things belong to all men* and there is nothing a man can call *his own* that any other man cannot claim by the same right as *his* (for where all things are *common*, nothing can be the *proper* to any one man); it follows from this that *property* and commonwealths came into being together (*), and a person's property is what he can keep for himself by means of the laws and the power of the whole commonwealth, i.e. by means of the one on whom its *sovereign power* has been conferred. This implies that individual citizens hold *their property*, over which none of their fellow citizens has any right, because they are bound by the same laws; but he does not hold any property on such terms that the holder of sovereign power has no right over it, since his commands are the laws themselves, his will comprehends the will of individuals, and individuals have appointed him their sovereign judge. There are indeed many things permitted to citizens by the commonwealth, and legal action may sometimes be taken against the holder of *sovereign power*; but such action is not a matter of *civil law* but of *natural equity*; and the question is not (*) what the holder of *sovereign power may* rightly do, but what he *willed*; hence he himself will be the judge, as if he could not give an unfair judgement, when equity is taken into account.

Property and commonwealths came into being together, etc.] *The objection sometimes made that property in things existed in fathers of families before the institution of commonwealths, fails, because I have already said that the family is a small commonwealth. For sons of the family hold their property as a concession from their father; it is distinct from the property of other sons of the family, but not from the father's. Fathers of different families, who share no common father or master, have a common right to all things.*

And the question is not what the holder of sovereign power may rightly do etc.] *Whenever a citizen is given a legal action against the Sovereign, i.e. against the commonwealth, the question of the action is not whether the commonwealth may rightly possess the thing which is the object of the action, but whether in its existing laws it has willed to possess it. For law is the declared will of the Sovereign. The commonwealth can exact money from the citizen on two grounds, namely as a tax or as a debt. In the former case, no legal action is given because it cannot be contested that the commonwealth has the right to exact taxes. In the second case an action is given, and the reason is that the commonwealth does not want to take anything from the citizen in underhanded ways, and yet is willing to take everything from him in an open fashion. Hence the facile criticism that on the basis of this doctrine princes could release themselves from the obligation of debts, misses the point.*

16. *Theft, Murder, Adultery* and all *wrongs* [*injuriae*] are forbidden by the laws of nature, but what is to count as a *theft* on the part of a citizen or as *murder* or *adultery* or a *wrongful act* is to be determined by the *civil*, not the *natural, law*. Not every taking of an object which is in the possession of another is a *theft*, but only the taking of something *that belongs to another*; what counts as *ours*, what as *another's* is a question for the *civil law*. Similarly, not every killing of a man is *Murder*, but only the killing of someone whom the *civil law* forbids us to kill; and not every act of intercourse is *adultery*, but only what the *civil laws* forbid. Finally, the breaking of a promise is a *wrong*, when the promise itself is legitimate; but where there is no *right* to make an agreement, no *right* passes; hence no *wrong* follows, as was said in II.17. What we may make agreements about and what we may not, also depends on the *civil law*. The commonwealth of the *Lacedaemonians* was therefore right to decree that young men who took certain things from others without being caught, would not be punished. For that was simply to make a law that anything so acquired *belonged to them* not to *the other*. Similarly, it is everywhere right to kill anyone in war from the need to defend yourself. Likewise a relationship which in one commonwealth is *marriage* will be considered *adultery* in another and vice versa. And again, agreements which constitute *marriage* for one citizen do not have the same effect for another even in the same commonwealth; the reason is that anyone who is forbidden to make any kind of agreement by the commonwealth (that is, by the *Man* or *Assembly* which holds *sovereign Power*) does not have the right to make agreements, hence his agreement is not valid; no *marriage* therefore occurs. But an agreement made by anyone who is not forbidden to do so is valid, and is a *marriage*. The addition of an oath (*) or Sacrament does not give validity to an illicit agreement, for it adds nothing to the strength of the agreement, as we said above at II.22. Thus one learns what *Theft* is, what *Murder* is and *Adultery*, and

generally what a *wrong* is, from the *civil law*, that is from the commands of the holder in that commonwealth of *sovereign power*.

The addition of an oath or Sacrament etc.] *Whether Marriage is a Sacrament or not (in the sense of the word used by Theologians) is beyond my scope to discuss here. I say only that a legal contract (i.e. a contract permitted by civil law) between a man and a woman to live together is certainly a legal marriage, whether it is a Sacrament or not. But a kind of cohabitation forbidden by the commonwealth or cohabitation between forbidden partners is not a marriage, because it is of the essence of marriage to be a legal contract. There have been marriages in many places, as among the Jews, the Greeks and the Romans, which were legal despite the fact that they could be dissolved. But among those who do not allow such contracts except on condition of indissolubility, a marriage cannot be dissolved; and the reason is that the commonwealth has forbidden it to be dissoluble, not because marriage is a Sacrament. Hence it will perhaps be the responsibility of the Clergy alone to perform the wedding ceremonies which have to be carried out in the Church* [Templum], *and to bless the couple, or consecrate them if that is what it should be called. Everything else, namely, who, when, and by what agreements marriages are made, is a matter for the laws of the commonwealth.*

17. To most men this *sovereignty* and *absolute power* [*potentia*] seems so harsh that they hate the very name of it. This is mostly due to ignorance of *human nature* and of the *natural laws*, but is also partly the fault of those who misuse their authority for their own greed when they are appointed to such a position of power. To avoid a sovereign power of this kind, some take the view that their commonwealth is well formed, if its future citizens, as they unite, agree upon certain articles which have been proposed, discussed in the group and approved; and they require observance of the articles and prescribed penalties for violators. For this purpose, and to repel external enemies, they authorize a fixed and limited revenue on the understanding that if it is insufficient, one must go back to a new meeting of the group. Who does not see that in a commonwealth so organized, the group which gave these instructions had *absolute power*? If then the *group* remains in being, or holds meetings from time to time on set days at set places, its *power* will be continuous.

But if they dissolve themselves completely, either the common-wealth is dissolved with them, and so they return to a *state of war*, or there is a devolution elsewhere of the power to punish those who shall break the laws, whoever they may be and however many; and this cannot be done without *absolute power* [*potestas*]. For he who has been granted *by right* all the power needed to coerce any number of citizens by penalties, has as much power as the citizens can confer upon him.

18. It is evident therefore that in every commonwealth there is some *one man* or *one assembly* [*concilium*] or *council* [*curia*], which has by right as much power over individual citizens as each man has over himself outside of the commonwealth, that is, *sovereign* or *absolute* power, which is to be limited only by the strength of the commonwealth and not by anything else. For if its power is to be limited, it has to be by a greater power; for the one that sets the limits must have greater power than the one restrained by limits. The restraining power therefore is either without limit, or is restrained in its turn by a greater power; and so it will come down at last to a power without other limit than that set by the strength of all the citizens together in its full extent. This is the so-called *sovereign power*, and if it is committed to an *assembly*, that assembly is called the *sovereign assembly*, and if it is given to one man, he is called the *sovereign Lord* of the commonwealth. The marks of *sovereign power* are: *to make and repeal laws*; to make decisions of *War and peace*; *to hear and decide* all *disputes* either in their own persons or through *judges* whom they appoint; *and* to choose all *Magistrates, Ministers* and *Counsellors*. Finally if there is anyone who can rightly do any action whatsoever which is not allowed to any other citizen or citizens besides himself, he holds *sovereign power* in the common-wealth; for the commonwealth alone can do what cannot rightly be done by an individual citizen or by several citizens together. He therefore who does these things is exercising the commonwealth's right, which is *sovereign power*.

19. Almost everyone who makes the comparison of common-wealth and citizen with the body and its members says that the holder of *sovereign power* in the commonwealth is to the whole commonwealth what the head is to the whole man. But it appears from what has been said that the recipient of such power (whether *Man* or *council*) has the relation to the commonwealth not of the head

but of the soul. Because man has a soul, he has a will [*voluntas*], that is, he can assent [*velle*] and refuse [*nolle*]; similarly a commonwealth has a will, and can assent and refuse through the holder of *sovereign power*, and only so. The appropriate analogy for the head is rather the corps of counsellors or (if he consults only one man) the single counsellor whose advice the holder of *sovereign power* makes use of in the most important matters of government.

20. *Sovereign power*, then, is established by force of the agreements into which individual subjects or citizens mutually enter one with another; and all agreements get their force from the will of the contracting parties, and likewise may lose their force and be dissolved by consent of the same parties. Someone will perhaps make the inference that *sovereign power* can be abolished by the simultaneous consent of all the subjects. Even if this were true, I cannot see what danger to *sovereigns* could *rightly* arise. For as the assumption is that each man has obligated himself to every other man, if any one of the citizens does not wish it to happen, all the rest will be bound whatever they may have agreed to. Nor can any one of them do without *wrong* what he has bound himself not to do by his agreement with me. By no stretch of the imagination could it ever happen that all the citizens together would unite in conspiracy against the *sovereign power*, without one single exception. There is therefore no danger that *sovereigns* can be *rightly* stripped of their authority. But there might easily be an appearance of *right* that they could be stripped of their power, if it were allowed that their right depends only upon the agreement which each one makes with each of his fellow citizens. For most people believe that whether subjects are summoned by authority of the commonwealth or gathered seditiously, the consent of all resides in the consent of the majority. This is in fact false; for it is not a natural rule that the consent of the majority should be taken for the consent of all, nor is it true of seditious gatherings. Rather the rule has its origin in civil institution, and is only true when the *man* or *council* which has sovereign power, summons the citizens and in view of their large numbers decides that selected men should receive authority to speak on behalf of those who select them, and that a majority of speakers on the proposals he puts forward for discussion is to stand for all of them. But a holder of *sovereign Power* is not understood to have summoned the citizens to debate about his own right, unless, in

absolute disgust, he abdicates power in explicit terms. Many men, however, in their ignorance, take for an agreement of the commonwealth, the consent of a majority of the citizens or even of a very few of them if they share their views; hence it could seem to them that *sovereign power* was rightly terminated provided it was done by the votes of a majority in some great convention of the citizens. But although power is constituted by the agreements of individuals with each other, that is not the only obligation on which the right of government rests. There is also the obligation towards the holder of power. For this is what each citizen says as he makes his agreement with each of his fellow citizens: *I transfer my right to this man on condition that you transfer your right to him also*. Hence the right which each man once had to use his strength for his own benefit is wholly transferred to some man or assembly for the public benefit. Thus by the agreements made between individuals which bind them to each other and by the gift of right which they are obliged to the ruler to respect, the power of government is secured by a double obligation on the part of the citizens, an obligation to their fellow citizens and an obligation to the ruler. Therefore no number of citizens can rightly strip the ruler of his power unless he gives his own consent as well.

Chapter VII

On the three kinds of commonwealth: democracy, aristocracy and monarchy

1. There are only three kinds of commonwealth, Democracy, Aristocracy, Monarchy. *2.* Oligarchy *is not a form of commonwealth distinct from* Aristocracy, *and* Anarchy *is not a form of commonwealth at all. 3.* Tyranny *is not a form of commonwealth distinct from legitimate* Monarchy. *4. There is no form of commonwealth which is a* mixture *of the kinds mentioned. 5. A* Democracy *is dissolved unless fixed times and places for meeting are established. 6. In a* Democracy *the intervals between meetings must be short, or the exercise of the sovereign power has to be given to some one person for the intervals. 7. In a* Democracy *individuals make agreement with each other to obey the* people; *the* People *itself has no obligation to anyone. 8. By what acts an* Aristocracy *is established. 9. In an* Aristocracy *the* Optimates *make no agreements; nor do they have obligation to any citizen or to the whole people. 10. A schedule of meetings is necessary to* Optimates. *11. By what acts a* Monarchy *is established. 12. A* Monarchy *is not bound by agreement to anyone as a consequence of accepting power. 13. A* Monarchy *is always in a position to perform all the acts necessary to government. 14. What kind of sin it is, and who is responsible, when commonwealths and citizens fail to perform their duty to each other. 15. A* Monarch *appointed without limitation as to time, can choose his own successor. 16. On* time-limited Monarchs. *17. So long as a* Monarch *retains the right of government, no promise of his is understood as having transferred the right to the necessary means of Government. 18. In what ways a citizen is released from being a subject.*

1. So far we have been speaking of the *commonwealth by design* in general. Now we must speak of its kinds. The differences between commonwealths are derived from the difference in the persons to whom *sovereign power* is committed. *Sovereign power* is committed either to *one man* or to *one Assembly* or *council* of many men. Again, an *Assembly of many men* is either an assembly of all the citizens (so that each of them has the right to vote and can participate in debating issues if he so wishes) or of only a part of the citizens. This is the origin of three kinds of commonwealth: The first is where *sovereign power* lies with an *Assembly* in which any citizen has

the right to vote; it is called DEMOCRACY. The second is where *sovereign power* lies with an *Assembly* in which not all but only a certain part have a vote; it is called ARISTOCRACY. The third is where sovereign power lies with *one man*; it is called MONARCHY. In the first, the dominant power is called the PEOPLE (Δῆμος [*POPULUS*]; in the second, the NOBILITY [*OPTIMATES*]; in the third, the MONARCH [*MONARCHA*].

2. The ancient writers on Politics have introduced three other kinds of commonwealth in opposition to these: in opposition to *Democracy* is *Anarchy*, or confusion; to *Aristocracy*, *Oligarchy*, i.e. government by a few; to *Monarchy*, *Tyranny*. But these are not three further kinds of commonwealth, but three alternative names, which have been bestowed by people who were annoyed with a government or its members. For men not only indicate things by the names they use, but also their own *feelings*, e.g. *love, hatred, anger*, etc.; and so it happens that what one man calls a *Democracy*, another calls *Anarchy*; what one calls an *Aristocracy*, another will call an *Oligarchy*; and where one man speaks of a *King*, another will speak of a *Tyrant*. Thus it is not *different kinds* of commonwealth that are designated by these different names, but *different sentiments* on the part of the citizens about the ruler. In the first place, who does not see that *Anarchy* is equally opposed to all the kinds in the list? For the word means that there is no government at all, i.e. there is no commonwealth at all. And how can it be that a *non-commonwealth* is a kind of *commonwealth*? Then what is the difference between *Oligarchy*, which signifies the government of *the few* or of the *magnates*, and *Aristocracy* which is the government of the *optimates* or of *the better people*, except that men are different from each other, so that the same things are not good to them all, and consequently that those who seem to some to be *the best*, seem to others to be *the worst*?

3. But it will not be easy to persuade people that *kingship* and *Tyranny* are not different kinds. The reason lies in men's feelings. Though they may prefer the commonwealth to be subject to *one* man rather than to *several*, they still believe that it is not well governed unless governed according to their own prescription. But how a *King* differs from a *Tyrant*, is a question for reason not feeling. First the difference is not that the tyrant has more power than the king: there is no power greater than *sovereign power*. Nor because the King, but not the Tyrant, has his power limited; one whose

power is limited is not a *King* but a *subject* of the limiter. Nor do they differ in how they acquired power; for if a citizen in a *Democratic* or *Oligarchic* commonwealth has violently seized *sovereign power*, he becomes a legitimate *Monarch* if he receives the consent of the people; without that consent, he is not a *Tyrant*, but a *public enemy* [*hostis*]. They differ only in the way they exercise power; he is a *king* who rules well, a *Tyrant*, who rules badly. It comes back to this, that once a king is legitimately established in *sovereign power*, the citizens will feel that he should be called *King*, if he is viewed as exercising his power well; if not, he will be seen as a *Tyrant*. *Kingship* and *tyranny* therefore are not different conditions [*status*] of government; one and the same *monarch* is given the name *King* to honour him, the name of *Tyrant* to damn him. The things we find said everywhere in books against *Tyrants*, originated with the Greek and Roman writers, who were ruled, in some places by the *people*, in others by *optimates*, and therefore detested not only *Tyrants* but *Kings* too.

4. There are those who hold that while *sovereign power* must exist somewhere in a commonwealth, if it is concentrated in a *single* source [*penes unum*], whether *man* or *Assembly*, it would follow (they say) that all the citizens would be slaves. To avoid this situation, they take the view that there can be a kind of state [*statum*] *made up from a mixture* of the three kinds mentioned, but different from each one; this they call *mixed Monarchy*, or *mixed Aristocracy*, or *mixed Democracy*, according to which of the three kinds predominates. For example, if the appointment of Magistrates and Decisions of peace and war are with the king, if the courts are in the hands of the *magnates*, payment of taxes is the *people's* responsibility, and legislation is shared by all, they would call this condition *mixed Monarchy*. But if this condition could actually exist, it would not advance the liberty of the people at all. For as long as they are all in agreement with each other, the subjection of individual citizens is as great as it could possibly be; but if they disagree, civil war returns, and the right of the *private Sword*, which is worse than any subjection. But we have given sufficient proof that a division of *sovereign power* (*) along these lines is impossible in the previous chapter, articles 6–12.

That a division of sovereign power along these lines is impossible, etc.] *Most say that power should not be divided; but they do want it to be restrained and kept within some limit. That is fair enough. But if, when they say restrained and limited, they understand the term to mean 'divided', then their distinction will not hold. I myself would wish that not only kings but also assemblies that have sovereign power would want to refrain from wrongdoing, remember their duties and stay within the limits of the natural and divine laws. But those who make this distinction want sovereigns to be limited and constrained by others. And as this cannot occur without the limiters having to have some share in power by which to limit them, it is a division of power, not a restraint.*

5. Let us now see what the founders do in the formation of each kind of commonwealth. When men have met to erect a commonwealth, they are, almost by the very fact that they have met, a *Democracy*. From the fact that they have gathered voluntarily, they are understood to be bound by the decisions made by agreement of the majority. And that is a *Democracy*, as long as the convention lasts, or is set to reconvene at certain times and places. For a convention whose will is the will of all the citizens has *sovereign power*. And because it is assumed that each man in this convention has the right to vote, it follows that it is a *Democracy*, by the definition given in the first article of this chapter. But if they split up, and the convention is dissolved without deciding on a time and place for meeting again, the situation returns to *Anarchy* and to the condition in which they were before they convened, i.e. to the condition of the war of all against all. A people therefore retains *sovereign Power* only so long as a certain time and place is publicly known and appointed, on which those who so wish may convene. For unless that is known and settled, they can convene at various times and places in factions or not at all. And that is no longer a Δῆμος, i.e. a *People [Populus]*, but a disorganized crowd, to which no *action* or *right* may be attributed. Two things, then, constitute a *Democracy*, of which one (an uninterrupted schedule of meetings) constitutes a Δῆμος, and the other (which is majority voting) constitutes τὸ κράτος or authority [*potestas*].

6. But if a *People* is to retain *sovereign power*, it is not enough to have settled times and places for meeting. Either the intervals between the meetings must not be so long that something could happen in the meanwhile which (for lack of *sovereign Power*) would endanger the commonwealth, or the *People* must devolve at least

the exercise of sovereign power on some *one* man or *one* assembly for the intervening period. If this has not been done, no adequate provision has been made for the defence and peace of individuals; it should not be called a commonwealth since it provides no security, and the right of self-defence at one's own discretion is back.

7. *Democracy* is not constituted by agreements which individuals make with the *People*, but by mutual agreements of individuals with other individuals. The first part of the statement is evident from the fact that in every agreement the persons making the agreement must exist before the agreement itself. But prior to the formation of a commonwealth a *People* does not exist, since it was not then a person but a crowd of individual persons. Hence no agreement could be made between the *people* and a *citizen*. But after a commonwealth has been formed, any agreement by a citizen with the *People* is without effect, because the *People* absorbs into its own will the will of the citizen (to whom it is supposed to be obligated); it can therefore release itself at its own discretion; and consequently is in fact free of obligation. The second part of the statement (that individuals make agreements with other individuals) is an inference from the fact that the formation of a commonwealth would be pointless if the citizens were not bound by any agreement to do or not do what the commonwealth bids them do or not do. Since therefore such agreements are understood to take place as a matter of necessity in the formation of a commonwealth, but (as has been shown) no agreement is possible between a *citizen* and a *people*, it follows that each of the citizens makes an agreement to submit his will to the will of the majority, on condition that the others also do likewise; as if each man said: *I transfer my right to the people, for your benefit, on condition that you transfer your right to the people for my benefit.*

8. An *Aristocracy*, or a *council of optimates* with sovereign power, has its origin in a transfer of right from a *Democracy*. This implies that certain men who are distinguishable from the rest by name or family or some other mark are put before the *people* and elected by a majority vote, and the total right of the whole *people*, or of the commonwealth, is transferred to those who have been elected, with the effect that the *council* of elected *optimates* may now rightly do what the *people* could rightly do before. Once this is done and the *sovereign power* has been transferred into their hands, it is evident that the people, as a single person, no longer exists.

95

9. In an *Aristocracy* the *council of optimates* is as free of all obligation as the *people* is in a *Democracy*. For the citizens were obligated, not by agreements with the *people*, but by reciprocal agreements with each other, to accept everything that the *people* might do; and therefore they were also obligated to accept the *people's* action in transferring the right of the commonwealth [*ius civitatis*] to the *optimates*. Nor could the *optimate council*, although elected by the people, be bound to anything by the people; for the *people* is dissolved at the instant of the council's formation, as was just said above, and the basis on which it was a *Person* ceases to exist. Hence the obligation owed to the *person* also ceases and is dissolved with it.

10. *Democracy* and *Aristocracy* have other points in common. First, without a fixed schedule of the times and places at which the *council of optimates* may meet, there is no longer a *council* or a single person, but a disorganized crowd without sovereign power. Secondly, the times of meetings may not be separated by long intervals, without destroying sovereign power, unless its exercise is transferred to some one man; the reasons for this are the same as we gave in article 5.

11. *Monarchy*, like *Aristocracy*, is derived from the power of the *people*, viz., by the transfer of its *right* (i.e. *sovereign power*) to *one man*. Here too the implication is that *one* specific *man* who is distinguished from all the rest by his name or some other mark, is put forward, and the whole right of the *people* is transferred to him by a majority of votes; with the effect that, once elected, he may rightly do all that the *people* could do before his election. Once this has been done, the *people* is no longer one *person*, but a disorganized crowd, since it was one person only by virtue of its *sovereign power*, which they have transferred from themselves to him.

12. It also follows that a *Monarch* is not binding himself by any agreement to anyone as a consequence of accepting power; for he accepts power from a *people*; and, as has just been shown, the instant that is done, a *people* ceases to be a *person*; and once the *person* has ceased to exist, all obligation to the *person* also ceases. The ground therefore of the citizens' obligation of obedience to their *Monarch* is simply the agreement by which they reciprocally committed themselves to all that the *people* might resolve to do, including obedience to a *Monarch* if the *people* should appoint one.

13. *Monarchy* differs from both *Aristocracy* and *Democracy* in that the latter require specific times and designated places for deliberation and decision, i.e. for the actual exercise of power; in the case of monarchy deliberation and decision occur at any time and in any place. *Optimates*, and the *people*, need to assemble, because they are not *one thing by nature*. A *Monarch*, who is one by nature, is always ready and able [*in potentia proxima*] to perform acts of government.

14. Since it has been shown above (articles 7, 9, 12) that those who have obtained *sovereign power* in a commonwealth are not bound by any agreements to anyone, it follows that they can do no *wrong* [*iniuria*] to the citizens. For by the definition given in chapter III, article 3, a *Wrong* is simply the violation of an agreement, hence there can be no *wrong* where there has been no agreement. There are however many ways in which a *people*, a *council of optimates* and a *Monarch* can sin against natural laws, by *cruelty*, for example, or by *unreasonableness*, by *insolence* and by other vices, which do not come under the strict and accurate signification of *wrong*. By contrast if a citizen fails to show obedience to the sovereign power, he is a *wrongdoer* [*iniurius*], and even in strict language will be called so, both against his fellow citizens on the ground that each man has agreed with every other man to show obedience, and against the *sovereign* because wrongdoers are taking back without his consent the right which they had given to him. And if a decision contrary to a *natural law* is made in the case of a *people* or a *council of optimates*, the offender is not the commonwealth itself, i.e. the civil person, but the citizens who voted for the decision. For an offence issues from an expression of natural will, not from a political will, which is artificial; because if it were the latter, those who voted against the decision would also be offenders. But in a *Monarchy* if the *Monarch* makes a decision contrary to the *natural laws*, he is himself at fault, because in him the civil will is the same as the natural.

15. A people which is to appoint a *Monarch* can transfer sovereign power to him either simply, without time limit, or for a fixed and determinate period. In the case of simple transfer the power of the recipient is as the power of the *people* which gave it to him. This is the reason why a *people* can *rightly* make *someone* a Monarch and why he can rightly make *another person* a monarch; with the effect

that a monarch to whom power is transferred simply, has not only the *right of possession* but also the *right of succession*, so that he has discretion to appoint his own successor.

16. But if power is transferred only for a limited time, other factors beside the transfer need to be taken into account. First whether when the *people* conferred the government upon him, it left itself the right of assembly at scheduled times and places, or not. Secondly, if it did leave itself this power, whether it left itself the authority to meet before the term they set for the *Monarch*'s possession of sovereign power should expire. Thirdly, whether it was their will to be summoned only at the discretion of the time-limited *Monarch*. Let us suppose that the *people* had already handed over *sovereign power* to some one man tenable only for his lifetime. When it had done this, let us suppose, first, that the assembly [*coetus*] had split up and members had gone their separate ways without deciding about the place where (after his death) they would meet for a new election. In this case it is clear from article 9 of this chapter that the *people* is no longer a *person* but a disorganized crowd, any one of whom may rightly meet with any of the rest at different times and at any place they choose, or, with equal right, i.e. natural right, seize power for himself if he can. Any *Monarch* who holds power on such terms is obliged by the natural law contained in chapter III, article 8, *on not returning evil for good*, to ensure that the commonwealth is not dissolved by his death, and he would do so by appointing a certain day and place on which the citizens who so wish may assemble, or by naming a successor himself – it is for him to determine which seems to be most in the public interest. Thus one who has received sovereign power for his lifetime in the manner described above, holds it absolutely and can determine the succession. Let us now suppose a second case: that the *people* leave the assembly after the election of a *time-limited Monarch* with the decision already made to meet at a certain time and place after his death; in this case, on the Monarch's death, power resides firmly in the *people* by their previous right, without any new act on the part of the citizens; for in the whole intervening period *sovereign power* (like *Ownership*)[1] remained with the *people*; only its *use* or

---

[1] *Dominium*, normally translated 'dominion', is here given its legal sense in reference to the people's ownership of 'sovereign power' by contrast with the Monarch's usufruct in it.

exercise was enjoyed by the time-limited *Monarch*, as a *usufructuary*. But if after the election of a *time-limited Monarch*, the *people* has departed from the council with the understanding that it would hold meetings at fixed times and places while the term set for the Monarch is still running, (as *Dictators* were appointed among the Romans), such a one is not to be regarded as a *Monarch* but as the first minister of the *people*, and the *people* can, if it shall see fit, deprive him of his office [*administratio*] even before his term is finished, as the Roman *people* did when they gave Master of the Horse *Minutius* equal power with *Quintus Fabius Maximus* whom they had previously made *Dictator*.[2] The reason is that it is unthinkable that a man or assembly which has direct and immediate power of action should hold power in such a way that it cannot actually give any commands; for power [*imperium*] is simply the right to give commands [*imperandi*] whenever it is possible by nature. Finally if the *people* leaves their council after appointing a *time-limited Monarch* without leave to meet again except on the orders of the appointee, the *people* is understood to be thereupon dissolved; and power belongs absolutely to anyone appointed on these terms. The reason is that it is not in the citizens' power to revive the commonwealth except at the will of the sole holder of power. And it does not matter that he may have promised to summon the citizens at certain times, since the *person* to whom the promise was made no longer exists except at his discretion. What we have said about these four cases of the *people* electing a *time-limited Monarch* will be more fully developed by a comparison with an *absolute Monarch* who has no heir apparent; for the *people* is a *Lord* [*Dominus*] of the citizens in such a way that it cannot have an heir unless it nominates one itself. Besides, the intervals between meetings of the citizens may be compared to the times when a *Monarch* is asleep; for the power is retained though there are no acts of commanding. Finally, the dissolution of a meeting on the terms that it may not reconvene is the death of a *people*, just as sleeping without waking is the death

---

[2] An incident from the Second Punic War. Quintus Fabius Maximus Cunctator was elected *dictator* (a temporary, emergency position) for the second time in 217 during the war against Hannibal. He quarrelled with his *magister equitum*, Minucius Rufus, and was effectively replaced before the period of his dictatorship had expired. Minucius attacked Hannibal and was disastrously defeated at Cannae (216). Fabius returned to power, this time as consul. He is the subject of the famous line of Ennius: 'unus homo nobis cunctando restituit rem'.

of a man. If a King without an heir is about to go to sleep and not wake up again (i.e. is about to die) and hands sovereign power to someone to exercise until he awakes, he is handing him also the succession; likewise if *people* in choosing a temporary Monarch, at the same time abolishes its own power of reconvening, it is passing dominion over the commonwealth to him. Further, a king who is going to sleep for a while gives sovereign power to someone else to exercise, and takes it back when he wakes up; just so *a people, on the election of a temporary Monarch*, retains the right of meeting again at a certain time and place, and on that day resumes its power. A king who has given his power to someone else to exercise, while he himself stays awake, can resume it again when he wishes; just so a *people* which duly meets throughout the term set for a *time-limited Monarch* can strip him of power if it so wishes. Finally a king who gives the exercise of his power to another person while he sleeps, and can wake up again only with the consent of that person, has lost his life and his power together; just so a *people* which has committed power to a *time-limited Monarch* on the terms that it cannot meet again without his command, is radically dissolved, and its power rests with the person it has elected.

17. If a *Monarch* makes a *promise* to a citizen – or to several citizens together – which has the consequence of frustrating the exercise of his sovereign power, that *Promise* or *Agreement*, whether made with an oath or not, is void. For an *Agreement* is a transfer of right which (by what was said in chapter II, article 4) requires appropriate indication of his will on the part of the transferor; and anyone who gives an adequate sign of his intention [*voluntas*] to retain the end, is also giving an adequate sign that he is not ceding his right to the means necessary to that end. One who has promised an essential element of *sovereign power* but keeps a hold on the *power* itself is giving a perfectly adequate indication that he has not promised anything but what the retention of *sovereign power* requires. Whenever therefore it becomes apparent that he cannot follow through on his promise without loss of *sovereign power*, the promise must be taken as not promised, i.e. as invalid.

18. We have seen how citizens, at the behest of nature, have bound themselves by mutual agreements to obey the *sovereign power*. We must look next at how it can happen that they are released from the bonds of such obedience. This happens first by *abdication*, i.e.

if one does not transfer his right to govern [*ius imperii*] to someone else but gives it up or abandons it; for when a thing is given up, it is made equally available for anyone to seize; and by right of nature each citizen may provide for his own preservation as he sees fit. Secondly, if a commonwealth has fallen into the power of enemies and resistance is impossible, it is recognized that the previous holder of *sovereign authority* has already lost it. For when the citizens have made every effort not to fall into the hands of an enemy, they have fulfilled the agreements they made with each other as individuals to offer obedience. And they must now make every effort to fulfil the promises which they made to avert death when they were conquered. Thirdly, in a *Monarchy* (for neither a Δῆμος nor a *Council of optimates* can cease to exist) all the citizens are released from their obligations if no successor is apparent. For no one is thought to be obligated when he does not know to whom he is obligated, because performance would be impossible in such a case. And in these three ways all the citizens together retreat from civil subjection into the liberty of all men to all things, i.e. into natural liberty, which is the liberty of the beasts. (For the state of nature has the same relation to the civil state, i.e. liberty has the same relation to subjection, as desire has to reason or a beast to a Man.) But in addition, individual citizens may rightly be released from subjection by the will of him who holds sovereign power; namely if they go to live abroad. This can happen in two ways: either by permission, as when one gets leave and voluntarily departs to live elsewhere, or by command, as an *Exile*. In both cases he will be free of the laws of his former commonwealth, because he is now bound by the laws of his new country.

Chapter VIII
On the right of Masters over slaves[1]

1. Master & slave, what they are. 2. The distinction between slaves who enjoy natural liberty on a basis of trust, and Workhouse slaves or those slaves who are held in prison or bonds. 3. The obligation of a slave arises from the physical liberty granted to him by his Master. 4. Bound slaves are not obligated by an agreement with their Masters. 5. Slaves do not have property in their goods against the Master. 6. A Master can sell a slave, or leave him to someone in his will. 7. A Master can do no wrong to a slave. 8. The Master of a Master is the Master of his slaves. 9. In what ways slaves are freed. 10. Dominion over animals is of the natural law.

1. In the last two chapters we have been speaking of the *commonwealth by design* [*civitas institutiva*], the commonwealth which is initiated by an accord between a number of men, binding themselves to each other by agreements and by pledging their faith to each other. The next topic to discuss is the *natural commonwealth* [*Civitas naturalis*], which may also be called the commonwealth *by Acquisition* [*Acquisita*] since it is acquired by natural power and strength. The most important things to know here are the ways by which the right of *Dominion* [*Dominium*] is acquired over men's *persons*. Where such a right has been acquired, there is a kind of *little kingdom*. For to be a *King* is simply to have *Dominion* over many *persons*, and thus a *kingdom* is a *large family*, and a *family* is a *little kingdom*. To return once again to the natural state and to look at men as if they had just emerged from the earth like mushrooms and grown up without any obligation to each other, there are only three ways by which someone can have *Dominion* over the *person* of another. The first is if, for the sake of peace and mutual defence, they put themselves under the sway [*ditio*] and *Dominion* of some one man or group of men by means of reciprocal agreements made with each other. We have already spoken of this way. The second way is if, on being captured or defeated in war or losing hope in one's own strength, one makes (to avoid death) a promise to the victor or the stronger party, to *serve* him, i.e. to do all that he shall

---

[1] On *servus* and *dominus*, see the introduction, pp. xlii–xliii.

command. In this contract the good which the defeated or weaker party receives is the sparing of his life, which could have been taken from him, in men's natural state, by right of war; and the good which he promises is service and obedience. By virtue of this promise, the vanquished owes the victor service and obedience, as absolute as may be, except for what is contrary to the divine laws. For anyone who is obligated to obey someone's commands before he knows what those commands will be, is bound to all his commands simply and without restriction. From this point on one who is so bound is called a SLAVE [*SERVUS*], the one to whom he is bound is called a MASTER [*DOMINUS*]. The third way of acquiring a right over a person is by generation [*generatio*]; this will be dealt with in the next chapter.

2. Not every captive in war whose life has been spared is understood to make an agreement with a master, because not everyone is trusted to be left with enough natural liberty to be able to run away or refuse service or cause trouble or loss for his *master* if he should take it into his head to do so. These people also perform services, but do so inside workhouses or in chains, and so they were not only called by the general name of slave, but also by the particular appellation of *workhouse slaves* [*ergastuli*]. Similarly in our day, *serviteur*, and *serf* or *esclave*, have different meanings.[2]

3. The obligation, therefore, of a *slave* to a *Master* does not arise simply because he spared his life but because he does not keep him bound or in prison. For an obligation arises from an agreement, and there is no agreement without trust as is clear from II.9, where an Agreement is defined as a promise from one who is trusted. Hence in addition to the benefit of sparing his life there is also the trust by which the *Master* leaves him in physical liberty, so that he could not only run away but could even take the life of the *Master* who saved his, if it were not for the obligation and bonds of agreement between them.

4. *Slaves* [*servi*] of the sort that are held in prison, workhouses, or bonds, are not included in the definition of *slaves* [*servi*] given above, because they serve in order to avoid beatings, not on the basis of an agreement. Hence if they run away, or kill their *Master*,

---

[2] This illustration from French usage may be an indication that in writing *de Cive* Hobbes kept a French audience in mind. Cf. the introduction, pp. xii–xv.

they are not acting against the natural laws. For confinement in bonds [*vinculis ligare*] indicates a presumption on the part of the man who binds him that he is not adequately held by any other bond of obligation [*obligatione*].[3]

5. A *Master* therefore has no less right and dominion over the *unbound* slave than over the *bound*, for he has supreme dominion over both; and he may say of his slave no less than of any other thing, animate and inanimate, *This is mine*. It follows that anything that belonged to the slave before enslavement belongs to his *Master* afterwards, and anything the *slave* may acquire is acquired for the *Master*. For he who has the right to dispose of a man's *person* as he pleases also disposes of all the things the *person* could dispose of. There is therefore nothing that the *slave* can keep as *his own* against his *Master*. By allotment from his *Master* however, he does have *property* and *Dominion* over things that are *his own* in the sense that he can keep and protect them against a *fellow slave*; in the same way in which it was shown above that a citizen has nothing which is properly *his own*, against the will of the *commonwealth*, or of the holder of sovereign power; but each citizen does have *things that are his own* against his fellow citizens.

6. Since therefore the *slave* himself and all that he has are the *Master*'s, and every man by natural right may dispose of his own as he wishes, the *Master* will be able to sell his *Dominion* of the slave, or pledge it or pass it by will, at his own discretion.

7. Moreover, the point demonstrated above about subjects in a *commonwealth by design*, that the holder of sovereign power can do them no *wrong*, is also true of slaves, because they have submitted their will to the will of the *Master*. Hence whatever he does, is done with their consent, and no wrong can be done to one who consents to it.

8. But if it happens, whether by capture or by voluntary submission, that a *Master* becomes a *slave* or *subject* to someone else, the latter will become *Master* of the other's *slaves* as well as of his person; he will be the *supreme Master* of the *slaves*, the *immediate Master* of their former *Master*. For since a *slave*'s possessions as well as his person belong to his *Master*, the *slaves* of the original owner

---

[3] A play on the words *ligare* ('bind' normally in a physical sense) and *obligare* ('bind', 'obligate', normally in a legal or moral sense).

become the new man's *slaves*; the *Master in-between* can do nothing
about them except as the *supreme Master* directs. This is the reason
why whenever the *Master*'s power over their *slaves* in a commonwealth is absolute, it is thought to derive from a right of nature,
not established by the civil law but prior to it.

9. A *slave* is freed from *servitude* in the same ways as a *subject* in
a *commonwealth by design* is freed from subjection. First, if the
Master grants him his liberty; for the right which the *slave* transferred to his *Master*, the *Master* can return again to the *slave*. Such
a gift of liberty is called MANUMISSION. It is analogous to a commonwealth giving a citizen the right to move to another commonwealth.
Secondly, if the *Master* expels the *slave*; in a commonwealth this is
called *banishment*. It does not differ in effect from *manumission*, but
in manner; for in the one case freedom is given as a punishment,
in the other as a favour. In either case *Dominion* is renounced.
Thirdly, if a *slave* is captured, the *new* servitude will cancel the *old*;
for *slaves* are acquired by war just like other things, and it is reasonable for the *Master* to protect them, if he wants them to be his.
Fourthly, a *slave* is freed by ignorance of the successor, for example,
if his *Master* dies with neither will nor heir; for no one is thought
to have an obligation if he cannot know to whom he should perform
the service due. Finally, a *slave* who is thrown into chains, or is
deprived of his physical liberty in any way, is released from the
other obligation, the one that depends on agreement. For no agreement exists except where there is trust in the party who makes the
agreement; and a trust cannot be violated which is not given. A
Master who is in service to another man, cannot liberate his *slaves*
from continuing for ever in the power of the *supreme Master*. For,
as shown above, such slaves are not his, but the *supreme master's*.

10. Right over non-rational animals is acquired in the same way
as over the *persons* of men, that is, by natural strength and powers.
In the natural state, because of the war of all against all, any one
may legitimately subdue or even kill Men, whenever that seems to
be to his advantage; much more will this be the case against animals.
That is, one may at discretion reduce to one's service any animals
that can be tamed or made useful, and wage continual war against
the rest as harmful, and hunt them down and kill them. Thus
Dominion over animals has its origin in the *right of nature* not in
Divine positive right. For if no such right had existed before the

publication of holy scripture, no one could rightly have slaughtered animals for food except someone to whom the divine will had been revealed in the holy scriptures; and the condition of mankind would surely have been very hard, since the beasts could devour them in all innocence, while they could not devour the beasts. Since therefore it is by natural right that an animal kills a man, it will be by the same right that a man slaughters an animal.

Chapter IX
On the right of parents over children, and on the Patrimonial Kingdom

1. Paternal Dominion *does not arise from* Generation. *2. Dominion over* infants *belongs to the person who first has them in his or her authority. 3.* Dominion *over* infants *originally belongs to the* mother. *4. An exposed infant belongs to the person who saves it. 5. The child of a private citizen and a holder of sovereign power belongs to the sovereign. 6. In a union of* Male *and* female *in which neither rules the other, the Children belong to the* mother, *unless it is otherwise determined by* agreement *or* civil law. *7.* Children *are subject to* Fathers *no less than* slaves *to* Masters *and* citizens *to the* commonwealth. *8. On the Honour due to* Parents *and* Masters. *9. What constitutes* liberty, *and the difference between* citizens *and* slaves. *10. There is the same right over the citizens in a* Patrimonial Kingdom *as in a kingdom by design. 11. The question about the right of succession is only in place in a* Monarchy. *12. A* Monarch *can dispose by will of the* sovereign power *of a commonwealth. 13. Or* give it away *or sell it. 14. An intestate* Monarch *is always understood to intend that his successor will be a* Monarch. *15. And one of his own* children. *16. And a* male *rather than a* female. *17. And the* oldest *of his sons in preference to the* younger. *18. And a* brother, *if he lacks offspring, before all others. 19. The succession to the* right *of succession* goes by the same route as succession to *power.*

1. Socrates is a man, therefore also an animal, is a valid reasoning and utterly evident, since all that one needs, to recognize the truth of the conclusion, is to understand the word *man*, because *animal* is in the definition of *man*; and everyone supplies the missing proposition, *man is an animal. Sophroniscus is the father of Socrates, therefore also his Master [Dominus] is also perhaps a valid inference, but not totally evident, because Master is not in the definition of father.* To make it evident, one needs to explicate the relation between *father* and *Master.* Those who have attempted in the past to assert the Dominion of a *father* over his *children* have only come up with the argument of *generation [parenthood]* as if it were self-evident that what I have *generated* is mine. This is the same as supposing that if

something is a triangle, it is immediately apparent, without any reasoning, that its angles are equal to two right angles. Besides, since *Dominion*, i.e. *sovereign power*, is indivisible, so that no one can serve two masters, but generation requires the cooperation of two persons, a Male and a female, it is impossible for Dominion to be wholly acquired by generation alone. At this point therefore we must take a more careful look at the origin of *Paternal Dominion*.

2. And so we must return to the natural state, in which because of the equality of nature, all adults are to be taken as equal to each other. There by *right of nature* the victor is *Master* of the conquered; therefore by *right of nature* Dominion over an *infant* belongs first to the one who first has him in their power [*potestas*]. But it is obvious that a *new-born child* is in the power of his *mother* before anyone else, so that she can raise him or expose him at her own discretion and by her own right.

3. If then she raises him, she is understood to be doing so on the condition that he shall not be her enemy (seeing that the state of nature is a state of war) when he grows up; i.e. her condition is that he obey her. For since by natural necessity we all *wish* what appears *to us good*, it cannot be supposed that anyone has given life to anyone that he may both acquire strength as he gets older and have the right to be an enemy. Now everyone is an enemy to everyone whom he neither obeys nor commands. And in this way in the state of nature every woman who gives birth becomes both a *mother* and a *Mistress* [*Domina*]. The allegation some make that it is not the *mother* in this case but the *Father* who becomes *Master*, because of the superiority of his sex, is groundless; for reason is against it, because the inequality of natural strength is too small to enable the *male* to acquire dominion over the *female* without war. And custom is not against [the mother's dominion], because *women*, in the person of the *Amazons*, did at one time wage wars against their enemies and handled their *offspring* as they pleased, and there are several places today where women have *sovereign power*. And decisions about their *children* are not made by their *husbands* but by the *women themselves*; and they undoubtedly do this by *natural right*, because holders of sovereign power are, as shown above, not bound by civil laws. Add that in the state of nature, it cannot be known who is a *child's father* except by the *mother's* pointing him out; hence he belongs to whomever the *mother* wishes, and therefore he belongs to the

mother. The original Dominion over *children* therefore is the *mother's*; and among men no less than other animals, the offspring goes with the womb.

4. *Dominion* passes from the *mother* to others in various ways: first, if she rejects or relinquishes her right by abandoning her child. The person who raises the abandoned child will have the same Dominion as the *mother* had. For the life which the *mother* gave him (not by *generation* but by *looking after* him) she takes away by *abandoning* him; hence the obligation which arose from the gift of life is cancelled by the *abandonment*. He has been saved, and owes everything to the one who saved him by looking after him; he has a foster-child's debt as to a *mother* and a *slave's* debt as to a *Master*.[1] For even though in the state of nature where all things belong to all men, the *mother* can reclaim the child (by the same right, of course, as anyone else), still the *child* cannot rightly transfer himself to his *mother*.

5. Secondly, if a *mother* has been captured in war, her *offspring* belongs to her captor, because he who has *Dominion* over a *person* has *Dominion* over everything that is hers; and that includes the *child*, as was said in the last chapter, article 5. Thirdly, if the *mother* is a citizen of a commonwealth, the holder of sovereign power in that commonwealth will have *Dominion* over her child; for he is Master also of the *mother*, and she is obliged to obey the sovereign in all things. Fourthly, if a *woman* gives herself to a man to share her life with him, on the terms that power be in the hands of the *man*, their common *children* belong to the *father* because of his power over the *mother*. But if a *woman who holds power* has *children* by a *subject*, the children so born belong to the *mother*. For otherwise a woman cannot have children without loss of power. And in general if the relationship of a *Man* and a *woman* is a *union* in which one is subject to the power of the other, the *children* belong to the *partner with power*.

6. But in the state of nature if a *man* and a *woman* enter into a partnership [*societas*] in which neither is subject to the power of the other, their *children* belong to the *mother* for the reasons given in article 3 above, unless the agreement provides otherwise. For a

---

[1] A double play on words: he has the debt of a 'foster-child' (*alumnus*) as to the one who 'looked after' him (*alendo*) and the debt of a 'slave' (*servus*) as to the one who 'saved' (*conservavit*) him.

woman can dispose of her right as she pleases by means of an agreement, as the *Amazons* once did; they conceived children by their
neighbours, restored the *male* children to them, and kept the *females*
for themselves, all by agreement. But in a commonwealth, if a *man*
and a *woman* make a contract to live together, any children born
belong to the *father*, because in all commonwealths, because they
are established by the *Fathers* not the *mothers* of the *family*, the
power of domestic government belongs to the man; and such a contract, if made in accordance with the civil laws, is called a MARRIAGE.
But if they only agree to concubinage, the *children* belong to either
mother or *father* according to the different civil laws of different
commonwealths.

7. By article 3, the *mother* is *originally the Mistress of the children*,
and the father or anyone else is their *Master* by derivative right
from her; it is therefore evident that *children* are no less subject to
those who look after them and bring them up than *slaves* are to
Masters, or *subjects* to the holder of *sovereign power* in the commonwealth; and that a parent is incapable of wronging [*injurius*] a *child*
so long as he is under his authority. *Children* are also released from
subjection in the same ways as *subjects* and *slaves*. *Emancipation* is
the same thing as *manumission* and *disowning* is the same as *banishment*.

8. An *emancipated child* or a *manumitted slave* has less fear of the
father of the family, once he is bereft of authority as father and
Master, and gives him less *honour* (meaning true internal *honour*)
than he did before. For *honour*, as was said in the previous section,[2]
is simply putting a high value on another man's power. One must
not suppose that the *manumittor* or the *emancipator* intended to raise
the *emancipated* child or the *manumitted* slave quite to his own level
so that he would not be liable to service, but would behave in every
way as his equal. One must therefore always assume that anyone
freed from subjection, whether *child* or *slave* or *colony*, promises at
least the external signs by which superiors are normally honoured
by inferiors. It follows that the precept about *honouring parents* is
of the *natural law*, on grounds not only of *gratitude* but also of
agreement.

---

[2] For the meaning of 'section' here, see V.4 n. 3.

9. Well, what is the difference, someone will ask, between a *free man* or a *citizen* on the one hand and a *slave* on the other? For, so far as I know, no writer has explained what *liberty* and *servitude* are. *Liberty* is commonly thought of as doing everything of our own freewill and with impunity; not to be able to do so is reckoned to be *servitude*. But this cannot be so in a commonwealth, or coexist with the peace of the human race; because there is no commonwealth without the power of government [*imperium*] and the right to coerce. LIBERTY (to define it) is simply the *absence of obstacles to motion*; as water contained in a vessel is not *free*, because the vessel is an obstacle to its flowing away, and it is *freed* by breaking the vessel. Every man has more or less *liberty* as he has more or less space in which to move; so that a man kept in a large jail has more *liberty* than a man kept in a small jail. And a man may be *free* in one direction but not in the other, as a traveller is prevented by hedges and walls from trampling on the vines and crops adjacent to the road. Obstacles of this kind are external and absolute; in this sense all *slaves* and *subjects* are *free* who are not in bonds or in prison. Other obstacles are discretionary; they do not prevent motion absolutely but incidentally, i.e. by our own choice, as a man on a ship is not prevented from throwing himself into the sea, if he can will to do so. Here too the more ways one can move, the more *liberty* one has. And this is what civil *liberty* consists in; for no one, whether *subject* or *child* of the family or *slave*, is prevented by the threat of being punished by his *commonwealth* or *father* or *Master*, however severe he may be, from doing all he can and trying every move that is necessary to protect his life and health. I find no reason for a *slave* to complain on the ground that he lacks *liberty*, unless it is an affliction to be restrained from harming himself and to keep the life which he had lost by war or ill fortune or even by his own idleness, together with all his food and everything needful for life and health, on the condition of being ruled. Anyone so restrained by threats of punishment from doing all he wants to do is not oppressed by servitude; he is governed and maintained. In every commonwealth and household where there are slaves what the *free citizens* and children of the family have more than the *slaves* is that they perform more honourable services in commonwealth and family, and enjoy more luxuries. And this is where the difference lies between a *free citizen*

and a *slave*, that the FREE MAN is one who serves only the commonwealth, while the SLAVE serves also his fellow citizen. All other *liberty* is exemption from the laws of the commonwealth, and is reserved to rulers.

10. *The father of the family, the children and the slaves*, united in one civil person by virtue of paternal power is called a FAMILY. If a family increases and grows so big with large numbers of *children* and the acquisition of more *slaves* that it cannot be subdued without a war of uncertain outcome, it will be called a PATRIMONIAL KINGDOM. This differs from a *Monarchy by design* in origin and manner of formation in that it was acquired by force, but when formed it has all the same properties, and both have the same right of government; they do not need to be discussed separately.

11. We have explained the right by which sovereign powers are formed; now we must speak briefly of the right by which they continue. The right by which they continue is called the right of SUCCESSION. In a *Democracy*, sovereign power is with the *people*, and therefore sovereignty rests with the same person so long as there are citizens. For a people has no *successor*. Similarly in an *Aristocracy*, when one of the *optimates* dies, another is appointed by the rest to take his place, hence there is no *succession*, unless they all die off at the same time, which I suppose never happens. The question then of the right of *succession* only arises in an *absolute Monarchy*. For *Monarchs* who exercise sovereign power only for a time are not actually monarchs but *ministers* of the commonwealth.

12. Firstly, if a *Monarch* has instituted a *successor* to himself by will, the person so instituted will *succeed*; for if he was instituted by the *people*, he will have the whole of the right to the commonwealth which the people had, as shown at VII.11. By the same right therefore by which the *people* could choose him, he can choose someone else. There are the same rights in a *Patrimonial kingdom* as in a *kingdom by design*. Hence every monarch can appoint his *successor* by will.

13. But what one can transfer to another by will, one can also, while living, give or sell; to whoever therefore he passes the sovereign power, whether by gift or sale, it is passed by right.

14. But if he did not make his wishes about his *successor* known, by Will or otherwise, while he was still alive, one makes a first assumption that he did not wish the commonwealth to revert to

Anarchy or a state of war, that is, to the ruination of the citizens. One makes this assumption both because he could not do that without breaking the natural laws by which he was bound in the court of conscience to do everything that necessarily contributes to peace, and also because if he had so wished, it would not have been difficult to make it publicly known. Next, one must think about a *successor* in the light of indications about his wishes, because the right passes according to the wishes of the father. That is why it is assumed that he wished his *subjects* to be under a *Monarchical* régime rather than any other, because he had recommended that condition by his own example of reigning, and did not condemn it later by contrary words or actions.

15. Further by natural necessity all men prefer the advancement of those who will reflect honour and glory on themselves rather than on others; and after his death a man has more honour and glory from the power of his *children* than from any other man's power; it follows that a father wants the advancement of his own children more than of anyone else. It is understood therefore to have been the wish of a father who dies intestate that one of his own children be his *successor*. This however is only to be understood if no more evident signs point the other way. After several *successions* custom may be a guide of this kind; if someone says nothing about the *succession*, he is assumed to agree with the custom of the kingdom.

16. Among children, males are preferred to females; at first perhaps because usually (though not always) they are better equipped to manage great affairs and especially wars; but later when it has become a tradition, as a matter of not going against the tradition; hence the *Father's* wishes are to be interpreted in their favour, unless a different tradition or other sign explicitly counters it.

17. Of the *sons* the eldest will *succeed*, because sons are equal and the power cannot be divided. For if there is a difference of age, the elder is more deserving; for in nature's judgement the older in years is the wiser (for this is usually the case). And there is no other judge. But if all the brothers are regarded as equal, the *successor* will be chosen by *lot*. There is a natural lottery, *primogeniture*, by which the eldest is preferred; and no one has the authority to judge whether the matter should be decided by this kind of lottery or another. The same argument works for the oldest born female as the oldest born male.

18. But if there are no children, then power will pass to brothers and sisters for the same reason for which the children would *succeed* if there were any; for the nearest by nature are assumed to be the nearest in affection; and the *succession* is to brothers before sisters; similarly to the older before the younger. The reason is the same here as in the case of the children.

19. *Succession* to the right of *succession* goes by the same route as *succession* to power. If the first-born dies before his father, he will be assumed to have passed his right of *succession* to his own children, unless his father had determined otherwise; hence grandsons and granddaughters are to succeed before their uncles. All these things hold, I say, unless the custom of the place (which the father will be regarded as consenting to by not having contradicted it) is a bar to them.

Chapter X
Comparison of the disadvantages of each of the three kinds of commonwealth

1. Comparison of the natural *state with the* civil *state. 2. The advantages and disadvantages of the* ruler *and of the* citizens *are the same. 3. In praise of* Monarchy. *4. The government of one man is not unfair simply on the ground that one man has more power than all the rest. 5. Rejection of the view of those who say that a commonwealth cannot consist of a* Master *with* slaves. *6. Exactions are worse under the rule of the* people *than under a* Monarch. *7. Innocent citizens are less liable to punishment under a Monarch than under the people. 8. The liberty of individual citizens is no less under a* Monarch *than under the* people. *9. It is not a disadvantage to the citizens that they are not all allowed to take part in public deliberations. 10. It is a bad thing to entrust civil deliberations to large gatherings because of most men's* ignorance. *11. Because of* eloquence. *12. Because of* faction. *13. Because of* instability *in the laws. 14. Because of a lack of* discretion. *15. These disadvantages are integral to* Democracy, *because men naturally love to have a reputation for sagacity. 16. The disadvantages for a commonwealth from a* boy-king. *17. An indication of the superiority of Monarchy is the authority of the generals of an Army in the field. 18. The best state of the commonwealth is when the citizens are the inheritance of the ruler. 19. The nearer* Aristocracy *is to* Monarchy, *the better it is; the further away, the worse.*

1. We have explained what *Democracy*, *Aristocracy* and *Monarchy* are. We must now compare them to see which of them is more suited to preserve the citizens' peace and secure advantages for them. But first let us compare the advantages and disadvantages [*commoda & incommoda*] of the commonwealth in general, so that no one will believe it would be better for everyone to live at his own discretion than to make a commonwealth at all. Outside the circumstances of a commonwealth [*statum civitatis*] each man does indeed have the most complete liberty, but it does him no good. And the reason is that he who does all things of his own free will because he has his liberty, also suffers all things at the will of others,

because they have their liberty. But once a commonwealth is formed, every citizen retains as much liberty as he needs to live well in peace, and enough liberty is taken from others to remove the fear of them. Outside the commonwealth every man has a right to all things, but on the terms that he may enjoy nothing. In a commonwealth every man enjoys a limited right in security. Outside the commonwealth anyone may be killed and robbed by anyone; within a commonwealth by only one person. Outside the commonwealth, we are protected only by our own strength; within by the strength of all. Outside the commonwealth, no one is certain of the fruits of his industry; within the commonwealth all men are. To sum up: outside the commonwealth is the empire of the passions, war, fear, poverty, nastiness, solitude, barbarity, ignorance, savagery; within the commonwealth is the empire of reason, peace, security, wealth, splendour, society, good taste, the sciences[1] and good-will.

2. *Aristotle* (*Politics*, 7.14) says that there are two kinds of régime, one directed to the advantage of the *ruler* and the other to the advantage of the *subjects*. As if it were *one* kind of a commonwealth when the citizens are treated harshly, and, a *different* kind, when they are treated gently. We must not allow him this. For all the advantages and disadvantages of the régime itself are the same for *ruler* and *subjects* alike and are shared by both of them. The disadvantages which occur to a particular citizen by his own misfortune, stupidity, negligence, ignorance, or extravagance, may be separate from the disadvantages of the Ruler, but they are not disadvantages of the Régime, because they can occur in any commonwealth. If the same things happen as a result of the way the commonwealth was originally set up, they will indeed be called disadvantages of the Régime, but they will be common to ruler and citizen alike, just as their advantages will be common also. The first and greatest advantage is Peace and defence, and it is the same for both. For both the ruler and the ruled employ the united forces of all their fellow citizens for the defence of their own lives. And the greatest disadvantage that can occur in a commonwealth, namely, massive slaughter of the citizens, arises from Anarchy, and overwhelms both the

---

[1] Reading *scientiae* as in all the printed editions. Warrender notes that the presentation copy reads *scientia*.

holder of sovereign power and every one of the citizens. Secondly, if the holder of sovereign power exacts so much money from the citizens that they cannot feed themselves and their families and maintain their physical strength, it is as big a disadvantage for the ruler as for themselves, since however rich he may be, he cannot protect his own wealth and Power without the physical aid of the citizens. But if he exacts only what the administration of government requires, that is equally advantageous for himself and the citizens for their common peace and defence. One cannot imagine how *public* wealth can be disadvantageous to *private* citizens, provided that private citizens are not so exhausted that it is impossible for them to get by hard work what they need to sustain the strength of body and soul. For this would also affect the interests of the ruler himself, and it would not arise from the bad design of the political order (because citizens can be oppressed in any kind of commonwealth), but from the poor administration of a well-designed commonwealth.

3. *Monarchy* is the best of the listed kinds of commonwealth, *Democracy, Aristocracy,* and *Monarchy.* This is to be shown by a comparison of their advantages and disadvantages in detail. We will therefore ignore certain arguments which present *Monarchy* to us as the preferred form, because they work not by reason but by example and testimony: namely, that the *universe* is ruled by *one God*; that the *Ancients* preferred the *Monarchical* form to the others, ascribing the government of the Gods to *Jupiter* alone; that in the early stages of affairs and of nations the decisions of princes were the law; that the *Paternal* government instituted by God at the Creation was *Monarchical*; that the other régimes have been cobbled together by human artifice (*) from the rubble of *Monarchy* after it had been destroyed by sedition; and that the people of God lived under kings.

Cobbled together by human artifice, etc.] *This seems to have been the point of the fable the Ancients have made for us about Prometheus.*[2]

---

[2] Ovid, *Metamorphoses*, I.82 and others refer to Prometheus making man from mud. The theft of fire occurs at Hesiod, *Works and Days*, 50ff. The important detail that the fire he stole came from the Sun occurs in late sources, e.g. Servius' commentary on Vergil, *Eclogues* 6.42. Hobbes's account is reminiscent of the version in Boccaccio, *Genealogie deorum gentilium libri*, IV.44.

They say that Prometheus stole fire from the Sun and made man out of mud: and for that deed was punished by angry Jupiter by having his liver constantly torn. That is, by human intelligence (that is what Prometheus signifies) laws and justice were copied from Monarchy; by their means (like the theft of fire from its natural source) the crowd (as the mud and dregs of mankind) were given life and form as one civil person, which is called Aristocracy or Democracy. The men who were found to inaugurate and support this régime (who might have lived securely and at leisure under the natural rule of kings) pay the penalty, on their exposed eminence,[3] of perpetual torment by worry, suspicion and dissension.

4. There are those who object to a Government of *one* man precisely because it is by one man; as if it were unfair, among so many, that any *one* man should be so preeminent in power that he can determine the fate of all the rest at his own discretion. Evidently, they would like, if they could, to sneak away from the government of the *one* God. It is envy that suggests this objection to *one*; they see that one man has what all men want. The same people would think it unfair on the same grounds if a *few* ruled, unless they either were or expected to be in the number; for if it is unfair that there is not an equal right for all, then the régime of the optimates is also unfair. But it has been shown that the state of equality is a state of war, and therefore inequality has been introduced with everyone's agreement. So one should no longer regard inequality as an unfair condition, when the one who has more is the one to whom we have voluntarily given more. Thus the disadvantages consequent on the rule of *one man*, are a consequence not of the rule of *one* but of the rule of a *man*. The question therefore is whether the rule of one *man* or of several *men* causes more disadvantages to the citizens.

5. But first one must refute the view which denies that a commonwealth made up of any number of slaves under one common Master is a commonwealth at all. At v.9 a *commonwealth* was defined as one *person* formed from several men, and his will is to be regarded by their own agreement as the will of all of them, so that he may

---

[3] Reading *alto* here, with the 1647 edition and the English translation of 1651, for Warrender's *alio*.

make use of individuals' strength and resources for the common peace and defence. By the same article of the same chapter, *one Person* exists, when the wills of several men are contained in the will of one man. But the will of each slave is contained in the will of his Master, as was shown at VIII.5, so that he may make use of their strength and resources as he pleases. It follows that it is a commonwealth which is formed from a *Master* and a number of *slaves*; and any argument which can be made against this tells equally against a commonwealth formed by a *father* and his *children*. For *slaves* have the place of *children* in the case of a *childless Master*. For they are his honour and his protection, and *slaves* are no more subject to their *Masters* than *children* to *fathers*, as was shown at VIII.5.

6. One of the disadvantages of sovereign power is that the sovereign may exact other monies apart from those needed for public expenses, i.e. for maintaining public ministers; for building and defending garrisons; for making war; and for maintaining his household in an honourable manner. He may if he wishes also exact monies at his pleasure to enrich his *children*, *relatives*, *favourites* and even *flatterers*. One must admit that this is a disadvantage, but it is a type of disadvantage found in every kind of commonwealth, and is more tolerable in a *Monarchy* than in a *Democracy*. For if a *Monarch* does choose to enrich them, there are not many of them, because they depend on one man. But in a *Democracy* the large numbers of *Demagogues*, i.e. the orators who have influence with the people (and there are a lot of them and new ones come along every day), are so many men who have *children*, *relatives*, *friends* and *flatterers* to be enriched. For individuals desire not only to make their families rich, powerful and illustrious, so far as they can, but also want to bind others to them with favours in order to strengthen their own position. Because a *Monarch's* ministers, slaves and friends are not numerous, he can more or less satisfy them without expense to the citizens, by conferring on them the offices of war and peace; in a *Democracy* where there are many to satisfy and always new ones coming along, it cannot be done without exploiting the citizens. Though a *Monarch* can promote unworthy candidates, he will not want to do it often; but in a *Democracy* all the Orators are acknowledged to be always trying it, for the simple reason that

they have to. Otherwise the power of the few who were doing it would grow to become formidable not only to the orators but also to the commonwealth.

7. Another disadvantage of sovereignty is the constant fear of death which every man inevitably experiences as he reflects that the holder of sovereign power may not only set any penalty he pleases for any offence he wishes, but may also, from anger and greed, put innocent citizens to death who have done nothing against the laws. This is in fact in every kind of commonwealth a great disadvantage where it occurs (it is its occurrence that is the disadvantage, not the possibility that it may occur), but the fault is the Ruler's, not the Régime's. Not all the deeds of *Nero* are of the essence of *Monarchy*. However the fact is that citizens are less often condemned unde-servedly when a *Man* reigns than when the *people* does. For the wrath of Kings is directed only at those who cause trouble by ill-judged advice or insolent language, or are personally opposed to them. And they ensure that the superiority which one citizen can have over another in point of power does no harm. Hence when a *Nero* or a *Caligula* is in power, no one can suffer undeservedly, except those who are known to him, namely Courtiers, or those who hold some conspicuous position; and not all of them, but only those who have something that he covets; for those who are trouble-some or insolent towards him deserve their punishment. In a *Mon-archy* therefore anyone who is prepared to live quietly is free of danger, whatever the character of the ruler. Only the ambitious suffer, the rest are protected from being wronged by the powerful. But where there is *popular control* [*dominatio*], there may be as many *Neros* as there are *Orators* who fawn on the *people*. For every Orator wields as much power as the *people* itself, and they have a kind of tacit agreement to turn a blind eye to each other's greed (*my turn today, yours tomorrow*), and to cover up for any of them who put innocent fellow citizens to death arbitrarily or because of private feuds. Besides, private power has a certain limit beyond which it will ruin the commonwealth; because of it monarchs must some-times take steps to see that no harm comes to the Country [*Respub-lica*][4] from that direction. When the source of that power has been

---

[4] Hobbes adapts the formula of the *senatus consultum ultimum*, the charge of the Senate to the consuls in a crisis to take whatever measures the safety of the country required.

wealth, they have decreased it by decreasing the wealth; if it has been popular *favour*, they have got rid of the powerful man himself without making any other charge against him. The same thing regularly happens in *Democracies*. The *Athenians* used to send powerful men into exile by *ostracism* without a charge, simply because of their power, and at Rome those who sought popularity with the plebs by favours were put to death on the ground that they were aiming for kingship. *Democracy* and *Monarchy* have been on a par in this, but their reputations have not been on a par. For reputation comes from the people, and what is done by many is approved by many. Hence if a *Monarch* does something which would be policy [*politia*] if done by the *people*, he is said to have done it from envy of their virtues.

8. Some think that *Monarchy* has fewer advantages than *Democracy*, because it has less liberty than *Democracy*. If by *liberty*, they mean exemption from the subjection due to the laws, i.e. the commands of the *people*, there is no *liberty* anywhere, either in a *Democracy* or in any other form of commonwealth. If they understand *liberty* to mean few laws, few things forbidden, and those the sorts of things without which there would be no Peace, then I deny that there is more *liberty* in a *Democracy* than in a *Monarchy*. For *Monarchy* can rightly coexist with such *liberty* as well as *Democracy*. For even if *liberty* is inscribed on the gates and towers of a city in the largest possible letters, it is not the *liberty* of the individual *citizen* but of the *city*; and there is no better right to inscribe it on a *popularly* governed than on a *Monarchically* governed city. When private citizens, i.e. subjects, demand *liberty*, what they are demanding in the name of *liberty* is not *liberty* but *Dominion*; but in their ignorance, they never see this. For if each man allowed to others, as the law of nature requires, the *liberty* which he demands for himself, the state of nature would return, in which all men may rightly do all things; and they would reject that state as worse than any civil subjection, if they knew it. If anyone demands that he alone should be free and everyone else restricted, what else is he demanding but *Dominion*? For the one who is free of all bonds, is *Master* [*dominus*] of all who are in bonds however many they are. Thus the citizens have no greater *liberty* in a popular state than in a Monarchical. What gives the impression that they do is equal *participation* in public offices and in power [*imperium*]. For where Power belongs to the *people*, individual citizens participate in it insofar as they are

part of the sovereign *people*. And they participate equally in public offices in so far as they have equal votes in electing magistrates and public ministers. And this is what *Aristotle* meant when, in the manner of his times, he spoke of power as liberty (*Politics* 6.2): *In a popular state there is liberty by definition. This is what they commonly say, as if no one was free outside this state.* From which one may infer in passing that those citizens who deplore their loss of liberty in a *Monarchy* are only annoyed because they are not called to play a role in the government of the Country.

9. But for this reason perhaps someone will say that the *popular state* is immensely preferable to *Monarchy*, because in that state, in which of course everyone manages public business, everyone has been given leave to publicly display his prudence knowledge and eloquence in deliberations about matters of the greatest difficulty and importance; and because the love of praise is innate in human nature, this is the most attractive of all things to all those who surpass others in such talents or seem to themselves to do so; but in *Monarchy* that road to winning praise and rank is blocked for most of the citizens. What is a disadvantage, if this is not? I will tell you. To see the proposal of a man whom we despise preferred to our own; to see our wisdom ignored before our eyes; to incur certain enmity in an uncertain struggle for empty glory; to hate and be hated because of differences of opinion (which cannot be avoided, whether we win or lose);[5] to reveal our plans and wishes when there is no need to and to get nothing by it; to neglect our private affairs. These, I say, are disadvantages. But to lose the opportunity to pit your wits against another man, however enjoyable such contests may be to clever debaters, is not such a disadvantage for them, unless we shall say that it is a disadvantage for brave men to be forbidden to fight, for the simple reason that they enjoy it.

10. There are also many reasons, why deliberation does not go as well in large assemblies as among a few counsellors. One is that right deliberation on any matter affecting the commonwealth's security requires a knowledge of external as well as internal affairs. Internal affairs concern the resources by which

---

[5] The apparently awkward placing of the parenthesis in the Latin text is paralleled by XVII.15.

the commonwealth is provisioned and defended and their sources; what places are suitable for defensive positions; how soldiers are to be recruited and maintained; the state of the *people*'s feelings towards the prince or governors of the commonwealth, and such like. External affairs concern the size and power bases of each neighbouring country; the advantages and disadvantages each one provides for us; their attitude toward us and toward each other; and the daily development of their policy. Very few people have any knowledge of these things in a large assembly of men who are for the most part inexperienced, not to say incompetent; so what can that large number of debaters contribute to policy with their inept views but a nuisance?

11. Another reason why a large group is ill suited to deliberation is that each member has to make a long, continuous speech to express his opinion; and deploy his eloquence to make it as ornate and attractive as possible to the audience, in order to win a reputation. The task of eloquence is to make the *Good* and the *bad*, the *useful* and the *useless*, the *Honourable* and the *dishonourable* appear greater or less than they really are, and to make the *unjust* appear *Just*, as may seem to suit the speaker's purpose. For this is what persuasion is; and however much reasoning they put into it, they do not begin from true principles but from ἐνδόξοις, i.e. from commonly accepted opinions, which are for the most part usually false, and they do not try to make their discourse correspond to the nature of things but to the passions of men's hearts. The result is that votes are cast not on the basis of correct reasoning but on emotional impulse. This is not the fault of the *man* but of *Eloquence* itself, whose end (as all the masters of Rhetoric point out) is not truth (except by accident) but victory; and its task is not to teach but to persuade.

12. The third reason why deliberation in a large assembly is unprofitable is that it is a source of *factions* in the commonwealth, and *factions* are the source of sedition and civil war. For when well-matched orators confront each other with conflicting proposals and adversarial speeches, the defeated speaker resents the victorious speaker and with him all those who accepted his point of view, as if they had despised his own advice and good sense; he makes every effort to ensure that his opponent's policy works out badly for the country; for so he sees that his opponent will

lose his glory and he will recover his. Besides, when the votes are sufficiently close for the defeated to have hopes of winning a majority at a subsequent meeting if a few men swing round to their way of thinking, their leaders get them all together, and they hold a private discussion on how to revoke the measure that has just been passed. They resolve among themselves to attend the next meeting in large numbers and to be there first; they arrange what each should say and in what order, so that the question may be brought up again, and the decision that was made when their opponents were there in strength may be reversed when they fail to show. This sort of effort and hard work, which they use to *fashion* a people, is usually called *faction*. When a *faction* is short of votes but superior or not much inferior in strength, then they try to get by arms what they could not get by eloquence and intrigue; and a civil war is born. But this, one will say, does not happen necessarily or often. One may also say that Orators are not necessarily greedy for glory, nor do great orators often disagree with each other on great issues.

13. It follows from this that where the supreme power to make laws is lodged in such assemblies, the laws are unstable, and are not changed to follow an alteration in the state of affairs or a change of sentiment, but according to whether a larger number of men from one *faction* or the other has found its way into the council; so that the laws there are tossed this way and that as on the waves of the sea.

14. In the fourth place, deliberations of large assemblies have the disadvantage that the commonwealth's policies which it is normally of the highest importance to keep secret, are revealed to enemies before they can be put into effect; and foreigners have as profound a knowledge as the *sovereign people* itself of what it can do and what it cannot, of what it plans to do and what it does not.

15. These disadvantages found in the deliberations of large assemblies prove that *Monarchy* is better than *Democracy* in so far as in *Democracy* questions of great importance are more often passed to such assemblies for discussion than in a *Monarchy*; it cannot easily be otherwise. There is no reason why anyone would not prefer to spend his time on his *private business* rather than on *public affairs*, except that he sees scope for his eloquence, to acquire a reputation for intelligence and good sense, and to return home and

enjoy the triumph for his great achievements with friends, parents and wife.[6] The whole pleasure which *Marcus Coriolanus* drew from his deeds in war was seeing that his mother was pleased with the praise he received.[7] But if in a *Democracy* the *people* should choose to concentrate deliberations about war and peace and legislation in the hands of just one man or of a very small number of men, and were happy to appoint magistrates and public ministers, i.e. to have authority without executive power, then it must be admitted that *Democracy* and *Monarchy* would be equal in this matter.

16. Nor do the comparative advantages or disadvantages of different types of commonwealth result from the fact that government [*imperium*] itself or the administration of government business is better entrusted to one man rather than to more than one, or on the other hand to a larger rather than a smaller number. For government [*imperium*] is a *capacity* [*potentia*], administration of government is an *act* [*actus*]. *Power* is equal in every kind of commonwealth; what differs are the acts, i.e. the *motions* and *actions* of the commonwealth, depending on whether they originate from the deliberations of many or of a few, of the competent or of the incompetent. This implies that the advantages and disadvantages of a régime do not depend upon him in whom the authority of the commonwealth resides, but upon the ministers of government. Hence it is no obstacle to the good government of a commonwealth if the *Monarch* is a woman, a boy or an infant, provided that the holders of the ministries and public offices are competent to handle the business. The saying, *Alas for the kingdom whose king is a boy*, does not mean that the state of *Monarchy* is inferior to the popular state, but the opposite. It means that it is an accidental disadvantage of Kingship, that when the *King is a boy*, it sometimes happens that many men force their way by ambition and violence into the public counsels, and the commonwealth is administered *Democratically*, and that is the origin of those unhappy conditions that for the most part go with *government by the people*.

---

[6] Reading *uxorem* for *uxores* of all the editions.
[7] Gnaeus Marcus Coriolanus, legendary Roman leader in the wars against the Volscians. Charged with tyrannical conduct towards his fellow citizens, he went over to the Volsci and led them against Rome. The pleas of his mother Veturia and his wife Volumnia deterred him from attacking the city (491 BC). Hobbes's text is a close translation from Plutarch, 'Life of Coriolanus', 4.

17. The most evident sign that the most absolute *Monarchy* is the best of all conditions for a commonwealth, is that not only kings but also commonwealths which are subject to the *people* and the *optimates* invariably confer full power to conduct a war on one man alone; and that power is the most absolute power possible; (note in passing that no King can rightly grant a General more power over an army than he can himself exercise over the citizens). A *Monarchy* therefore is the best government of all in an army camp. And what else are countries but so many camps fortified against each other with garrisons and arms, and their state (since no common power restrains them, even though an uncertain peace, as fragile as a short truce, exists between them) is to be regarded as a natural state, i.e. a state of war?

18. Finally, since it was necessary to our preservation to be subject to some *man* or *assembly*, our best situation is to be subject to someone who has an interest in our safety and health. This situation occurs when we are the sovereign's inheritance; for everyone has a strong natural inclination to preserve his own inheritance. The wealth of princes is not estates and monies but the citizen's physical and mental vigour. Anyone will readily grant this who notices how highly the lordships of small commonwealths are valued in monetary terms, and how much more easily men bring in money than money brings in men. No example readily comes to mind of a subject robbed of life and property by his prince from sheer caprice without any fault on his part.

19. The comparison so far has been between the *Monarchic* and the *popular* state; we have said nothing about *Aristocracy*. From what has been said about the other two regimes, it seems we may conclude that the form of *Aristocracy* which is hereditary, and, content with the election of Magistrates, devolves deliberation on the few men who are best fitted to it, and which (to put it simply) imitates government by *Monarchs* most closely and government by the *people* least closely, is better for individual citizens than the other forms of *Aristocracy*, and is longer lasting.

Chapter XI

Passages and examples from holy scripture about the right of Kingship, which appear to support our account

1. The origin of a commonwealth by design is from the consent of the people. 2. Judgements *and* Wars *depend on the will of sovereigns. 3. Holders of sovereign power cannot rightly be punished. 4. Without sovereign power there is no* commonwealth *but* Anarchy. *5. Slaves and Sons owe simple obedience to Masters and Parents. 6. Absolute power is supported by clear passages from both Old and New Testaments.*

1. At VI.2 we derived the origin of a commonwealth by design, or political commonwealth, from an agreement by a number of men, in such terms that it is apparent that all must consent or be regarded as enemies. Such was the origin of God's Kingdom over the Jews instituted by *Moses. If you shall hear my voice,* etc. *you will be to me a Priestly kingdom,* etc. *Moses came, and calling together the elders of the people,* etc. *and all the people replied together: we will do all that the Lord has spoken* (Exod. 19.5–8). Such too was the beginning of *Moses'* power under God, or his viceregal power. *The whole people saw the voices and the lights,* etc. *saying to Moses: 'speak to us and we will hear'* (Exod. 20.18–19). The beginning of the reign of Saul was similar. *But, seeing that Naas, King of the sons of Ammon, had come against you, you said to me, 'No way, but a king shall command us', although your Lord was reigning over you. Now therefore your king is here whom you have chosen and asked for* (1 Sam. 12.12). And when they did not all give their agreement, though the majority did, (for there were *the sons of Belial,* who *said, Surely he won't be able to save us? and they despised him,* 1 Sam. 10.27), those who did not agree were put to death as enemies. *Who is it,* (said the people to Samuel) *who said, 'Saul will not reign over us? bring the men and we will kill them'* (1 Sam. 11.12).

2. In the same chapter VI, articles 6 and 7, it was shown that both legal *Judgements* and *Wars* depend on the will of the holder of sovereign power in the commonwealth; that is, in a *Monarchy,* on the one man who is *Monarch* or *King.* This is confirmed by the

people's own judgement. *'We too will be as all the nations are, and our king shall* JUDGE us, and shall go out before us, and fight our *WARS* for us' (1 Sam. 8.20). And by the testimony of King Solomon, with respect to *judgements*, and all subjects which can be argued to be *good* or *bad*. *Give therefore to your servant a teachable heart, so that he may be able to* JUDGE your people, and tell GOOD from EVIL (1 Kings 3.9). And of Absalom, *there is no one appointed by the King to hear you* (2 Sam. 15.3).

3. King David confirms that Kings cannot be punished by their subjects, as shown above at VI.12. Although Saul was seeking him to put him to death, David still refrained from killing Saul and forbade Abisaeus to do so saying: *Do not kill him; for who shall stretch out his hand against the Anointed One of the Lord, and be guiltless?* (1 Sam. [26].9).[1] And when he had cut off the hem of Saul's cloak, *May the Lord*, he said, *be merciful to me, lest I do this thing to my Lord, the Anointed One of the Lord, to lift my hand against him* (1 Sam. 24.7). And he ordered the death of the *Amalekite* who had killed *Saul*, although he had done it to win his favour (2 Sam. 1.15).

4. The statement at Jud. 17.6, *In those days there was no king in Israel, but each man did what seemed to him to be right*, (as if where there is no *Monarchy*, there is *Anarchy*, or universal chaos) could be used to prove the superiority of kingship to all other forms; except that by the word *King*, might perhaps be meant not *one man* but *one council*, provided it were the seat of sovereign power. But even so the point still emerges that in the absence of sovereign and absolute power (as we attempted to prove in the whole of the sixth chapter) anyone may do whatever he pleases, or whatever seems right to him; and that is inconsistent with the survival of the human race, which is why in every commonwealth sovereign power is understood to exist somewhere by the law of nature.

5. We said (at VIII.7, 8) that *slaves* owe simple obedience to their *Masters*, and at IX.7 that *children* owe simple obedience to their *fathers*. St Paul says the same thing: in the case of servants, *Servants, obey your Lords in the flesh in* ALL THINGS, *not serving them to make a good impression, as men-pleasers, but fearing the Lord in the simplicity of your heart* (Col. 3.22). And on children, *Children, obey your par-*

---

[1] Reference given incorrectly in all editions. Corrected by Warrender.

ents in ALL THINGS; *for this is pleasing in the Lord* (Col. 3.20). And just as in the case of simple obedience we take it as ALL THINGS that are not against the laws of God, so in the passages quoted from St. Paul, we must understand after ALL THINGS the phrase, *except for what is against God's laws.*

6. To avoid going through the right of princes point by point, I will quote the passages which establish all their power at once (namely that their subjects owe them simple and absolute obedience). And first from the new Testament: *The Scribes and the Pharisees sit on the seat of Moses; therefore observe and do* ALL THINGS *that they say to you* (Matth. [23].2). Do *all things*, he says, that is, *simply* obey. Why? Because they sit on the *seat of Moses*, the seat, that is, of the *civil prince*, not of *Aaron*, the Priest. *Let every soul be subject to the higher powers; for there is no power that is not of God. And the powers that be have been ordained by God. Therefore he who resists a power, resists the ordination of God. And those who resist, earn damnation for themselves*, etc. (Rom. 13.1ff). Since therefore the powers that were at the time of St. *Paul* were ordained by God, and all kings at that time demanded complete obedience from their subjects, it follows that such power was ordained by God. *Be subject to every human creature for God's sake, whether to the King as supreme, or to governors as sent by him to take vengeance on evildoers, and to commend good men; for such is the will of God.* (1 Pet. 2.13). Again, St. Paul to Titus: *Remind them to be subject to princes and powers, to do what they are told* (3.1). Which Princes? Surely the Princes of those times who required simple obedience? To come next to Christ's own Example: the kingdom of the Jews was due to him by hereditary right derived from David, but since he lived as a subject, he paid taxes to *Caesar* and declared that they belonged to *Caesar: Pay what are Caesar's to Caesar* (he said) *and to God what are God's* (Matth. 22.21). And when it pleased him to act as a King, he required complete obedience. *Go*, he said, *into the village which is in front of you, and straightway you will find an ass tied up, and a foal with her. Untie them and bring them to me, and if anyone says anything, say that the Lord has need of them* (Matth. 21.2). This he did, then, by his right as Lord, or King of the Jews. To take away a subject's property on the ground that *the Lord has need* is absolute Power. The clearest passages to the same effect in the old Testament are the following. *Approach and hear* ALL THINGS *that the Lord our God*

shall say to you, and you shall tell us, and we will listen and do them
(Deut. 5.27). Complete obedience is contained in that phrase *all
things*. Again, to *Joshua: And they answered Joshua and said, 'We will
do ALL the things that you have instructed us, and we will go wherever
you send us; as we obeyed Moses in ALL THINGS, so we will obey you
also; only may the Lord your God be with you as he was with Moses.
Anyone who speaks against your face, and does not obey ALL the instructions that you give him, let him die'* (Josh. 1.16). And the parable of
the Thorn-bush: *And all the trees said to the Thorn-bush, 'Come and
rule over us', and it answered them, 'If in truth you are making me
your King, come and rest under my shade; but if you do not so wish,
let fire come out from the Thorn-bush, and consume the cedars of Leb-
anon'* (Jud. 9.14). The point of these words is that we must accept
the instructions of those whom we have truly set as Kings over us,
if we do not want to be consumed by the fires of civil war. Royal
power is more particularly described by God himself through
Samuel: *Warn them of the right of the King who will reign over them,*
etc. *This shall be the right of the King who will command you, he will
take your Sons and put them in his chariots,* etc. *he will make your
Daughters his unguent makers,* etc. *he will take your best Olive orchards
and give them to his servants,* etc. (1 Sam. 8.[9ff.]). Surely such power
is absolute? Yet God himself calls it THE RIGHT OF THE KING. And
no one seems to have been exempt from it, not even the *high Priest*
of the Jews. For when *the King* (namely Solomon) said to *Abiatharus
the priest, 'Go to your estate at Amathot, you are truly a man of death,
but I will not kill you today, because you carried the ark of the Lord
God before my father David, and suffered toil in all the things in which
my father was afflicted'*, and Solomon dismissed *Abiatharus as the Priest
of the Lord* (1 Kings 2.26), it cannot be shown from any account
that this was displeasing to God; for we do not read that Solomon
was rebuked or that his person at that time was unacceptable to
God.

Chapter XII

On the internal causes which tend to dissolve a commonwealth

1. That judgements of good and evil belong to individuals, is a seditious opinion. 2. That subjects sin in obeying their Princes, is a seditious opinion. 3. That tyrannicide is permitted, is a seditious opinion. 4. That the holders of sovereign power are also subject to the civil laws, is a seditious opinion. 5. That sovereign power can be divided, is a seditious opinion. 6. That faith and holiness are not acquired by effort and reason but are always supernaturally infused and inspired in men, is a seditious opinion. 7. That individual citizens have absolute property or ownership of their goods, is a seditious opinion. 8. Men are disposed to sedition by not knowing the difference between a people and a crowd. 9. Men are disposed to sedition by too strict an exaction of taxes, however justified and necessary it may be. 10. Men are disposed to sedition by the hope of success. 11. Men are disposed to sedition by the hope of success. 12. The quality which is needed to excite seditions is eloquence without wisdom. 13. How the stupidity of the vulgar and the eloquence of the ambitious conspire to dissolve the commonwealth.

1. To this point we have been speaking of the causes of the formation of commonwealths, of the agreements on which they rest, and of the rights of sovereigns over citizens. Now we must speak briefly of the causes of the dissolution of commonwealths, or the causes of sedition. In the motion of natural bodies we have three things to consider: the *internal disposition* by which bodies are capable of making motion; the *external Agent*, by which a certain, specific motion is actually produced; and the *action itself.* So likewise in a commonwealth, there are three things to look at when the citizens are in an uproar: first, the *doctrines* and *passions* inimical to peace, by which the minds of individuals are given a certain disposition; second, what sort of men take people who are already disposed to rebellion and violence, and incite, assemble and direct them; and third, the means by which it is done, or *faction* itself. Of doctrines that dispose men to sedition, the first, without question, is: *that knowledge of good and evil is a matter for individuals.* We allowed that this was true in the natural state; in fact we proved it (1.9); for in a

natural state, individuals live by equal right, and have not submitted by their own agreement to other men's power. But in the civil state it is false. For it has been shown (VI.9) that the civil laws are the rules of *good* and *evil*, of the *just* and the *unjust*, the *honourable* and the *dishonourable*, and that therefore one must accept what the legislator enjoins as *good*, and what he forbids as *evil*. The legislator is always the holder of sovereign power – in a Monarchy, the Monarch. We confirmed this by the words of *Solomon* [11.2].[1] For if it were the case that the good to be followed and the evil to be avoided were what individuals decided they are, what is the meaning of these words (1 Kings 3.9): *You will give your servant a docile heart, that he may be able to judge your people and distinguish between good and evil?* Since it is for kings to distinguish between good and evil, it is wicked to say, though it is said every day, *He who does rightly is a King*, and, *Kings need not be obeyed unless their commands are just*, and other phrases of that kind. *Just* and *unjust* did not exist until commands were given; hence their nature is relative to a command; and every action in its own nature is indifferent. What is *just* or *unjust* derives from the right of the ruler. Legitimate kings therefore make what they order just by ordering it, and make what they forbid unjust by forbidding it. When private men claim for themselves a knowledge of *good* and *evil*, they are aspiring to be as Kings. When this happens the commonwealth cannot stand. The oldest of God's commands is (Gen. 2.17): *Do not eat of the tree of the knowledge of good and evil*, and the oldest of the devil's temptations is (3.5): *You will be as gods knowing good and evil*. The first reproach God made to men is (v. 11): *Who told you that you were naked, unless you have eaten of the tree of which I told you not to eat? as* if he were saying, how did you decide that the nakedness in which it seemed good to me to create you, was dishonourable, except by usurping for yourselves a *knowledge* of good and evil?

2. Whatever one does against conscience is a sin [*peccatum*]; for to do such a thing is to reject the law. But a distinction must be made: my sin is what I as agent regard as a sin on my part; but what I regard as a sin in someone else, I may sometimes do without committing sin myself. For if I am told to do something which it

---

[1] All the Latin editions give the reference here as 2.6; Warrender follows the English translation in referring to 11.2.

is a sin for the person to tell me to do, I commit no sin in doing it, provided that the person who tells me to do it is my Lord by right. For I am not acting unjustly if I go to war at the order of my commonwealth though I believe that it is an unjust war; rather I act unjustly if I refuse to go to war, claiming for myself the knowledge of what is just and unjust which belongs to the commonwealth. Those who do not observe this distinction will find themselves committed to sin whenever they are ordered to do anything illicit – or which seems so to them. For if they obey, they will be acting against conscience; if they do not obey they will be acting against right. If they act against conscience, they show that they do not fear the penalties of the life to come; if they act against law, they are doing what one man can to undermine human society and the civil life of this world. Hence those who teach that *subjects commit sin in obeying a command of their Prince which seems to them unjust*, hold an opinion which is not only false but one of those opinions which are inimical to civil obedience; it depends upon the original error noted in the previous article. For by judging of good and evil for ourselves we ensure that we commit a sin whether we obey or disobey.

3. The third seditious doctrine sprung from the same root, is that *tyrannicide is licit*. In fact certain Theologians in our own day and all the Sophists of the past – *Plato, Aristotle, Cicero, Seneca, Plutarch* and the rest of the champions of Anarchy in Greece and Rome – have supposed that it is not only licit, but deserves the highest praise. By the word *tyrants* they mean not only Monarchs but all who exercise sovereign power in any kind of commonwealth: at Athens not only *Pisistratus* who ruled alone, but also the Thirty men who later held power together, were spoken of individually as *Tyrants*. Now anyone whom they want killed as a *Tyrant*, rules either by right or without right. If without right, he is a public enemy [*hostis*] and is rightly killed, though this should not be called *Tyrannicide* but *hosticide*. If he holds power rightly, the divine question applies: *Who told you that he was a Tyrant, unless you have eaten of the tree of which I told you not to eat?*[2] For why do you call him a *Tyrant* whom God made a *King*, unless you, a private person, are claiming for yourself a knowledge of *good* and *evil*? One may easily see how dangerous this belief is to commonwealths, and particularly

[2] Cf. Genesis 3.11.

to *Monarchies*, by recognizing that it exposes any *King*, good or bad, to the risk of being condemned by the judgement, and murdered by the hand, of one solitary assassin.

4. The fourth opinion inimical to civil society comes from those who think that *holders of sovereign power are subject to the civil laws.* I have already shown at VI.14 that this is a false opinion. It is false because a commonwealth cannot be obligated either to itself or to a citizen. Not to itself, because one cannot be obligated to oneself. Not to a citizen, because the individual wills of citizens are contained in the will of the commonwealth in such a way that if the commonwealth wills to release itself from such an obligation, the citizens also will to do so, and it is accordingly free. What is true of the commonwealth is also understood to be true of the man or assembly of men which holds sovereign power; for they are the commonwealth; it exists only through their sovereign power. This opinion is obviously incompatible with the essence of a commonwealth because it would put the *knowledge of just and unjust*, i.e. the determination of what is, and what is not, contrary to the civil laws, back into the hands of individuals. As soon as an order is given which is thought to be contrary to the laws, there will be an end to obedience and to all coercive authority [*potestas coactiva*] too, and that cannot happen without destroying the essence of a commonwealth. This error has powerful supporters (among them *Aristotle*) who think that because men lack self-restraint, sovereign authority in the commonwealth should be lodged in the laws alone. But they do not seem to have looked at all deeply into the nature of a commonwealth, who suppose that coercive authority, legislation and the interpretation of laws (which are powers a commonwealth must necessarily have) should be left to the laws themselves. And although individual citizens can sometimes contend in judgement with the commonwealth itself and take legal action against it, this is appropriate only when it is not a question of what the commonwealth can do, but of what it intended by a certain law. For example, when there is a capital case against a citizen under a certain law, the question is not whether the commonwealth can take away his life by its own absolute right, but whether it intended that his life should be taken away under that law. If he broke the law, it did so intend; otherwise it did not so intend. Therefore, the argument that the citizen has legal action against the commonwealth is not

sufficient to prove that the commonwealth is bound by its own laws. To the contrary, it is evident that the commonwealth is not bound by its own laws, because no one is obligated to himself. Laws are made for *Titius* and *Gaius*,[3] not for the commonwealth, even though ambitious lawyers have got ignorant laymen to believe that the laws depend on lawyers' jurisprudence and not on the authority of the commonwealth.

5. Fifthly, the doctrine that *sovereign power can be divided* is absolutely fatal to commonwealths. There are different ways of making the division. The effect of one kind of division is to grant sovereign power to the civil authority on issues affecting peace and the good things of this life; and to concede issues involving salvation of souls to others. But since the most essential prerequisite of salvation is justice, the result of this division is that citizens measure justice not, as they should, by the civil laws, but by the commands and teachings of people who are, in relation to the commonwealth, either private persons or foreigners. In superstitious terror they refuse to offer the obedience due to their Princes; falling by fear itself into what they fear. What can be more dangerous to a commonwealth than for citizens to be turned by the threat of eternal torment from obeying their princes, i.e. from obeying the laws, or from being just? Another division of sovereign power gives the supreme power of War and Peace to one man (whom they call the *Monarch*) but not the right to exact money, which they assign to others. Since money is the sinews of war and peace, this is either not a real division of the thing itself, in that it gives the power to those who have authority over the money and only the name to the other; or if it is a division, it dissolves the commonwealth, for neither War, if war is necessary, nor the public peace, can be sustained without money.

6. It is commonly taught that *Faith and holiness are not acquired by effort and natural reason, but are always supernaturally infused or inspired in men.* But if this were true, I do not see why we were bidden to give account of our faith[4] or why every true Christian is not a Prophet, or why in fact each man should not decide what he

---

[3] Stock names of Roman citizens from the *Digest* and other Roman law texts.
[4] Perhaps a reminiscence of I Peter 3.15: 'But sanctify the Lord God in your hearts: and be ready always to give an answer to every man that asketh you a reason of the hope that is in you with meekness and fear.'

should or should not do from his own inspiration rather than from the precepts of rulers or from right reason. We are back to *private knowledge of good and evil*, which cannot be conceded without the dissolution of commonwealths. This opinion is so widespread in the Christian world that the number of Apostates from natural reason is almost infinite. It began with crazy men, who got themselves a store of sacred words from reading scripture, and have developed the habit of stringing them together as they preach in such a way that what they say is meaningless, but seems divine to the ignorant; when a man has no rational capacity but his speech appears divine, he will inevitably be thought to be divinely inspired.

7. The seventh doctrine inimical to commonwealths is that *individual citizens have absolute Dominion [Dominium] over their possessions*; i.e. such a *property [proprietas]* in them as excludes the right of all their fellow-citizens and of the commonwealth itself to those things. It is not true. For those who have a *Lord [Dominus]* do not have *Dominion*, as was proved at VIII.5. And the commonwealth by its formation is the Lord of all the citizens. Before accepting the civil yoke no one had a property right in anything; all things were *common* to all men. Tell me, then, where this *property* came to you from, if not from the commonwealth? And from where did it come to the commonwealth, except that each man transferred his right to the commonwealth? You too therefore assigned your right to the commonwealth. Your *Dominion* therefore and your *property* are as extensive as the commonwealth wishes and lasts for just so long; as in a family, the father determines which goods are the *property* of the children and for how long. However, the vast majority of those who profess civil science take a different line. *We are*, they say, *equal by nature; there is no reason why anyone has a better right to take away my property than I have to take away his; we know that money is sometimes necessary for the public defence, but those who exact it must demonstrate the need and take the money on the basis of consent.*[5] Those who speak like this fail to realize that the procedure they suggest has already taken place at the beginning when the commonwealth was being formed; by speaking as if they were still in a disorganized crowd [*dissoluta multitudo*] and no commonwealth were

---

[5] Italics supplied by the translator.

yet formed, they are undermining the commonwealth that has been formed.

8. The last factor that is detrimental to a civil Régime, and particularly to a Monarchy, is that men do not make a clear enough distinction between a *people* and a *crowd*. A *people* is a *single* entity, with *a single will*; you can attribute *an act* to it. None of this can be said of a crowd. In every commonwealth the *People* Reigns; for even in *Monarchies* the *People* exercises power [*imperat*]; for the *people* wills through the will of *one man*. But the citizens, i.e. the subjects, are a *crowd*. In a *Democracy* and in an *Aristocracy* the citizens are the *crowd*, but the *council* is the *people*; in a *Monarchy* the subjects are the *crowd*, and (paradoxically) the *King* is the *people*. Ordinary people and others who do not notice this point, always speak of a *large number* of men as the *people*, i.e. as the *commonwealth*; they speak of the *commonwealth* having rebelled against the *king* (which is impossible) and of the *people* wanting, or not wanting, what malcontent and murmuring subjects want or do not want; under this label of the *people*, they are setting the *citizens* against the *commonwealth*, i.e. the *Crowd* against the *people*. These then are the main opinions which make the citizens ripe for unrest if they are steeped in them. Since the holder or holders of sovereign power in any commonwealth must preserve their majesty, the crime of lèse-majesté naturally attaches to these opinions.

9. What grieves and discontents the human spirit more than anything else is *poverty*; or *want* of the essentials for the preservation of life and dignity. And although everyone knows that wealth is got by industry and kept by thrift, the poor always shift the blame from their own idleness and extravagance onto the government of the commonwealth, as if their private property was exhausted by public exactions. But men should reflect that those who have no patrimony must not only labour to live but fight in order to labour. Every one of the Jews who built the wall of *Jerusalem* in the time of *Ezra* did the work with one hand and held a sword in the other. In every commonwealth, one has to recognize that the hand which holds the sword is the *King* or *supreme council*, and it must be maintained by the citizens' industry no less than the hand with which each man builds his private fortune. *Taxes* and *tributes* are simply the wages of

those who keep watch under arms, so that the citizens' industry will not be hampered by enemy invasion. It is no more just a complaint to blame their poverty on payment of taxes than to say that they are getting poorer by paying their debts. But most men never think of any of this; they are in the same condition as people afflicted by the disease called *Incubus*; this is caused by over-eating, but it makes them feel that they are being assaulted and oppressed and suffocated by a heavy weight. It is pretty obvious that those who believe themselves to be carrying the whole massive burden of the commonwealth are prone to sedition; and those who are hurting in current conditions are glad for revolution.

10. Another grievance that hurts the commonwealth is the discontent felt by those who with ample leisure at their disposal, fail to achieve a position of dignity. By nature all men compete for honours and reputation, but those most of all who are least distracted by worry about ordinary necessities. They are driven by leisure sometimes to discuss politics with each other, and sometimes to superficial reading of books of History, Oratory, Politics and other things. And so they come to believe that they are well equipped by their intelligence and learning to handle affairs of the highest importance. But many of them have to be passed over; for they are not all what they believe themselves to be, and even if they were, there are too many of them to be all employed in public office. They take this as a personal insult; they envy those who got ahead of them, they still hope to make it themselves, and the failure of current public policies becomes their dearest wish. Hence it is not surprising if they passionately expect opportunities for revolution.

11. *Hope of winning* must also be included among the seditious passions. For men can be as steeped as may be in opinions inimical to peace and civil government; they can be hurt and exasperated by injuries and insults from those in authority; but if they have little or no *hope of winning*, no sedition will follow; individuals will hide their feelings and put up with a bad situation rather than risk a worse. Four things are indispensable to this *hope*: *numbers*, *tools*, *mutual trust* and *Leaders*. To resist the public Magistrates without heavy *numbers* is not sedition but desperation. By *tools* I mean *arms* and *provisions*; without these, *numbers* have no value, and neither do

arms without *mutual trust*; and none of these things has value without union[6] under a *leader*. He must be a *leader* whom they willingly obey, not because they are obligated by having submitted to his command (for we have argued in this very chapter that men in this situation do not know that they are obligated beyond what seems right and good to themselves), but because they value his courage and military skill, or because they share his passions. If these four things are available to men who can barely tolerate their present conditions and who measure the rightness of their actions by their own judgement, the only other thing needed to create sedition and turmoil in the commonwealth is *someone to rouse them and incite them to action*.

12. No one was more made for sedition than *Catiline*; he is portrayed in *Sallust* as having *adequate eloquence but little wisdom*.[7] *Sallust* separates *wisdom* from *eloquence*, attributing the latter to him as essential to a born rabble-rouser, denying him wisdom because wisdom dictates peace. But there are two kinds of *Eloquence*: one is a lucid and elegant exponent of thought and conceptions, which arises partly from observation of things and partly from an understanding of words taken in their proper meanings as defined. The other *eloquence* is an agitator of the passions (e.g. *hope, fear, anger, pity*), and arises out of a metaphorical use of words, adapted to the passions. The former fashions speech from true principles, the latter from received opinions of whatever kind. The art of the one is Logic, of the other Rhetoric. The end of one is truth, of the other victory. Both have their uses, the one in deliberation, the other in exhortation. For one is never separated from *wisdom*; the other almost always is. From the actual work which they have to do it is easy to see that a *powerful eloquence* of this kind, divorced from a knowledge of things, i.e. from wisdom, is the true feature of those who agitate and incite the people to revolution. For they could not infect the people with those absurd opinions inimical to peace and civil society, unless they held them themselves; and that indicates a greater ignorance than can belong to a wise man. For who can be thought to be even moderately wise, who does not know whence the laws derive their force; what are the rules of *justice* and *injustice*,

---

[6] Reading, for *sive* of the Latin editions, *sine*, as implied by the English translation of 1651 and preferred by Warrender.

[7] Sallust, *Catiline*, 5.4.

honour and *dishonour*, *good* and *evil*; what achieves and preserves peace among men and what destroys it; what is *one's own* and what is *another's*; and what he wants done for himself (so that he may do the same to another)? But their ability to render their hearers insane (who were merely stupid before); to make men believe that a bad situation is worse than it is, and that a good situation is bad; to exaggerate hopes and to minimize risks beyond reason, is due to eloquence; not the eloquence which expounds things as they are, but the other eloquence, which by communicating the excitement of the speaker to the minds of others makes everything appear as he had seen it in his own excited mind.

13. Even many of those who are loyal to the commonwealth unwittingly cooperate in disposing the citizens' minds towards sedition, by infecting the young people in the schools and the rest of the population from the pulpit with teaching that follows the opinions we have spoken of. But those who want to turn that disposition into action devote the whole thrust of their effort first to uniting the disaffected as a *faction* and a *conspiracy*; and then to getting the leading role in the *faction* themselves. They unite them into a faction by making themselves mediators and interpreters of individuals' plans and actions, and by appointing persons and places for meeting and discussing those issues by which the government of the commonwealth may be reformed according to their ideas. For them to control the *faction*, they must form a *faction* within the *faction*; that is, they must hold secret meetings separately with a handful of people, where they may arrange what proposals are to be made in the general assembly later, and what each of them is to say and in what order, and how to draw to their position those who have most power and most influence with the rank and file of the *faction*. And in this manner when they have a large enough *faction*, which they dominate by their eloquence, they incite it to take control of affairs, and thus they sometimes succeed, if there is no opposing faction, in overthrowing the government, but more often they only wound it and provoke civil war. Thus *stupidity* and *eloquence* unite to subvert the commonwealth; in the manner in which once upon a time (as the story goes)[8] the daughters of *Pelias*, king of Thessaly conspired with *Medea* against their father. Wishing to

---

[8] Cf. Ovid, *Metamorphoses*, 7.297–349.

restore a decrepit old man to his youth, they cut him in pieces by the advice of *Medea* and placed him on the fire to cook, in the vain hope that he would be rejuvenated. In the same manner the mob in their stupidity, like the daughters of *Pelias*, desiring to renew their old commonwealth and led by the *eloquence* of ambitious men as by the sorcery of *Medea*, more often split it into *factions* and waste it with fire than reform it.

Chapter XIII
On the duties of those who exercise sovereign power

1. The right of sovereign power is distinguished from its exercise. 2. The safety of the people is the supreme law. 3. It is the duty of rulers to look to the common interest of many, not to the private interest of this man or that. 4. By safety is meant all advantages. 5. The question whether it is the duty of Kings to provide for the safety of the souls of their citizens, as seems best to them according to their own conscience. 6. What constitutes the safety of the people. 7. Intelligence agents are necessary to the defence of a country. 8. It is also necessary to the defence of a people to make ready in time of peace soldiers, arms, fortifications and money. 9. The right instruction of the citizens in civil doctrine is necessary to the preservation of peace. 10. Fair distribution of public burdens assists the preservation of peace. 11. It is naturally fair that tax assessments should be related to what each person consumes not what he possesses. 12. It conduces to peace to keep a check on ambitious men. 13. And to dissolve factions. 14. The citizens' prosperity is favoured by laws which encourage profitable skills and restrain expenditure. 15. The laws should determine no more than the interest of the citizens and the commonwealth requires. 16. No greater penalties should be inflicted than the laws specify. 17. Redress should be given to citizens against corrupt judges.

1. From what has been said so far, the *duties* of citizens and subjects in each kind of commonwealth and the *powers* of sovereigns over them are now clear. We have not yet spoken of the *duties* of sovereigns [*imperantium*] and of how they should behave towards citizens. We must distinguish between the *right* and the *exercise* of sovereign power; for they can be separated; for instance, he who has the *right* may be unwilling or unable to play a personal role in conducting trials or deliberating issues. For there are occasions when kings cannot manage affairs because of their age, or when even though they can, they judge it more correct to content themselves with choosing ministers and counsellors, and to exercise their power through them. When *right* and *exercise* are separated, the government of the commonwealth is like the ordinary government of the world, in which God the first mover of all things, produces natural

effects through the order of secondary causes. But when he who has the right to reign wishes to participate himself in all judgements, consultations and public actions, it is a way of running things comparable to God's attending directly to every thing himself, contrary to the order of nature. So we shall speak briefly and summarily in this chapter of the *duties* of those who exercise sovereign power whether in their own right or by someone else's. For it is not my plan to descend to particular points in which princes may do things differently from each other; this must be left to experts in the practical politics of individual commonwealths.

2. All the duties of sovereigns are implicit in this one phrase: *the safety of the people is the supreme law*. For although those who hold sovereign power among men cannot be subject to laws properly so called, i.e. to the will of men, because sovereignty and subjection to others are contradictory, it is nevertheless their *duty* to obey right reason in all things so far as they can; right reason is the natural, moral and divine law. And since governments were formed for the sake of peace, and peace is sought for safety, if the incumbent in power used it otherwise than for the people's safety, he would be acting against the principles of peace, that is, against natural law. And just as the people's safety dictates the law by which Princes come to know their *duty*, it also teaches them the art by which they look after their own interest. For the power [*potentia*] of the citizens is the power of the commonwealth, that is, his power who holds the sovereignty in the commonwealth.

3. By people here is meant not one civil person, namely the commonwealth itself which rules, but the crowd of citizens who are ruled. For a commonwealth is formed not for its own sake but for the sake of the citizens. Not that notice should be taken of *this* or *that individual* citizen. The sovereign as such provides for the citizens' safety only by means of laws, which are universal. Hence he has done his duty if he has made every effort, to provide by sound measures for the welfare of as many of them as possible for as long as possible; and to see that no one fares badly except by his own fault or by unavoidable circumstances; and it is sometimes good for the safety of the majority that bad men should do badly.

4. By *safety* one should understand not mere survival in any condition, but a happy life so far as that is possible. For men willingly entered commonwealths *which they had formed by design* [*institutivus*]

in order to be able to live as pleasantly as the human condition allows. Those who have taken it upon themselves to exercise power in this kind of commonwealth, would be acting contrary to the law of nature (because in contravention of the trust of those who put the sovereign power in their hands) if they did not do whatever can be done by laws to ensure that the citizens are abundantly provided with all the good things necessary not just for life but for the enjoyment of life. And those who have acquired power by arms all want their subjects to be fit to serve them with the strength of both mind and body; hence they would be acting against their own aim and purpose if they made no effort to see that they are provided not only with what they need to live but also with what they need to be strong.

5. And in the first place, all Princes believe that the kind of opinions people hold about God and the kind of worship they offer him are of the highest significance for their *eternal salvation*. On this assumption, one may question whether sovereigns and the ministers of sovereign power in a commonwealth (whoever they may be, whether one man or several) are not offending against the law of nature, if they do not ensure instruction in the doctrine and practice of the worship which they themselves believe is indispensable to the citizens' *eternal salvation*, or if they permit a contrary teaching or practice. It is evident that they are acting against conscience and, so far as they can, are intending the citizens' eternal damnation. For if that was not their intention, I do not see why (being sovereign and uncompellable) they would allow teachings and practices among their citizens which they believe will damn them. But we will leave this problem aside.

6. Regarding this life only, the good things citizens may enjoy can be put into four categories: 1) defence from external enemies; 2) preservation of internal peace; 3) acquisition of wealth, so far as this is consistent with public security; 4) full enjoyment of innocent liberty. Sovereigns can do no more for the citizens' happiness [*felicitas*] than to enable them to enjoy the possessions their industry has won them, safe from foreign and civil war.

7. Two things are necessary to a people's defence: to be *Forewarned* and to be *Forearmed*. For the state of commonwealths towards each other is a *natural* state, i.e. a state of hostility. Even when the fighting between them stops, it should not be called Peace,

but an intermission during which each watches the motion and aspect of its enemy and gauges its security not on the basis of agreements but by the strength and designs of the adversary. And this is by natural right, as has been shown from the fact that agreements are invalid in the natural state, whenever justified fear is a factor (II.10).[1] The first requirement therefore of a commonwealth's defence is that there be someone to collect *intelligence* and so far as possible *forecast* the plans and movements of all those who have the capacity to do it harm. Reliable *intelligence agents* are to those who exercise sovereign power as rays of light to the human soul; and it is more correct to say of political sight than of natural sight that perceptible and intelligible appearances of things are carried invisibly through the air to the soul (that is, to those who exercise the sovereign power of the commonwealth). Hence they are as necessary to the safety of a commonwealth as rays of light to the safety of a man. Or we may use the analogy of spiders' webs, whose incredibly fine threads spread out in all directions and convey outside movements to the spiders sitting in their little cavities inside. Without *intelligence agents* sovereigns have no more idea what orders need to be given for the defence of their subjects than spiders can know when to emerge and where to make for without the threads of their webs.

8. The second essential requirement of a people's defence is to be *forearmed*. To be forearmed is to be equipped with troops, weapons, a navy and fortifications in a state of readiness before danger threatens, and with funds already accumulated. For it is late, and may be impossible, to conscript soldiers and procure armaments after suffering a defeat. Similarly not to build fortifications and install garrisons at appropriate points before your territory is invaded is to behave like the clowns in Demosthenes, who know nothing about sword fighting and shift the shield from one part of the body to another wherever the blows fall.[2] Those too who think it is time enough to exact the funds for provisioning the troops and other army expenses when danger begins to appear, are surely failing to consider how difficult it is to scrape together such an amount of money all at once; people are so tight-fisted. For almost all men

---

[1] The reference should be to II.11.
[2] Cf. Demosthenes, *Philippic*, I.40–1.

regard anything that they have once got their hands on as so much their own private property, that they believe they are being wronged when they are compelled to pay out even a tiny part of it to the community. Nor is it possible suddenly to find the large sums necessary to defend the commonwealth from the revenue to the treasury from excise or sales tax. Hence money for war must be accumulated in time of peace if we want the commonwealth to be secure. Since therefore, for the citizens' safety, sovereigns need to get intelligence of enemy plans, to maintain weapons and garrisons, and to have money readily available; and since princes are obliged by the law of nature to make every effort to secure the citizens' safety; it follows not only that they are permitted to send out spies, maintain troops, build fortifications and to exact money for the purpose, but also that they may not do otherwise. They may also do anything that seems likely to subvert, by force or by craft, the power of foreigners whom they fear; for the rulers of commonwealths are obliged to do all they can to ensure that the calamities they fear do not happen.

9. Many things are required to preserve internal Peace, because (as was shown in the last chapter) many things conspire to disturb it. We showed there that there are things which dispose men's minds to sedition and other things which move and incite men so disposed. We named certain evil doctrines as the most influential factors in creating this disposition. It is therefore a duty of those who administer sovereign power to root these doctrines out of the citizens' minds and gently instil others. But as opinions are sown in men's minds not by command but by teaching, not by threat of penalties but by clarity of argument, laws to resist this evil should be directed not against the people in error but against the errors themselves. The errors which we maintained in the previous chapter to be incompatible with the quiet of the commonwealth have crept into the minds of uneducated people partly from the pulpits of popular preachers and partly from daily conversation with men whose easy circumstances give them leisure for these pursuits and who in their turn got these errors into their heads from those who taught them in their young days at the Universities [*Academiae*]. Hence, vice versa, anyone who wants to introduce a sound doctrine has to begin with the Universities. That is where the foundations of civil doctrine, which are true and truly demonstrated, have to be

laid; after the young men are steeped in them, they can instruct the common people in private and in public . The more certain they are of the truth of what they teach and preach, the more vigorously and forcefully they will do so. For as everyday exposure has given current acceptance to propositions which are false and no more intelligible than if you took words by lot from an urn and strung them together, how much more would men imbibe true doctrines conforming to their own understanding and to the nature of things, if they were similarly exposed to them. I hold therefore that it is a duty of sovereigns to have to have the true Elements of civil doctrine written and to order that it be taught in all the Universities in the commonwealth.

10. The second factor, we have shown,[3] which disposes men to sedition is the discontent that arises from *poverty*; even if their poverty results from their own extravagance or idleness, nevertheless they blame it on those who govern the commonwealth, claiming they are oppressed and exhausted by taxes. Yet it may sometimes happen that their complaint is justified, namely when the burdens of the commonwealth are imposed on the citizens unequally. For a burden which would be light if all shared it, becomes heavy, and indeed intolerable, for the rest when many wriggle out of it. And it is not so much the burden itself that men object to as the inequality. The most contentious struggles are about tax exemptions, and in those struggles the less successful envy the more successful as if they had been defeated in battle. It is in the interest of the public peace to remove a justified complaint, and consequently it is a duty of sovereigns to ensure that public burdens are equally borne. Besides, since the citizens' contributions to the community are simply the price they pay to purchase peace, it is logical that those who equally enjoy the peace should pay equal shares, by contributing either money or service to the commonwealth. And the natural law (by III.15) is that in assessing others' rights every man should treat himself as equal to every other man; hence sovereigns are obliged by natural law to impose the burdens of the commonwealth upon the citizens equally.

11. Equality here does not mean monetary equality, but equality of burden, i.e. proportionate equality between burdens and benefits.

---

[3] XII.9.

For although all men equally enjoy peace, the benefits of peace are not equal for all. For some acquire more property and some less. And again, some consume more and others less. The question can be asked therefore whether citizens should contribute to the public purse in proportion to their gains or to their consumption, that is, whether persons should be taxed so that they contribute in proportion to their wealth, or whether things should be taxed, so that each man contributes in proportion to his consumption. We should reflect that people who have made equal amounts do not possess equal amounts, because one man is thrifty and keeps what he has made while the other wastes it in extravagant living, and hence, where they pay taxes in proportion to their wealth, they equally enjoy the benefit of peace, but do not bear the burdens of the commonwealth equally. On the other hand, where the things themselves are taxed, each man in spending his own money, without noticing it fully pays the portion due to the commonwealth, which is proportionate not to what he possesses but to what, by virtue of the commonwealth, he did possess. There is therefore no longer room for doubt that the first method of exacting money is against equity and likewise against the duty of sovereigns, and that the latter method is consistent with reason and with their duty.

12. Thirdly, we have said[4] that the sense of grievance [*aegritudinem animi*] that arises from *ambition* is an obstacle to public peace. There are those who believe they know better than other people, and are more fit to govern than the present ministers. They have no way of showing how much their talents could help the commonwealth but by hurting it. Ambition and longing for honours cannot be removed from men's minds, and sovereigns have no duty to attempt to do so. They can however ensure by a consistent employment of rewards and punishments that the road to honours does not lie through criticism of the current régime nor through factions and popular favour, but through the opposite. Good men are those *who respect the decisions of the senate, and respect laws and rights.*[5] If we saw a consistent pattern on the part of those who administer sovereign power of distinguishing them with honours and punishing the factious and branding them with contempt, there would be more

---

[4] XII.10.
[5] Horace, *Epistles* 1.16.41.

ambition to obey than to oppose. It does sometimes happen that just as one must coax a horse because he is fierce, so one must conciliate a defiant citizen because he is powerful. But that is what a rider or a ruler would do who was almost thrown off, and here we are speaking of those whose authority and integrity are intact. It is their duty, I say, to encourage obedient citizens, and to suppress factious citizens as forcefully as they can; for it is the only way by which public power [*potentia publica*], and with it the citizens' quiet, can be preserved.

13. But if sovereigns have a duty to control factious individuals, much more is it their duty to break up and disperse the factions themselves. By FACTION[6] I mean a crowd [*multitudo*] of citizens, united either by *agreements* with each other or by the power of one man, without authority from the holder or holders of sovereign power. A *faction* is like a commonwealth within the commonwealth; for just as a commonwealth comes into being by men's union in a natural state, so a faction comes into being by a new union of citizens. By this definition a number of citizens who have bound themselves in obedience to a foreigner, whether he be a prince or simply a citizen, or who have made an agreement or alliance of mutual defence with each other against all men not excepting those who hold sovereign power in the commonwealth, is a *faction*. Popularity too implies faction, when it reaches the point that an armed force could be founded upon it, unless guarantees are given in the form of hostages or other pledges. And the same is to be said of immoderate private wealth; for everything obeys money. Since therefore it is true that the state of commonwealths towards each other is a natural state and a state of hostility, Princes who permit faction are as good as admitting an enemy within the walls. This is against the citizens' safety and therefore against the natural laws.

14. Two things are necessary for the citizens to prosper: *hard work* and *thrift*; a third contributing factor is the *natural produce* of earth and water; and there is also a fourth, *military activity*, which sometimes increases the citizens' wealth but more often erodes it. For a commonwealth set on an island in the sea, with only just enough room for habitation, can grow rich by trade and manufacture alone, without sowing and without fishing; but there is no

---

[6] Cf. XII.13.

doubt that if they have territory, the same number of them can be richer or a larger number can be equally well off. The fourth factor, *military activity*, was once regarded as a gainful occupation under the name of *piracy* or *raiding*. And before the formation of commonwealths, when the human race lived dispersed in families, it was considered just and honourable. For raiding is simply making war with small forces. And great commonwealths, particularly *Rome* and *Athens*, at certain times so enlarged their country from the spoils of war, foreign tribute and the acquisition of territory by arms, that they did not impose taxes on the poorer citizens; in fact they actually distributed money and land to individuals. But we should not take enrichment by these means into our calculations. For as a means of gain, military activity is like gambling; in most cases it reduces a person's property; very few succeed. As there are only three things then which enable the citizens to increase their prosperity – *products of earth and water*, *hard work* and *thrift* – they are the only objects of a sovereign's duty. Laws which promote the skills which improve returns from the products of earth and water, such as *agriculture* and *fishing*, will be useful in the first category. Conducive to the second are all the laws by which idleness is prohibited, industry is stimulated and various arts are given recognition: *the art of navigation* (by which the products of the whole world, which cost virtually no more than the labour, are gathered into one commonwealth); *the mechanical arts* (in which I include all the arts of the superior crafts) and the *mathematical sciences*, which are the sources of the nautical and mechanical arts. Conducive to the third are all those laws which forbid extravagant expenditure on food and clothes, and generally on all things consumed by use. And since such laws are useful for the ends described, it is part of the duty of the sovereign to endorse them.

15. Liberty for citizens does not mean exemption from the laws, or that those who hold sovereign power may not make whatever laws they please. But since all the movements and actions of the citizens have never been brought within the scope of law, and cannot be because of their variety, the things that are neither commanded nor forbidden must be almost infinite; and each man can do them or not at his own discretion. In these each man is said to enjoy his own liberty, and liberty here is to be understood in this sense, viz. as that part of natural right which is allowed and left to

the citizens by the civil laws. Water stagnates and corrupts when it is closed in by banks on all sides; when it is open on all sides it spreads, and the more outlets it finds the freer it is. So with the citizens: they would be without initiative if they did nothing except at the law's command; they would be dissipated if there were no legal restrictions, and the more things left unregulated by the laws, the more liberty they enjoy. Both extremes are faulty; for laws were invented not to extinguish human actions but to direct them; just as nature ordained banks not to stop the flow of the river but to direct it. The extent of this liberty is to be measured by the good of the citizens and of the commonwealth. Hence it is, in the first place, contrary to the duty of those who rule and have authority to make laws that there be more laws than the good of the citizens and of the commonwealth essentially require. For since men more often deliberate about what they should or should not do by natural reason than by knowledge of laws, where there are more laws than we can easily remember and where they forbid things which reason by itself does not forbid, men must necessarily fall foul of the laws as they fall into traps, through ignorance and without any bad intention; and this is incompatible with the innocent liberty, which sovereigns are obliged by natural law to preserve for their citizens.

16. A major part of the *liberty* which is harmless to the commonwealth and essential to happy lives for the citizens, is that they have nothing to fear but penalties which they can anticipate or expect. This is the case either when the laws define no penalties at all, or when the penalties actually inflicted are no greater than those defined. Where none is defined, the first law-breaker anticipates an undefined or discretionary penalty and his fear (one assumes) is unlimited because it is a fear of unlimited suffering. But (by what we have said at III.11) the law of nature instructs those who are not subject to civil laws – and therefore instructs sovereigns – that in vengeance and punishment one must not look at past evil but at future good. And it is an offence against natural law to have any other measure of discretionary punishment than the public interest [*utilitas publica*]. But a penalty may be defined or prescribed by law, as when it is laid down in explicit words: *he who does this will suffer this*, or may be defined in practice, as when a penalty (not being prescribed by law) is discretionary at first, and then defined by the punishment of the first offender (for natural equity tells us that

equal offenders should be equally punished); in either case it is contrary to the law of nature to require a greater penalty than that defined by law. For the purpose of punishment is not to force a man's will but to form it, and to make it what he who fixed the penalty desires it to be. Now deliberation is simply weighing up the advantages and disadvantages of the action we are addressing (as on a pair of scales), where the weightier consideration necessarily goes into effect by its own natural inclination. If the penalty which a legislator attaches to a crime is too small to make fear weigh more heavily than greed, the legislator, i.e. the sovereign is responsible for the fact that the greed outweighs fear of the penalty (the excess of greed over fear being the cause of the crime). If he then inflicts a greater penalty than he had previously defined in the actual laws, he is punishing in another a fault he committed himself.

17. Another element of the innocent *liberty* which is essential to the citizens is that each man may enjoy without fear the rights which he is granted by the laws. For it is pointless to distinguish *mine* from *another's* by law if they are confounded again by false judgement, robbery or theft. And it is a fact that false judgements, robberies and theft occur when judges are corrupt. For the fear by which men are deterred from doing wrong is not caused by pre-scribing penalties but by inflicting them. For we gauge the future from the past, rarely expecting what rarely happens. If judges often remit the penalties due by law, whether corrupted by gifts, influence or even pity, and so give wicked men the expectation that they will not be punished, good citizens will be beset by murderers, robbers and swindlers, unable to communicate freely with each other or move about at all; in fact the commonwealth itself is dissolved, and each man recovers his right to protect himself at his own discretion. The law of nature therefore instructs sovereigns not only to practise justice themselves, but also to use penalties to compel the judges they have appointed to do the same; this implies that they lend an ear to the complaints of citizens, and, whenever necessary, appoint a special court of inquiry into the regular judges.

Chapter XIV
On laws and sins

1. Those who do not scrupulously weigh the force of words at times confuse *law* [*lex*] with *advice* [*consilium*], at times with *Agreement* [*Pactum*] and sometimes with *right* [*jus*]. They confuse *law* with *advice* when they think that it is the monarch's duty not only to listen to advisors but also to obey them. As if there was no point in seeking advice unless one were to follow it. The distinction between *advice* and *law* is to be sought in the difference between *advice* and *command* [*mandatum*]. ADVICE is an *instruction or precept* [*praeceptum*] in which the reason for following it is drawn *from the matter itself*. But a COMMAND is an *instruction* in which the reason for following it is drawn from *the will of the instructor*. For one can only properly

say: *This is what I want, this is my order*, if *will* stands for reason. But since laws are obeyed not for their content, but because of the will of the instructor, *law* is not *advice* but *command*, and is defined thus: LAW is *a command of that person (whether man or council) whose instruction is the reason for obedience.* So that the following are to be called laws: God's precepts with respect to men, the commonwealth's to its citizens, and in general the instructions of all powerful people to those who are unable to offer resistance. *Law* and *advice*, then, differ from each other in many ways. For *law* comes from one who has power over those whom he instructs, *advice* from one who does not have power. To do what one is instructed by *law* is a matter of *duty*; to take *advice* is *discretionary*. *Advice* is directed to the purpose of *the person instructed*, *law* to the purpose of *the instructor*. *Advice* is addressed only to *those who want it*, *law* also to *those who do not want it*. Finally the right *to give advice* is cancelled at the discretion of *its recipient*; the right of the *lawgiver* is not cancelled at the discretion of the person on whom *law* is imposed.

2. They confuse *law* with *agreement* when they take the view that laws are nothing but ὁμολογήματα[1] or agreed formulae for living determined by the common consent of mankind. Aristotle is among them. He defines law as follows: Νόμος ἐστι λόγος ὡρισμένος καθ᾽ ὁμολογίαν κοινὴν πόλεως, μηνύων πῶς δεῖ πράττειν ἕκαστα,[2] that is, *Law is an utterance, determined by the common consent of the commonwealth, which declares how things are to be done.* This is not a definition of *law* simply, but of *civil law*. For it is evident that *divine laws* do not arise from the consent of men, nor do *natural laws*; for if they originated in human consent, they could also be abolished by human consent; but they are immutable. But in fact it is not an acceptable definition of *civil law* either; for commonwealth in that passage may mean either one civil person having one will or a crowd of men each of whose own private wills is free. If it is taken as one person, *by common consent* is not well put; for one person does not have a *common consent*. Nor should he have put *declaring* what needed to be done, but *ordering*. For what the commonwealth declares to its citizens it is ordering them to do. By

---

[1] 'Agreements'.

[2] *Rhetoric to Alexander*, Introduction, 1420a25; cf. II, 1422a2 and III, 1424a10. This work, which has come down to us in the works of Aristotle, is not now normally attributed to him.

commonwealth, then, he understood a crowd of men declaring rules for living by common consent (fixing the wording by a vote, for example). But these are nothing but mutual agreements, which do not obligate anyone and are therefore not laws, until by the establishment of a sovereign authority with the power to compel, each man is given a guarantee against the others who would not otherwise observe them. By this definition of *Aristotle's*, therefore, *laws* are nothing other than bare agreements without force which will or will not become *laws* only when there is someone who exercises power by the right of the commonwealth, and it will be at his discretion . Thus Aristotle confuses *laws* with *agreements* as he should not; for an *agreement* is a *promise*, a *law* is a *command*. In *agreements* one says, *I will do*; *laws* say, *Do*. We are obligated by an *agreement* (*); we are kept to our obligation by a *law*. An *agreement* obligates of itself; a *law* keeps one to one's obligations in virtue of the universal *agreement* to render obedience. And hence in an *agreement*, we must settle what is to be done before we are obligated to do it; but in a *law* the obligation to do comes first, and we determine afterwards what is to be done. *Aristotle*, therefore, should have defined *civil law* thus: *a civil law is an utterance prescribed by will of the commonwealth, which commands the things one should do*. And this is the same definition as we gave at VI.9 above, viz. that *civil laws are commands about the future actions of the citizens from the one* (man or council) *which is endowed with sovereign power in the commonwealth*.

We are obligated by an agreement, etc.] *Some have thought that being obligated and being kept to one's obligation are the same thing and that consequently this is a verbal not a substantial distinction. So I will put it more clearly. A man is obligated by an agreement, i.e. he ought to perform because of his promise. But he is kept to his obligation by a law, i.e. he is compelled to performance by fear of the penalty laid down in the law.*

3. They confuse *law* [*lex*] with *right* [*jus*] when they persist in doing what is permitted by *divine right*, though forbidden by the *law of the commonwealth*. The civil law cannot permit what is prohibited by *divine law*, nor can it prohibit what is commanded by *divine law*. However nothing stops the prohibition by *civil law* of what is permitted by divine right, i.e. what by divine right may be done,

for *lower laws* can restrict the liberty left by *higher laws*, though they cannot extend it. And a *right* is a *natural liberty* not created by laws but left by them. Take away laws and there is complete liberty. It is restricted first by *natural* and *divine law*; what is left is then restricted by *civil laws*; and what survives the civil law can be restricted by the *decisions* of particular cities and associations. There is then a great difference between *law* and *right*; for a *law* is a *bond*, a *right* is a *liberty*, and they differ as contraries.

4. All *law* can be divided first according to its different sources into *divine* and *human law*. Then following the two modes by which God makes his will known to men, *divine law* is twofold: *natural* (or *moral*) and *positive*. *Natural law* is the law which God has revealed to all men through his *eternal word* which is innate in them, namely by *natural reason*. And this is the law which I have been attempting to expound throughout this little book. *Positive law* is that law which God has revealed to us through the *prophetic word* by which he spoke to men as a man; such are the laws which he gave to the *Jews* about their constitution [*politia*] and divine worship; and they can be called *divine civil laws*, because they were particular to the commonwealth of Israel, his own particular people. *Natural law* can again be divided into the natural law of *men*, which alone has come to be called the *law of nature*, and the natural law of *commonwealths*, which may be spoken of as the *law of nations* [*lex gentium*], but which is commonly called the *right of nations* [*ius gentium*]. The precepts of both are the same: but because commonwealths once instituted take on the personal qualities of men, what we call a *natural law* in speaking of the duties of individual men is called the *right of Nations*, when applied to whole commonwealths, peoples or nations. And the Elements of *natural law* and *natural right* which we have been teaching may, when transferred to whole *commonwealths* and *nations*, be regarded as the Elements of the *laws* and of the *right of Nations*.

5. All *human law* is *civil law*. For the state of man outside the commonwealth is a state of enmity; and because in that state no one is subject to anyone else, there are no laws beyond the dictates of right reason, which is divine law. But in a commonwealth, the commonwealth alone, that is the man or council [*curia*] to whom the sovereign power of the commonwealth is committed, is the legislator, and the laws of the commonwealth are civil laws. *Civil*

laws can be divided, according to their different subject matters, into *sacred* and *secular*. *Sacred laws* are those to do with religion, that is, with the ceremonies and worship of God, (namely, what persons, things and places are to be consecrated and by what rite; what beliefs about the deity are to be publicly taught; and with what words and rituals prayers are to be offered; and such like); in so far as they are not prescribed by any divine positive law. For *sacred civil laws* are *human* laws (and are also called *ecclesiastical*) about *sacred* things; *secular civil laws* are normally given the general name of *civil laws*.

6. Again *civil law* has two parts, in accordance with the two duties of the legislator, of which one is to *give judgement* and the other is to *compel* acceptance of the judgements; one part is *distributive*, the other *vindicative* or *penal*. *Distributive civil law* is the law by which his own right is distributed to each man, that is, the law which lays out the rules for all things, by which we may know what belongs to us and what to others, so that others may not obstruct us in the use and enjoyment of our own, and we may not obstruct them in the use and enjoyment of theirs; and what it is legal for each to do or not to do, and what is illegal. *Vindicative civil law* is the law by which the penalties to be imposed on those who break the law are prescribed.

7. *Distributive* and *vindicative* are not two *kinds* of law but two *parts* of the same law. For if a law says nothing more than, for example, *let that be yours which you have caught with your own net in the sea*, it is useless. For though someone else may take from you what you have caught, that does not prevent it from still being yours; for in the state of nature where all things are common to all men, the same thing is both yours and another's so that what the law defines as yours was also yours before the law, and does not cease to be yours after the law, even though it is in the possession of another; the law achieves nothing therefore, unless it is taken to mean that a thing is yours in the sense that all are prohibited from obstructing your ability to use and enjoy it at all times in security and at your discretion. What is required for a man to have property in goods is not that he may be able to use them, but that he alone may be able to use them, and that is achieved by prohibiting others from obstruction: But it is useless even to prohibit, unless you instil the fear of punishment; hence a law is useless, unless it contains

both parts, the part which forbids wrongs to be done and the part which punishes those who do them. The first of these, which is called *distributive*, is *prohibitive*, and is addressed to all men; the second, which is called *vindicative* or *penal*, is imperative, and is addressed only to the public ministers.

8. It follows from this that *there is a penalty attached to every civil law*, explicitly or implicitly. For where no penalty is prescribed, either in writing or by the example of someone who has previously been punished for breaking the law, there it is implied that the penalty is discretionary, i.e. depends upon the discretion of the legislator, i.e. of the sovereign; for any law that can be broken with impunity is useless.

9. The principles that each man has *his own* right proper to him and distinct from *another's*, and that he is forbidden to violate the rights *of others*, have their source in the civil laws. And therefore the following precepts are civil laws: *You shall not refuse your parents the honour prescribed by the laws; you shall not kill a man whom the laws forbid you to kill; you shall avoid intercourse forbidden by the laws; you shall not take away another's goods against the will of the owner; you shall not frustrate the laws and the courts by false testimony.* Natural laws give the same precepts, but implicitly; for natural law (as explained at III.2) commands that *agreements* be kept, and hence also commands men to show obedience when they have agreed to obey, and to keep their hands off what is another's, when what is another's has been defined by civil law. And (by VI.13) all citizens *agree* at the very formation of the commonwealth to show obedience to the commands of the holder of sovereign power, i.e. to the civil laws, even before they can be broken. For the natural law did give rise to obligation in the natural state, where, first, nothing was another's (because nature gave all things to all men), and it was consequently not possible to encroach on what was another's; where, secondly, all things were in common, for which reason also all sexual unions were licit; where, thirdly, it was a state of war, and hence licit to kill; where, fourthly, the only definitions were those of each man's own judgement, and that would include the definition of the honours due to parents; finally where there were no public courts and therefore no practice of giving testimony whether true or false.

10. Since therefore the obligation to observe those laws is older

than the promulgation of the laws themselves, because contained in the actual formation of the commonwealth, natural law commands that all civil laws be observed in virtue of the natural law which forbids the violation of agreements. For when we are obligated to obey before we know what orders will be given, then we are obligated to obey universally and in all things. From this it follows that no civil law can be contrary to natural law (except a law which has been framed as a blasphemy against God; for in relation to Him commonwealths themselves are not *sui juris*, and are not said to make laws). For if, notwithstanding the law of nature's prohibition of theft, adultery, etc., the civil law commands such an infringement, the act does not count as theft, adultery etc. When in the old days the Lacedaemonians gave permission to boys by a specific enactment to pilfer other people's things, they laid it down that those things were not other people's but belonged to the pilferer; and so such pilferings were not thefts; similarly among the pagans sexual relationships were by their laws legal marriages.

11. It is necessary to the essence of a law that two things be known to the citizens: first, what man or council has sovereign power, i.e. the right of making laws; second, what the law itself says. For he who has never come to know to whom he is obligated or what his obligations are cannot obey, and is exactly as if he were not obligated. I do not say that it is necessary to the essence of a law that this or that be continuously known, but only that it once has been known, and if the citizen afterwards forgets either the legislator's right or the law itself, that is no bar to his obligation to obey, since he could have remembered if he had the will to obey, as natural law commands.

12. *Knowledge of the legislator* depends on the citizen himself; for without his personal consent and agreement, either explicit or implied, the right of legislation could not have been conferred on anyone. It is explicit when the citizens at the beginning determine the form for governing the commonwealth among themselves, or when by their promise they submit to the power [*imperium*] of some person; if it is not explicit, it must at least be implied, as when they accept the benefit of a person's power and laws for protection and preservation of themselves against others. For when we demand that our fellow citizens obey someone's power for our good, we admit by that very demand that his power is legitimate. And hence

one can never plead ignorance of his authority to make laws, for each man knows that he did what he himself did.

13. *Knowledge of the laws* depends on the legislator, who has a duty to promulgate them; for otherwise they are not laws. For a law is a command of a legislator; and a command is a declaration of will; there is no law therefore if the will of the legislator has not been declared; and this is done by *promulgation*. Two things have to be established in the promulgation: one is that he or they who promulgate the law either have the right to legislate themselves or do so by authority of those who do have. The other is the actual meaning of the law. The first thing – that the laws promulgated come from the holder of sovereign power – can be evident, i.e. known (in the strict and philosophic sense of the word 'known') only to those who hear it from the mouth of the sovereign himself; the rest have belief; but they have such strong reasons to believe that not to believe is scarcely possible. In a *democratic* commonwealth, in fact, when everyone can take part in making laws if he wishes, anyone who was absent has to believe those who were there. But in *monarchies* and *aristocracies*, because few men have permission to hear the commands of the monarch and the optimates by direct presence, it was necessary to give these few the authority [*potestas*] to publish them to the rest. And so we believe those to be *edicts* and *decrees* of princes, which are put before us as such either in writing or by the voice of those who have that responsibility. The reasons we have to believe are these: that we have seen that the prince or the supreme council has consistently made use of such *counsellors, clerks, spokesmen, seals* and tokens of that sort to declare his will; that he has never taken their authority from them; that punishment has been inflicted on those who have not believed such a promulgation and have broken the law; and that anyone who so believes and obeys the *edicts* and *decrees* published through them anywhere in his territory is held blameless, while he who does not believe and does not obey is punished. For to permit these things to be done consistently, is a sufficiently evident sign and a clear enough declaration of his will; provided there is nothing in the *law*, *edict* or *decree* which diminishes the ruler's sovereign power. For one must not believe that he wishes to have his authority clipped by any of his ministers, while he retains the will to rule. When there is a question about the *meaning of laws*, it is to be sought from those

whom the sovereign has charged with *the trial of cases*, or *the courts*. For *giving judgement* is simply the application of *laws* to individual cases by *interpretation*. We recognize those who have been entrusted with this responsibility in the same way in which we recognize who has been entrusted with the authority to promulgate laws.

14. As there are two ways of promulgating *civil* law, so there are two kinds of civil law: *written* and *unwritten*. By *written* law I mean law which requires the voice or some other sign of the will of the legislator to become law. For law as a species is coeval in nature and time with the human species, and for that reason is older than the invention of letters and the art of writing. So the requisite of *written law* is not *writing* but vocal expression [*vox*]; this alone is of its essence, writing is employed *to record law*. For we read that before letters were invented to help the memory, *laws* used to be put in metrical form and recited. *Unwritten law* is law which needs no promulgation but the voice of nature, or natural reason, such as are *natural laws*. For though natural law is indeed distinguished from civil in so far as it gives precepts to the will, it is still civil so far as actions are concerned; for example, the law, *thou shalt not covet*, which relates to a mental state is merely a natural law; but the law not to seize what is not yours, is both natural and civil. For as it is impossible to write down ahead of time universal rules for the judgement of all future cases which are quite possibly infinite, it is understood that in every case overlooked by the *written laws*, one must follow the *law of natural equity*, which bids us to give equal to equals. And this is by force of the *civil law*, which also punishes those who by their action knowingly and willingly transgress *natural laws*.

15. On this basis it appears first that although the *natural laws* have been written down in philosophers' books, they are not for that reason to be called written laws; nor are the writings of jurists, for lack of sovereign authority; nor the *responses of jurists*,[3] i.e. of the *judges*, except in so far as their responses have attained customary authority with the consent of the sovereign; and then they are to be accepted among the written laws, not because they are customary (custom does not constitute law in its own right) but because of the

---

[3] 'The responses of the jurists' (*responsa prudentium*) were one of the recognized sources of Roman law. See e.g. Justinian, *Institutes*, 1.2.8.

will of the sovereign, which is declared in the fact that he has allowed the opinion to become customary.

16. In the broadest sense a *sin* [*peccatum*][4] takes in everything *done*, *said* and *willed* against right reason. For each man uses reason to look for the means to the end which he proposes for himself; if he reasons rightly (that is, starting from the most evident principles he weaves a seamless discourse of necessary consequences), he will go the straightest way; if not, he will go astray; that is, he will *do*, *say* or *attempt* something contrary to his own purpose, and when he does that, he will indeed be said to have *erred* in reasoning, and to have *sinned* in acting and willing; for *sin* follows *error*, as *will* follows *understanding*. This is the widest understanding of the word, and it includes all *imprudent action*, whether contrary to law, as to wreck someone else's house, or not contrary to law, as to build one's own house upon sand.

17. But in the context of *law* the word *sin* is narrower; it does not mean every action against Right reason but only one *which is blamed* [*culpatur*], and for that reason it is called *a culpable evil* [*malum culpae*]. However, a thing should not be called a *sin* [*peccatum*] or a *fault* [*culpa*] just because it is blamed [*culpetur*], but only if it is blamed with reason. So one must ask what it is to *blame with reason* and without reason. Human nature is such that each man calls what he wants for himself *good*; what he avoids, he calls *bad*; because men's passions differ, what one calls *good*, another calls *bad*; the very same man will now call one thing *good*, and at another time *bad*; and what he calls *good* in himself, he will call *bad* in someone else. We all judge *good* and *bad* by our own delight and annoyance (either present or expected). Given that the successful achievements of enemies (because they increase their honour, property and power) and of equals (because of the competition for honours) are *annoying* for everybody, and thus are felt to be and are *bad*; given also that men are accustomed to regard as *evil*, i.e. to *find fault with*, those who are a source of *evil* for themselves; it is impossible that culpable and inculpable actions can be defined by agreement between individuals who are not pleased and displeased by the same things. They can indeed agree that certain generalities, such as *theft*, *adultery*, and so on are *sins*, as if they were saying that all men call

---

[4] *Peccatum*: 'sin' or 'moral offence'.

those things *bad* to which they attach names which are normally taken in a bad sense. But we are not asking whether theft is a sin; we are asking what is to be said to be theft, and the same with the others that are like it. Since therefore, amid such diversity of opinion, what is rationally to be blamed is not to be measured by one man's reason more than by another's, because of the equality of human nature; and since there exists no reason other than the reasons of *individuals* and the reason of *the commonwealth*, it follows that the commonwealth must determine what is *to be blamed with reason*; so that a *fault*, i.e. a SIN, is what anyone does, fails to do, says or wills contrary to *the reason of the commonwealth*, i.e. against the laws.

18. One can act illegally from human weakness; even though one may wish to keep the laws, yet one's action may be illegal, and therefore rightly blamed and called a *sin*. There are also those who disregard the laws and whenever they see an opportunity to make a profit and get away with it, no consciousness of agreements and pledged faith stops them from breaking them. In their case not only their actions but their attitude is in conflict with the laws. Those who sin only because of weakness are *good men* even when they are sinning; but the other sort are *bad men* even when not sinning. And although both things – both action and disposition – are in conflict with the laws, those conflicts are distinguished by different names. For lawlessness of actions is ἀδίκημα, *unjust action*; lawlessness of disposition is ἀδικία and κακία, *injustice* and *evil*. The former is the *weakness* of a disturbed mind; the latter is the *wickedness* of a settled disposition.

19. Now if in fact what is not contrary to any law is not a sin, and if there is no law which is not a command of the holder of sovereignty, and if no one holds sovereign power which has not been conferred upon him by our consent, how can one be said to have committed a sin by asserting either that God does not exist or that he does not govern the world, or by vomiting some other blasphemy over Him? For he will say *that he has never submitted his will to God's will because he has been of opinion that God does not exist. And though his belief was wrong, and hence would also be a fault, it would have to be numbered among the sins of imprudence or ignorance, which cannot rightly be punished*. This defence, it seems, will have to be admitted to the extent that a sin of this kind, though monstrous

and damnable, should still be classed among sins of imprudence
(*); but to excuse it on the grounds of imprudence or ignorance is
absurd. For the atheist is punished directly by God or by kings
appointed by God, not as a subject is punished by a king on the
ground that he has not kept the laws, but as an enemy is punished
by an enemy because he has refused to accept the laws; that is, by
right of war, like the giants who battled the gods. For men are
enemies to each other when they are not subject one to the other
or to any common ruler.

Should still be classed among the sins of imprudence] *Many critics
have taken me to task for classing atheism as imprudence not as injustice;
in fact some have taken it to prove that I have not shown myself a keen
enough adversary of atheism. They also raise the objection that as I
have said elsewhere that it can be known by natural reason that God
exists, I ought to admit that they do at least sin against the law of
nature, and therefore are guilty not only of imprudence but of injustice.
As a matter of fact I am such an enemy to Atheists that I have strongly
desired and diligently sought some law by which I could condemn them
for injustice. But since I have not found such a law, I have gone on to
ask what name God would give to men who are so exceedingly hostile
to him. This is what God says of the atheist:* 'The fool hath said in
his heart: there is no God.' *And thus I have placed their sin in the
same class as it was placed by God himself. And then I show that atheists
are enemies of God; and the name, enemy, I think, is sometimes stronger
than 'unjust man'. Finally, I insist that he may be justly punished on
this account both by God and by sovereigns. And thus I neither excuse
nor palliate this sin in any way. As for my contention that* God's existence *can be known by natural reason, this must be taken not as if I
thought that all men can know it – unless they think it follows that
because Archimedes discovered by natural reason the proportion of a
sphere to a cylinder, any Tom, Dick or Harry could have done the same.
I say therefore that although God's existence can be known by some men
by the light of reason, it cannot be known by men who are constantly in
pursuit of pleasure, wealth or honour, nor by those who do not have the
habit, the ability or the concern to reason correctly, nor, finally, by
fools – which is where the Atheist belongs.*

20. The obligation to obey individual civil laws is derived from the
force of the agreement by which individual citizens are obligated to

each other to offer absolute and universal obedience (as we have defined it above at VI.13) to the commonwealth, i.e. to the sovereign, whether that is one man or one council, so that that agreement contains within itself all the laws together; it is consequently evident that the citizen who renounces the general pact of obedience is renouncing all the laws together. This evil is more serious than any single sin as constant sinning is more serious than a *single* sin. And this is the sin which is called the CRIME OF LÈSE-MAJESTÉ, which is a deed or word by the citizen or subject by which he reveals that he no longer intends to obey the man or council to whom the sovereign power in the commonwealth has been committed. A citizen reveals such an intention by his action when he inflicts or attempts to inflict violence on the persons of those who hold sovereign power or are carrying out their orders; such are traitors, Regicides, those who bear arms against their country or desert to the enemy in wartime. People reveal the same intention in words when they plainly deny that they or the other citizens are obligated to offer such obedience, – either totally, as one would who (to protect the obedience which we owe to God) denied that one should obey rulers simply, absolutely and universally; or partially, as would one who said that rulers have no right to wage war or make peace at their own discretion, conscript soldiers, raise taxes, choose magistrates and public ministers, make laws, settle disputes, fix penalties or anything else that is essential to the existence of the commonwealth. These words and actions, and others like them, are crimes of lèse-majesté by natural (not civil) law. But it can also happen that an action committed before the introduction of a civil law was not the crime of lèse-majesté, but would be if it were done after its introduction. For instance, if it should be declared by law that forging money or counterfeiting the seals of the commonwealth is to be taken as a sign of renunciation of civil obedience (i.e. as the crime of lèse-majesté), anyone who does this after the introduction of the law is no less guilty of lèse-majesté than the former kind of traitor, but he is committing a lesser sin, because he is not violating all the laws together but only[5] one law; for calling something lèse-majesté which in its own nature is not, rightly fixes an invidious name, and perhaps a heavier penalty, on the sinner, but does not make the sin itself more serious.

---

[5] Reading *tantum* (edition of 1647) for *tantam* printed by Warrender.

21. The sin which is the crime of treason by natural law is a transgression of natural, not civil, law. For since the obligation to civil obedience, by force of which all civil laws are valid, is prior to every civil law, and the crime of treason is by nature simply violation of that obligation; it follows that it is the law which preceded civil law which is violated by the crime of treason; and that is the natural law, by which we are forbidden to break agreements and our pledged faith. If a sovereign prince made a civil law in the form: *do not rebel!*, he would achieve nothing. For unless the citizens are previously obligated to obedience, i.e. not to rebel, every law is invalid; and an obligation which binds one to do something which one is already obligated to do is superfluous.

22. It follows from this that *rebels*, *traitors* and others convicted of *treason* are punished not by *civil right*, but by *natural right*, i.e. not as *bad citizens*, but as *enemies of the commonwealth*, and not by the *right of government* or dominion, but by the *right of war*.

23. Some hold that their actions contrary to a civil law, where a penalty is prescribed in the law itself, are expiated if they willingly submit to punishment; they also hold that those who have paid the penalty required by law are not guilty before God of a violation of natural law (despite the fact that by violating civil laws, we also violate the natural laws which command that civil laws be kept). As if the law were not forbidding the action, but suggesting a penalty as the price of a licence to do what the law forbids! By the same reasoning they could infer that no transgression of the law whatsoever is a sin, but that every man has a right to the liberty which he has purchased at his own risk. It has to be recognised that the words of a law can be understood in two ways. One way is that it contains two parts (as stated above at article 7), viz. an absolute prohibition: *you shall not do it*, and a vindicative part: *anyone who does, shall pay the penalty*. The other way is that it consists of one conditional [sentence], viz. *You shall not do it, unless you wish to pay a penalty*. Taken this way, the law's prohibition is not simple but conditional. If it is understood in the first way, the agent is committing a sin, because he is doing what is forbidden by law. If in the second way, he is not committing a sin, because he was not forbidden to do the thing, provided he fulfilled the condition. For in the first sense all are forbidden to do it, in the second sense only those who avoid the penalty. In the first sense the vindicative part of the law does not

obligate the defendant, but obliges the magistrate to inflict the penalty. In the second sense the actual person who owes the penalty is obligated to exact the penalty; but he cannot be obligated to pay the penalty if it is capital or otherwise serious. The sense in which a law is to be understood is at the discretion of the holder of sovereign power. When, then, there is doubt about the meaning of a law, it will be a sin to act because if we do not act we are certain not to commit a sin, no matter how the law may be interpreted later. For to do something of which you are in doubt whether it is a sin or not, when you have the freedom to abstain, is a contempt for the laws; and so, by III.28, is a sin against natural law. The distinction therefore between *active* and *passive obedience* is an empty one, as if a sin against natural law, which is the law of God, could be expiated by penalties laid down by human judgement, or as if it were no sin to sin at one's own cost.

Religion

Chapter XV
On the Kingdom of God by nature

1. In the previous pages we have proved from reason and from the testimony of holy scripture that a state of nature, a condition, that is, of absolute liberty like that of men who are neither Sovereigns nor Subjects, is Anarchy and a state of enmity; that the precepts for avoiding such a state are the *laws of nature*; that a commonwealth cannot exist without sovereign power; and that the holder of sovereign power is owed simple obedience, that is, obedience in all things consistent with God's commands. Only one thing more is needed to complete our knowledge of our civil duty: we must know what the laws or commands of God are. Otherwise we cannot know whether what we are ordered to do by the authority of the civil power is against God's laws or not. And as a result, inevitably, we would either defy God's majesty by obeying the commonwealth too strictly, or slip into confrontation with the commonwealth in our anxiety not to offend God. To avoid both these rocks, we need to

know the Divine laws; but as knowledge of a Kingdom's laws depends on a knowledge of the Kingdom, we must speak in what follows of *the Kingdom of God*.

2. At Psalm 96.1 the Psalmist says: *The Lord Reigns, let the earth rejoice*. Again the Psalmist says (Psalm 98.1): *the Lord Reigns, though the peoples rage; he sits upon the Cherubim, though the earth be moved.* That is to say, whether men will or no, God is king of the whole earth; and he is not shaken from his throne if a few men deny his *Existence* or his *Providence*. God so rules all men through power that no man can do anything which He does not want done; yet this is not Reigning in the precise and proper sense. A ruler is said to reign if he rules through *speech* rather than *action*, i.e. if he rules by *precepts* and *threats*. In the kingdom of God therefore we do not count inanimate bodies or things without reason as subjects (though they are subject to divine power), because they *do not understand* God's *precepts* and *threats*. Nor do we count *Atheists*, because they do not believe that God exists, nor those who believe in God's existence but not in his governance here below; for though they too are ruled by the power of God, they do not accept his *precepts* or fear his threats. The only persons to be numbered in the kingdom of God are those who accept that he is ruler of all things, that he has *given precepts* to men and *set penalties* for transgressors. All the rest we should call not subjects but enemies of God.

3. A ruler can only be said to rule by *precepts* if he publicly declares his precepts to those who are to be ruled; for a ruler's *precepts* are laws for the ruled. But they are not *laws* unless they are promulgated clearly, so that there can be no excuse for ignorance. Men promulgate their laws by *word* or *voice*; they have no other way of universally signifying their will. God's *laws* however are declared in three ways. First, *by the silent dictates of right reason*. Secondly, *by direct revelation*, which is thought to be carried by a *supernatural voice*, or by a *vision* or *dream* or *inspiration* (the breath of God). Third, *by the voice of a man* whose credibility God has certified to other men by working true miracles through him. A man whose voice God uses in this way to signify his will to others is called a PROPHET. These three ways can be called the triple *Word of God*: namely, the *rational Word*, the *perceptible Word* and the *Prophetic Word*. Corresponding to these are the three ways by which

we are said to hear God: *right Reasoning, Perception* and *Faith.* To few men has the *Word* of God been made *perceptible*; and God has only spoken to men by Revelation on an individual basis, and has said different things to different men; this has never been a way in which the laws of a Kingdom have been published to a people.

4. A twofold Kingdom is attributed to God; which corresponds to the difference between his *Rational* and his *Prophetic Word.* There is the *Natural* Kingdom in which he rules through the dictates of right Reason. It is a universal kingdom over all who acknowledge the divine power because of the rational nature which is common to all. And there is the *Prophetic* Kingdom, where too he rules, but by his *Prophetic Word.* It is a particular kingdom, because he has not given positive laws to all men, but only to a particular people, and to certain specific men whom he himself chose.

5. In the *Natural Kingdom* God's right to Reign and to punish those who break his laws is from *irresistible power* alone. For all right over others is either from *Nature* or from *Agreement.* I have shown in chapter VI how the right to rule arises from *Agreement.* But the same right flows also from nature by the very fact that nature has not taken it away. For since by nature all men had a right to all things, each man had a right, as old as nature itself, to rule over all men. What caused men to abolish this right was simply their fear of each other, as shown above at chapter II, article 3; that is to say, at the dictation of reason, that right had to be given up for the preservation of the human race. For the inevitable consequence of men's being equal to each other in point of strength and natural powers was war; and the consequence of war is the ruin of mankind. However, if anyone had been so much more powerful than all the rest that they could not have resisted him with their united strength, there would have been no reason whatsoever for him to give up the right granted him by nature. His right of dominion over all the rest would have stayed with him because of his preeminent power, which would have enabled him to ensure their survival and his own. In those whose power cannot be resisted, and thus in God *omnipotent*, the right to dominion flows from the *power* itself. And when God punishes, or even kills, a sinner, even if he is punishing him because he sinned, one must not say that he could not justly have afflicted or killed him even if he had not sinned. And though the

will of God in punishing can be related to a preceding sin, it does not follow that his right to afflict or kill depends on *human sin*, not on *divine power*.

6. The question, famously disputed by the ancients, *why bad things happen to good men and good things to bad men*, is the same as our question here, *by what right God dispenses good and bad to men*. And its difficulty has staggered the faith in divine providence not only of the common people but also of philosophers and, more remarkably, of saints. At Psalm 72.1, *How good* (says David) *is the God of Israel to those of upright heart; but my feet had almost slipped, my steps had almost gone, because I was envious of the wicked, seeing the peace of sinners.* And how bitterly Job protested to God that, though he had been just, he was so afflicted by calamities. In Job's case God himself solved this difficulty with his own living voice, and justified his right with arguments drawn not from Job's sin but from his own power. So in the dispute between Job and his friends, the friends inferred his guilt from his punishment, while he rebutted their accusation by arguments from his own innocence. But God, when he had heard both parties, rejects his protest, not by convicting him of any injustice or sin, but by exhibiting his own power (Job 38.3ff). *Where were you*, he says, *when I laid the foundations of the earth?* etc. As for Job's friends, he says (Job 42.7) that *he is angry with them because they have not said the right thing in his presence, as his servant Job has.* Consistent with this is the view our Saviour expressed in the case of the man born blind: when his disciples asked whether it was the blind man or his parents who had sinned, he replied (John 9.3), *Neither this man nor his parents sinned; but that the works of God might be revealed in him.* And though it is said at Rom. 5.12 that *Death came into this world through sin*, it does not follow that God by his right could not have made men subject to disease and death even if they had not sinned, seeing that he has made the other animals mortal and liable to disease even though they cannot sin.

7. But if God has the right to reign on the basis of his omnipotence, it is evident that men incur the *obligation* to obey him because of their weakness (*). For the *obligation* which arises from agreement (discussed in chapter II) is out of place in a situation like this where the right to command arises from nature without the intervention of an agreement. There are two kinds of *natural obli-*

gation: one, where liberty is excluded by physical obstacles, as when we say that heaven and earth and all creatures obey the common laws of their creation. The other, where liberty is excluded by hope and fear; as when we say that a weaker man cannot disobey a stronger man whom he has no hope of being able to resist. It is this second kind of obligation, i.e. fear, or the awareness of one's own weakness (in the face of divine power), that in the natural kingdom of God gives rise to our obligation to obey him; that is to say that reason tells all men who acknowledge the power and providence of God *not to kick against the pricks*.[1]

Because of their weakness] *If anyone thinks this harsh, I ask him to reflect quietly, if there were two who were omnipotent, which one would be obligated to obey the other. It will be admitted, I believe, that neither is obligated to the other. If this is true, my point is also true, that men are subject to God primarily because they are not omnipotent. For when our Saviour warned Paul (who was at that time an enemy of the church) not to kick against the pricks, He seems to have required obedience from him on the ground that he did not have strength to resist.*

8. Since the *Word of God* (God reigning through nature alone) is defined simply as right reason; and since the laws of Kings can only be known from their *Word*, it is evident that the laws of God reigning through nature alone are the only *natural laws*. These are the laws which we enumerated in chapters II and III and deduced from the dictates of reason; they are *Humility*, *Equity*, *Justice*, *Mercy*, and the rest of the *moral virtues*, the bringers of *peace* [*virtutes morales pacis conciliatrices*], which relate to men's duties towards each other; as well as the other laws that right reason dictates about the honour and worship due to God's majesty. There is no need to repeat what those *natural laws* or *moral virtues* are. But we must look at the honours and worship of God that right reason dictates, i.e. the *sacred laws*.

9. Properly speaking, HONOUR [*HONOR*] is nothing other than the opinion one has of the union of *power* and *goodness* in another person. And to *honour* someone is the same as to put a high value on him. Thus Honour is not in the person honoured, but in the

---

[1] Cf. Acts 9.5, 26.14.

person who honours. Three passions are stirred by the opinion which is *Honour: Love*, which relates to *Goodness*, and *Hope* and *Fear* which relate to *power*. From these passions spring external actions, by which the powerful are commonly placated and propitiated, and which are the effects of honour itself, and hence are natural signs. But the word *Honour* has also been applied to these external effects of honour; in this sense we are said to *Honour* someone, when we give evidence by our words or actions that we have an exalted notion of his power; and thus *Honour* is the same as *Worship*. WORSHIP [*CULTUS*] is an external act, the sign of internal Honour. If we make serious efforts to win people's favour or to placate them when they are angry by doing services for them, we are said to be *Worshipping* [*Colere*] them.

10. All signs of a person's mind are either *words* or *actions*; hence all worship consists in either *words* or *actions*. There are three types of each: the first is *Praise* or *proclaiming* a person's *goodness*; the second is *proclaiming* a person's *present power*, which is to *Magnify* him [μεγάλυνσις]; the third is *proclaiming* his *felicity* or *power* as secure also *for the future*, which is called μακαρισμὸς.[2] Each kind of honour can be shown both by *Word* and *Action*. We *Praise* and celebrate a person with *Words* when it is done in a proposition or *descriptively*, i.e. by his *attributes* or *titles*, which can be said to be praising or celebrating him *by epithets & by predicates*, as when we say that the person we are honouring is *generous*, *brave* and *wise*. We praise and celebrate by *Actions*, through their *consequences* or *assumptions*, as, by *giving thanks*, which implies *goodness*; by *obedience*, which implies *power*; by *congratulation*, which implies *success*.

11. Whether we want to celebrate someone by *words* or by *actions*, we shall find some things which signify honour among all men. Among the *attributes* [of this kind] are the general names of *virtues* and *powers*, which cannot be taken in a bad sense, for example, *Good, Handsome, Brave, Just*, and so on. Among *actions* are *Obedience, Thanksgiving, Prayers*, and others of this kind, which always imply recognition of power and virtue. There are other terms and actions which for some people imply honour, for others insult, for others neither; among such *Attributes* are the words which are variously taken as virtues or as vices, as honourable or dishonourable,

---

[2] Blessing, congratulation.

in accordance with the variety of opinion. For example, killing a personal enemy; running away; being a philosopher or a politician, and so on, which are held in honour by some and in contempt by others; among such *actions* are those which depend on the custom of a place, or the rules of the civil laws; as, baring the head in greeting, or taking off one's shoes or bowing; making one's petitions standing, prostrate or on one's knees; standard forms of ceremonies, and so on. *Worship* which implies honour at all times and places can be said to be *natural*; worship which follows local custom can be said to be *Arbitrary*.

12. Next, *Worship* [*Cultus*] may be *Commanded* – that is to say, ordered by its object – or it may be *spontaneous*, i.e. expressive of the feelings of the worshipper. If it is *Commanded*, honour is implied not by the actions *as such*, but by the fact that they were *Commanded*; for what they signify directly is *obedience*, and obedience signifies *power*. And thus *worship on command* consists in obedience; while *spontaneous* worship gives honour by the nature of the actions alone; if on-lookers find them indicative of honour, it is *worship*; if not, it is *insult*. Again, *worship* may be either *public* or *private*; *public* worship cannot be *spontaneous* with respect to individual worshippers, but may be with respect to the commonwealth. For since spontaneous worship is offered at the discretion of the worshipper, it would not be offered in a uniform manner, but in as many different forms as there are worshippers, unless all their wills were united by the power of one man. But *private* worship may be *spontaneous*, if it is offered without the knowledge of others; for whatever is offered openly is constrained either by the laws or by shame before others, and that is against the nature of *spontaneity*.

13. What is the *end* and *aim* of *worshipping* others? To see this, we must ask why it is that a man enjoys being worshipped. We must take up the point we proved elsewhere, that his *Enjoyment* lies in his contemplation of his own virtue, force, knowledge, beauty, friends, wealth or any other *power* which he has or regards as his own. This is nothing other than *Glory*, or the feeling of triumph as he reflects that he is being honoured, i.e. loved and feared, i.e. that he has men's services and assistance at his command. Now since men believe that a man is powerful when they see him honoured, i.e. regarded as powerful by others, it comes about that honour is enlarged by worship; and real power accrues from a reputation for

power. So in ordering or allowing himself to be worshipped, his *purpose* is to make as many people as possible obedient to him either from love or from fear.

14. What *worship* does *natural reason* assign to God? To answer this question, let us start from his *attributes*; and in the first place, obviously, we must attribute *existence* to him. For there can be no will to honour one whom we do not believe to exist. It is also obvious that the philosophers who have said that the world itself or the soul (i.e. a part) of the world is God, have spoken unworthily of him; for they are giving him no attributes; they are denying his existence altogether. For by the name *God* is meant the *cause of the world*; and those who say that *the world is God*, are saying that *there is no cause of the world*, i.e. that *there is no God*. It is likewise obvious that those who assert that the world is not created but eternal, are (since the eternal cannot have a cause) denying that *the world has a cause*, i.e. that *God exists*. It is also obviously a poor opinion of God to take away from him the government of the world and of the human race by attributing inactivity to him. For if, despite his omnipotence, which they admit, he has no concern for things here below, the well-known aphorism applies: *What is above us is nothing to us*; and since they have no reason to love and fear him, he might just as well not exist as far as they are concerned. Then, among the *attributes* which signify *greatness* and *power*, those which signify anything finite or determinate, are not signs of a disposition to honour him, for we do not honour God worthily, if we attribute less *power* or *greatness* to him than we can. And every finite thing is less; for something greater than finite can always be assigned and attributed to him. We shall not therefore attribute *form* to God, for all *form* is *finite*; nor shall we say that he is conceived, or caught, by the imagination or any other faculty of the human soul; for whatever we conceive is *finite*. Although the word *infinite* signifies a concept of the mind, it still does not follow that we have any concept of an *infinite Thing*; for when we say that something is *infinite*, we are not signifying anything in reality [*aliquid in re*] but an incapacity of our own minds; as if we were saying that we do not know whether and where it ends. Nor does it reflect honour on God to say that the *idea of him* is in our minds, for an *idea* is a concept of ours, and there is no concept except of what is *finite*; nor that he has *parts* or

that he is *wholly* something or other, for those too are attributes of *finite* things. Nor that he is *in space*, for all things that are *in space* have *bounds* and limits of their size on all sides; nor that he *moves* or *is at rest*, which both imply that he is *in space*. Nor that there are several gods, because plural things are not infinite either. Further, with regard to the *attributes of happiness* [*felicitas*], attributes which signify *pain* are unworthy of God (unless they are understood, not of a feeling, but as standing by metonymy for the effect), such as *repentance, anger, pity*; so are attributes which signify need, like *desire, hope, want*, and the *love* which is also called *lust*; for they are signs of a *lack*, since one can only be understood as *desiring, hoping* or *wanting* what one *needs* and *lacks*; and thus are attributes which signify a *capacity to suffer*; for *suffering* is a sign of a limited power and one which depends on someone else. When therefore we attribute a *will* to God, it is not to be understood as like our will, which is called *rational desire*. For if God *desires*, he *lacks* something, and to say that is an insult; we must suppose that it is something analogous which we cannot conceive. Similarly when we attribute *sight* to him and other *sense-acts*, or *knowledge* and *understanding*, which in us are nothing other than an agitation of the mind caused by the pressure of external things on the organs, we must not think that anything like that happens to God; for it is a sign of a power which is *dependent* on another, and that is not the most blessed state. Anyone therefore who wishes to attribute to God only those names which reason directs, must use names which are either negative, as *infinite, eternal, incomprehensible*, or superlative, as *best, greatest, mightiest, highest*, etc., or indefinite, as *good, just, mighty, creator, king* and so on; in the sense that we are not trying to say what is (which would be to confine him within the limits of our imagination [*phantasia*]), but to confess our own admiration and obedience, which is a sign of humility and of a disposition to give as much honour as one can. For the reason of nature dictates only one significant name of God – *the existent*, or simply *that which is*, and one name of relationship to us, namely *God*, in which are contained both *King* and *Lord* and *Father*.

15. The most general precept of reason about *external actions* for the worship of God (as about *attributes*) is that they should be signs of a disposition to honour. The first thing which this precept

includes is prayers. *He who forms divine faces in gold or marble is not making gods; gods are made by prayers.*[3] For prayers are signs of hope; and hope is an acknowledgement of God's power and goodness.

Secondly, this precept includes *Thanksgiving*, which is a sign of the same feeling, except that *prayers precede the benefit, while thanksgiving follows.*

Thirdly, it includes *Gifts*, i.e. *offerings* and *sacrifices*, for they are *Actions* of *Thanks*.

Fourthly, *not to swear by any other.* For in taking an oath, a man is invoking against himself, if he should break it, the anger of one who has the power to know whether he has broken it and to punish even the most powerful. And that is true of God alone. If there really were a man from whom his subjects could not hide their wickedness, and whom human power could not resist, it would be enough to pledge one's faith without an oath; breach of faith could be punished by a man; and therefore there would be no need of an oath.

Fifthly, *to speak of God with due thoughtfulness.* For this is a sign of *Fear*; and Fear is an acknowledgement of *Power*. This precept implies that *one must not use the name of God rashly or in vain*; for both are thoughtless. *One must not use an oath, where there is no need*; for that is vain. And there is no need of oaths except between commonwealths to avert or end the armed conflict that must arise when promises are broken; and within the commonwealth for certitude in the courts. Likewise *there should be no arguing about the nature of God*. For our basic premise is that *in the natural kingdom of God all questions are examined by reason alone*, i.e. from the principles of natural knowledge. But we are so far from understanding the nature of God by this means that we cannot achieve a satisfactory knowledge of the properties of any created thing, not even of our own bodies. The only result of such arguments is that we rashly apply to God's majesty terms which have been fashioned to the feeble measure of our own conceptions. This precept also implies (as far as the right of the Kingdom of God is concerned) that those who say that *this* or *that is inconsistent with God's justice* are engaged in rash and thoughtless phrase-making. For men too take it as an insult if their children dispute their right, or measure justice other than by their own commands.

[3] Martial, *Epigrams* 8.24.4–5.

Sixthly, *it is appropriate that anything offered in Prayers, Thanks-givings and Sacrifices should be the best of its kind and indicative of honour*, i.e. that *speech* should not be extempore or frivolous or vulgar, but beautiful and well crafted; for although it was absurd for the pagans to worship God in the form of an image, it was not irrational to use songs and music in their rites. It is also appropriate that the *Victims* be *handsome*, the *Offerings magnificent*, the ritual indicative of submission or gratitude, or commemorative of benefits received; for all this comes from the passion to honour.

Seventhly, *it is appropriate to worship God not only in private, but openly and publicly in the sight of men*. For the most pleasing worship, as said above (article 13) is that which generates honour in others. If others do not see, the most pleasing aspect of worship is lost.

Finally, we must make every effort *to keep the natural laws*. For making light of the government of God surpasses all other insults; just as, by the contrary, obedience is more acceptable than any sacri-fice.[4] These are the principal natural laws about the worship of God, the natural laws (I mean) which are dictated by reason to individual men. For Commonwealths as wholes, each of which is one person, natural reason also prescribes *uniformity of Public Worship*. For actions done by individuals following their private reason are not actions of a commonwealth, and are not therefore the worship of the commonwealth; and the actions of the commonwealth are understood to be done by order of the holder or holders of sovereign power, and hence with the consent of all the citizens together, i.e. uniformly.

16. The *natural laws* on divine worship listed in the last article prescribe only the natural signs of honour which should be offered. But one must recognise that there are two kinds of signs: *Natural* signs, and *Conventional* signs, which are signs based upon explicit or tacit agreement [*constitutio*]. Now because in every language the use of *Names* or *Appellations* arises from decision, it will also be able to be altered by decision. For what depends upon and derives its force from men's will, can be altered or abolished by their will if they consent. Hence the *Names* which have come to prevail as the *attributes* of God by human decision, can also go out of use if men so decide; and what can be decided by a man, may also be subject

---

[4] Cf. Proverbs 21.3.

to decision by the commonwealth. The commonwealth therefore (that is, those who hold the power of the whole commonwealth) will have the right to judge which *names* or *appellations* bring *honour* to God and which do not, i.e. which doctrines of the nature and operations of God are to be publicly held or professed. Actions however have natural significance, not arising from human decision, just as effects are signs of their causes. Some actions are always signs of contempt for those in whose presence they are done, namely, actions by which the body's uncleanness is displayed, and anything we are ashamed to do in the presence of people we respect. Other actions are always signs of honour, as, to approach and address someone decently and respectfully, or to give him the right of way or any other privilege. The commonwealth can make no changes in these. But there is an infinite number of other actions, which are indifferent with regard to honour or insult; and they can be taken up as signs of honour by the commonwealth, and when so taken up really do bring honour. It may be understood from this that one must obey the commonwealth in whatever it has commanded as a sign of honour to God, i.e. as to be used for public worship, provided it may be taken up as a sign of honour; because whatever the commonwealth employs as a sign of honour is a sign of honour.

17. We have now spoken of God's laws, both sacred and secular, under the Reign of God through nature alone. But as anyone may make a mistake in reasoning, and consequently men may hold conflicting opinions about most actions, one may ask a further question: whom did God will to be the *interpreter* of *right reason*, i.e. of his laws? In the case of the *secular laws*, i.e. those which are concerned with justice and men's behaviour towards other men, we have already shown, on the basis of what we said previously about the formation of the commonwealth, that it is agreeable to reason that all *judgements* should be the responsibility of the commonwealth; and *judgements* are nothing other than interpretations of laws; and as a consequence the *interpreters of law* everywhere are the commonwealths, i.e. those who hold sovereign power in the commonwealths. In the case of *sacred laws*, one must remember that, as we demonstrated above (v.13), individual citizens have transferred all the right that they could transfer to the holder(s) of sovereign power. Now they could transfer the right to decide on the manner of honouring

God, and therefore they have transferred it. That they could transfer it is evident from the fact that before the formation of the commonwealth the manner of honouring God was to be sought by each
man's *private reason*; and each man can submit his *private reason* to
the *reason of the whole commonwealth*. Besides, if individuals followed their own reason in worshipping God, worshippers are so
different from each other that they would judge each other's
worship to be unseemly or even impious; and would not accept that
the others were worshipping God at all. And therefore it would not
be *worship*, and even the worship most agreeable to reason would
not be worship, because the nature of *worship* is to be a *sign of
inward honour*, but a thing is only a sign if it makes something
known to others; a thing is therefore not a sign of honour, unless
others accept it as a sign of honour. Again, a true sign is made a
sign by men's consent, and therefore an honorific sign is made by
men's consent, i.e. it becomes a sign of honour by order of the
commonwealth. It is not therefore contrary to the will of God, made
known through reason alone, to offer him the signs of honour which
the commonwealth shall command. Citizens can therefore transfer
the right to decide about the manner of worshipping God to the
holder(s) of sovereign power in the commonwealth. And in fact they
should do so; for otherwise every absurd opinion about the nature
of God and all the ridiculous rituals which have ever existed among
any people, might appear in the same commonwealth at the same
time; and every man would believe as a result that everybody else
was heaping scorn upon God. Therefore it could not rightly be said
of anybody that he was worshipping God, for no one worships God,
i.e. offers external honours, unless he is offering something which
others accept as honours. We may therefore conclude that the
interpretation of *natural laws*, both *sacred* and *secular*, where God
reigns through nature alone, depends on the authority of the commonwealth, i.e. of the man or council which has been granted sovereign power in the commonwealth; and whatever God commands,
he commands through its voice. And, conversely, whatever commonwealths command both about the manner of worshipping God
and about secular matters, is commanded by God.

18. Against this one could ask: first, does it not follow that one
must obey the commonwealth if it directly commands one to pour
insults upon God or forbids his worship? I say that it does not

follow, and that one must not obey; for no one could take a pro-
fusion of insults or total absence of worship as a mode of worship.
And again before the formation of the commonwealth no one who
acknowledged the reign of God had the right to deny the honour
due to him, and he could not therefore transfer the right to give
such an order to the commonwealth. Second question: must one
obey the commonwealth, if it orders something to be said or done
which is not a direct insult to God, but from which insulting consequences may be derived by reasoning? For instance, if an order
were given to worship God in the form of an image in the presence
of people who believe that to do so is a sign of honour? Certainly
it must be done (*). For worship is instituted as a sign of honour,
and to worship in this way is a sign of honour, and spreads the
honour of God among those who accept it as a sign. What if an
order were given to attribute a name to God whose meaning we do
not understand, and we cannot see how it is consistent with the
very name of *God*. That too must be done, because the things we
do to give honour (not knowing anything to the contrary), are signs
of honour if they are taken as such; and hence we are refusing to
advance God's honour if we refuse to do them. We should take the
same view of all *attributes* and *actions* in the purely natural worship
of God, which may be the subject of dispute or controversy. For
although such commands may sometimes be against right reason,
and are therefore sins in those who command them, yet they are
not against right reason nor sins in subjects, for in controversial
matters their right reason is reason subject to the reason of the
commonwealth. Final question: should one obey, if the man or
council to which sovereign power in the commonwealth has been
committed, gives an order to worship him or them with the *attributes* and *actions* with which God should be worshipped? There are
many things which can be attributed to God and men alike; for men
too can be *praised* and *magnified*; and there are many actions by
which both God and men can be worshipped. But we must look
only at the significance of the *attributes* and *actions*. Even against
the orders of Kings we must avoid *attributes* by which we signify a
belief that a man holds power independently of God, or is immortal,
or infinitely powerful, and so on; we must also avoid *actions* that
have this significance, as to pray to someone in his absence, to ask
for what God alone can give, e.g. rain and fine weather; to offer

him what God alone can accept, e.g. Burnt-offerings, or to offer him the highest form of worship, e.g. sacrifice. For these actions tend to imply a lack of belief in God's reign, which is contrary to the initial supposition. But genuflection, prostration or any other bodily act can rightly be employed even in civil ceremony, for they may signify no more than recognition of civil authority. For divine cult is distinguished from civil cult, not by movement, place, dress or gesture of body, but by the sentiment towards the object of worship which it proclaims. Consequently, if we prostrate ourselves before someone with the intention of proclaiming by that sign that we regard him as God, it is divine worship; if we do so as a sign of acknowledgement of civil authority, it is civil worship. *Divine worship* is not distinguished from *civil worship* by any action normally understood by the words λατρεία [service] and δουλεία [slavery]; for the first denotes a slave's *duty* and the latter a slave's *condition*, and so both words describe precisely the same activity.

Certainly it must be done] *We said in article 14 of the present chapter that those who attribute limits to God are acting against the natural law of the worship of God. But those who worship God in the form of an image, are setting limits to him. They are therefore doing what should not be done, and this passage seems to contradict the previous one. The first reply must be that it is not those who offer such worship under compulsion of authority who are assigning limits to God, but those who command such worship. For those who worship against their will do really worship, but they stand up or bow down in the places where they have been told to do so by the legal ruler. Secondly, I say that it [image-worship] should be done, not always and everywhere, but where the basic principle is that the only rule for worshipping God is the dictates of human reason; for then the will of the commonwealth acts as reason. But in the Kingdom of God by Agreement, whether it is the old or the new agreement, where Idolatry is expressly forbidden, it must not be done, even if the commonwealth so commands. If he reflects on these points, anyone who thought there was a contradiction between this article and article 14, will no longer think so.*

19. The conclusion of all this is that, under the Reign of God by natural reason alone, subjects commit sin in the following ways: first, if they violate the moral laws, those which were expounded in

chapters II and III; secondly, if they violate the laws or commands of the commonwealth in matters pertaining to justice, thirdly, if they do not worship God κατὰ τὰ νόμιμα;[5] Fourthly, if they do not confess among men by word and action that there is one God, most Good, most Great, most Blessed, supreme King of all the world and of the Kings of the world, that is, if they do not worship God. This fourth offence in the natural Kingdom of God is, by our account in the last chapter, article 20, the *crime of lèse-majesté against God*. For it is a denial of God's power, or *Atheism*. This is how they Sin in this case: it is as if we supposed that there was a supreme King, who in his absence ruled by a viceroy. They would offend against the king if they did not obey the viceroy in all things, unless he sought the kingdom for himself, or tried to transfer it to someone else. Those who gave the viceroy such absolute obedience that they would not make an exception even of this, would be said to be Guilty of treason.

---

[5] 'According to the laws' or 'according to the conventions'.

Chapter XVI
On the kingdom of God by the old Agreement

1. True religion was established by God through Abraham *(while superstition held sway over foreign nations). 2. By the agreement between* God *and* Adam, *dispute about the commands of superiors was forbidden. 3. The form of the agreement between God and* Abraham. *4. That agreement contains a recognition of God, not simply, but as he appeared to* Abraham. *5. The laws by which* Abraham *was bound were simply the laws of* nature, *and the law of Circumcision. 6.* Abraham *was the* interpreter *to his people of the* Word of God *and of* all the laws. *7.* Abraham's *subjects could not sin in obeying him. 8. The Agreement of God with the* Hebrew people *at* Mount Sinai. *9. From this time the government of God obtained the name of* Kingdom. *10. The laws which were imposed on the Jews by God. 11. What the* Word of God *is, and how it is known. 12. What the* written Word of God *was among the Jews. 13.* Authority to interpret the Word of God *and supreme* civil authority *were united in Moses while he was alive. 14. They were united in the high Priest during the lifetime of Joshua. 15. They were also united in the* high Priest *down to the time of* King Saul. *16. They were united in the* Kings *until the captivity. 17. After the captivity they were in the* Priests. *18. Among the Jews, denial of divine providence, and Idolatry, were the only crimes of divine lèse-majesté; in all other things they owed obedience to their Princes.*

1. Aware of their own weakness and in wonder at natural events, the human race has developed an almost universal belief that an invisible God is the Workman who has made all visible things; they also fear him, believing that they do not have adequate self-protection in themselves. But their imperfect use of reason and the vigour of their passions have prevented them from worshipping him rightly. The fear of the invisible, when separated from right reason, is superstition. Without special assistance from God, it proved almost impossible to avoid the twin rocks of *Atheism* and *superstition*; for the latter proceeds from fear without right reason, the former from an *opinion of reason* without fear. So the greater part of mankind has readily succumbed to *Idolatry*; and almost every Nation

has worshipped God by way of *images* and in the *shapes* of finite things, and has worshipped spectres or Phantoms, and called them demons.[1] But it pleased God's majesty (as we read it written in the sacred History) to call out of the human race one man, *Abraham*, in order to bring mankind through him to a true worship of himself; it pleased him to reveal himself to him supernaturally; and to enter into that famous agreement with him and his descendants which is called *the Old Agreement, the Old Covenant* and *the Old Testament. Abraham* therefore is the source of true religion; *he was the first after the Flood to teach that there is one God, Creator of the Universe.* And from him *the Kingdom of God by agreement* took its origin. Josephus, Antiquities of the Jews, book I, chapter 7.

2. It is true that at the beginning of the world God's rule over *Adam* and *Eve* was not only natural but also by *agreement*; from which it appears that any obedience other than that which natural reason dictated should be given only by agreement, i.e. from men's own consent. But as this *agreement* was immediately made void, and was never renewed, the origin of the *Kingdom of God* (which is our subject here) has to be found elsewhere. Note in passing that by the precept not to eat of the tree of the *knowledge of good and evil* (whether it is *judgement* of *Good* and *Evil* that is forbidden here, or eating some fruit from a tree) God required utterly simple obedience to his precepts, without argument as to whether the precept was *Good* or *Bad*; for without the command, the fruit of the tree has nothing in its nature by which its eating could be morally *bad*, i.e. a *sin*.

3. The agreement between *God* and *Abraham* was made in this form (Gen. 17.7–8): *I will set my agreement between me and you and your descendants in their generations after you with an everlasting covenant, that I be your God and the God of your descendants after you for ever. And I will give to you and to your descendants after you the land of your wanderings, the whole of the land of Canaan, as an everlasting possession.* So that *Abraham* and his seed would preserve the memory of this Covenant it was necessary to devise a sign.

---

[1] Warrender inserts the words *forte ex metu* ('perhaps from fear') from the presentation copy (see introduction, p. xiii). This was perhaps intended by Hobbes as an etymological gloss on *daemonia* ('demons'), as if he derived the word from δέος/δείδω 'fear').

Hence *Circumcision* was appended to the agreement, but only as a sign (v.10): *This is my agreement which you will keep between me and you and your descendants after you. Every male from among you shall be circumcised, and you shall circumcise the flesh of your foreskin, to be a sign of the Covenant between me and you.* The Agreement therefore is that *Abraham* acknowledge that *God* is his God and the God of his descendants, i.e. that he submit himself to be ruled by him; and that God give *Abraham* the inheritance of the land in which he was then living as a foreigner; and that *Abraham* arrange for the circumcision of himself and his male descendants as a sign to preserve the memory of this agreement.

4. But since even before the Agreement *Abraham* acknowledged God as creator of the world and king (for he never doubted either the *existence* of God or his *Providence*), surely it was superfluous for God to offer *Abraham* a price and a *contract* for the obedience which was due to him by nature, by promising him the Kingdom of the Land of *Canaan* on condition that he accepted him as his God, since he already was that before by natural law. Hence the words, *that I be your God and the God of your descendants after you*, do not mean that *Abraham* satisfies this *agreement* merely by acknowledging the power and Dominion that God has over men by nature, i.e. by the general recognition of God, which is a matter of *natural reason*, but by the specific recognition of him as the one who had said to him (Gen. 12.1): *Go out of your Land*, etc., and (Gen. 13.14), *Lift your eyes*, etc., as the one who appeared to him in the guise of the three heavenly figures (Gen. 18.1–2), and (Gen. 15.1) in a vision and (v.13)[2] in a dream; which *is a matter of Faith*. No account is given of the form in which God appeared to *Abraham*, and what sound he made to address him, but it is certain that *Abraham* believed that the voice was the voice of God and a true revelation, and that he wanted his followers to worship the one who had so addressed him as God, creator of the universe; and his faith lay not in believing that *God exists* or that his promises *are true* (which all men believe), but in not doubting that the one whose voice and promises he had heard was God. It is also clear that *God of Abraham* signifies not simply *God* but *God appearing to him*, just as the

---

[2] The references to 12.1, 18.1–2 and v.13 have been corrected following Warrender.

worship *Abraham* owed to God on that ground, was not the worship of *reason* but the worship of *religion* and *faith*; the worship which God, not reason, had revealed to him, *supernaturally*.

5. We do not read of any laws given to *Abraham* by God or by *Abraham* to his family, either then or later, either secular or sacred (with the exception of the one command about *circumcision*, which is in the *Agreement* itself). It is clear from this that there were no other laws or worship by which *Abraham* was bound, beyond the natural laws, rational worship and circumcision.

6. *Abraham* was also the *interpreter* of all the *laws*, both sacred and secular, for his own people, not only by nature in that he employed only natural laws, but also by the wording of the *agreement*, by which he promises obedience not only for himself but also on behalf of his descendants. *This* would have been pointless, if his children were not obliged to obey his commands. At Gen. 18.18 God says: *All the nations of the earth are to be blessed in him: for I know that he will command his children and his household after him, to keep the way of the Lord, and to do judgement and justice.* How can this be understood unless his children and his household were assumed to be obliged to give obedience to his commands?

7. It follows that *Abraham*'s subjects could not have offended in obeying *Abraham* himself, provided that *Abraham* did not command them to deny *God's existence* or *Providence*, or to do anything expressly against God's honour. In all other things *God's Word* was to be taken from his lips as the *interpreter* of all the *laws* and of the *words* of *God*. Only from *Abraham* could they learn who the God of *Abraham* was and how he was to be worshipped. But after *Abraham* those who were subject to the government of *Isaac* or *Jacob* obeyed them in all things for the same reason, and committed no offence, as long as they acknowledged and confessed the *God of Abraham* as their God and King. For they had submitted simply to *God* before submitting to *Abraham*; and to *Abraham* before the *God of Abraham*; and again to the *God of Abraham* before *Isaac*. Hence among the subjects of *Abraham* the only *crime of treason against God* was to deny God; but among their descendants it was also a crime of treason *to deny the God of Abraham*, i.e. to worship God other than as instituted by *Abraham*, i.e. in the form of images (*) made by hand, as the other nations did and were for that reason called *Idolaters*.

Down to this time subjects could easily distinguish among the commands of their princes, what was to be done and what avoided.

In the form of Images made by hand] *See XV.14, where we show that such worship is irrational. But if it is done by order of a commonwealth which does not know and has not received the written word of God, such worship, as we show at XV.18, is rational. But where God rules by an agreement in which there is an explicit provision against such worship (as in Abraham's agreement), then it is wrong, whether by order of the commonwealth or against its orders.*

8. To proceed now, following the lead of holy scripture, the same *Agreement* was renewed with *Isaac* (Gen. 26.3, 4) and with *Jacob* (Gen. 28.14), where God calls himself not simply *'God'*, which nature tells us he is, but gives himself a distinct name, *'the God of Abraham and Isaac'*, and later, he will, through *Moses*, renew the same *Agreement* with the whole people of *Israel. – I*, he says (Exodus 3.6), *am the God of your father, the God of Abraham, the God of Isaac, and the God of Jacob.* Then later when that people had halted in the desert near Mount Sinai, and was not only wholly free but also totally hostile to human subjection because of their recent experience of Egyptian slavery, it was proposed that they should all renew the *old Agreement* in these terms (Exodus 19.5): *If therefore you hear my voice and keep my Agreement* (i.e. the *Agreement* made with *Abraham, Isaac* and *Jacob*), *you shall be my particular property out of all the peoples, for the whole earth is mine, and you shall be to me a priestly kingdom, and a holy people.* And the whole people answered together (v.8): *We will do all that the Lord has spoken.*

9. In this covenant, note, among other things, the term *Kingdom*, not previously used. For although God was their king both by *nature* and by the *Agreement* with *Abraham*, they nevertheless owed him only natural obedience and natural worship, as his subjects, but the religious worship which *Abraham* had instituted they owed him as subjects of *Abraham, Isaac* or *Jacob*, their natural Princes. For the only *Word of God* that they had received was the natural word of right reason, and there was no *agreement* between God and themselves except in so far as their wills were included in the will of *Abraham*, as their Prince. But now, by the *agreement* made at Mount

Sinai, a *kingdom of God by design* [*institutivum*] comes into being over them, as each individual gave his consent. This is the point at which that *Kingdom of God* which is so famous in holy scripture and in the writings of Theologians comes into being, and this is what is referred to when God said to *Samuel*, as the *Israelites* were demanding a King (I Sam. 8.7): *They have not rejected you but me, lest I Reign over them*, and what *Samuel* said to the *Israelites* (I Sam. 12.12): *You said, A King will command us, when the Lord your God was Reigning over you*; as well as what is said at Jeremiah 31 [32]: *the Agreement which I made when I had dominion over them*. It is also the teaching of *Judas of Galilee*, mentioned at Josephus, Jewish Antiquities 18.2, in these words: *Judas of Galilee was the founder of the fourth sect of seekers of wisdom. They agree with the Pharisees in everything except that they burn with a constant passion for liberty, believing that God alone is to be regarded as Lord and Prince, and they will more readily bear the most exquisite forms of punishment, together with their families and loved ones, than call any mortal man Lord.*

10. Now that the right of the kingdom by the *Agreement* is established, we must next see what *laws* God made for them. Everyone knows them, they are the *Decalogue*, and the other *laws*, *judicial* and *ceremonial*, which are laid out from *Exodus* 20 to the end of the *Pentateuch* and the death of *Moses*. Of the whole body of *laws* given by the hand of *Moses*, some obligate by nature, because they were given by *God* as *God of nature*, and had validity even before *Abraham*. Others derive their obligation from the *agreement* made with *Abraham*, because they were given by God as the *God of Abraham*, and had validity before *Moses*, in virtue of the first *Agreement*. Others derive their obligation solely from the *agreement* which was made later with the people itself, because they were given by *God* specifically as *King of the Israelites*. Of the first kind are all the precepts of the *Decalogue* which relate to morals, as: *Honour your parents; do not kill; do not commit adultery; do not kill; do not steal; do not speak false witness; do not covet*. For they are natural laws. Also, the precept, *on not taking the name of God in vain*; for it is a part of natural worship as shown at article 15 of the last chapter. Likewise the second precept, *on not giving adoration through an image* made by themselves; for this too is of natural religion, as shown in the same article. Of the second kind is the first precept of the *Decalogue*, *on not having* foreign *Gods*, for this is the essence of the *agreement*

with Abraham, by which God demands precisely this, that he be his God and the God of his descendants. Likewise the precept *on keeping holy the sabbath*. For hallowing of the seventh day was instituted in memory of the six-day creation, as appears from these words (Exod. 31.17): *The agreement (the sabbath agreement* is meant*) is eternal between me and the sons of Israel, and a perpetual sign; for in six days the Lord made the heaven and the earth, and on the seventh day he ceased from his work.* Of the third kind are the *political, judicial* and *ceremonial* laws, which affected only the Jews. The laws of the first and second kind, written on the *tablets of stone*, i.e. the *Decalogue*, were preserved in the *Ark* itself; the others were written in the *volume* of the whole law and stored in *the side of the Ark* (Deut. 31.26).[3] For the latter could be changed, but the former could not without breaking the faith of *Abraham*.

11. Every *Law* of God is a *Word of God*, but not every *Word of God* (conversely) is a *law*. *I am the Lord your God, that brought you out of the land of Egypt* is a Word of God; it is not a law. Nor is just everything the *Word of God* which is said or written along with the word itself, for the purpose of proclaiming the *Word of God*. For *Thus saith the Lord*, is not an utterance of the Lord, but of a spokesman or a Prophet. The whole and sole Word of God is what a true Prophet has proclaimed that God has said. The books of the Prophets which include both what God says and what the Prophet himself says are called the Word of God because they contain the Word of God. But since the whole and sole *Word of God* is what is delivered as such by a true Prophet, one must know who is a true Prophet before one can know what the *Word of God* is; nor can one give credence to a *Word of God* before one gives credence to a Prophet. *Moses* was given credence by the people of *Israel* for two things, *miracles* and *faith*. However striking and evident his miracles were, they would not have given him credence, or at least ought not to have, if he had called them out of *Egypt* to some other worship than that of the God of *Abraham*, *Isaac* and *Jacob*, their fathers. For that would have been against the *Agreement* they had made with God. Similarly, God laid before the *Jews* two marks of a true Prophet, *supernatural prediction of the future*, which is a great miracle, and *faith in the God of Abraham, who liberated them from*

---

[3] Corrected reference from Warrender.

Egypt. Anyone lacking either of these is no true Prophet, and what he holds out as the *Word of God* is not to be taken as such. If faith is wanting, he is rejected in these words (Deut. 13.1–5):[4] *If there shall arise in the midst of you a Prophet, or one who says that he has seen a dream, and if he foretells a sign and a portent, and what he has spoken comes to pass, and if he says to you 'let us go and follow foreign gods', etc., that Prophet, or forger of dreams, shall be put to death.* If prediction of the future is missing, he is dismissed in these words (Deut. 18.21–2): *But if in silent thought you reply, 'How shall I know which word was not spoken by the Lord?', you shall have this sign. What that Prophet predicted in the name of the Lord, and it did not come about, was not spoken by the Lord; in the pride of his heart the Prophet forged it.* It is now beyond dispute that a *Word of God* is what is proclaimed as such through a true Prophet; and a true Prophet among the Jews was one whose faith was true, and whose predictions were confirmed by the event. But there may also be much dispute, what it is to follow alien Gods, and whether events which are said to confirm predictions really do so or not, especially in the case of predictions which presage the event in obscure and Enigmatic fashion; and most of the prophets' predictions are like this, because they do not *see God* openly, as *Moses* did, but *through enigmas and figures* (Numbers 12.8). They can only be judged by *natural Reason*; for that judgement depends on interpretation of the Prophet and comparison of it with the event.

12. The Jews accepted the book of the whole law (which is called *Deuteronomy*) as the *written Word of God*. And that was the only book they accepted down to the time of the captivity, so far as can be inferred from the sacred history. For the book was passed by *Moses* himself to the Priests, to be kept safe and deposited in the side of the Ark of the Covenant, to be copied out by the Kings, (Deut. [31].9, 26);[5] and long afterwards it was recognized by the authority of King Josiah as *Word of God* (2 Kings 23.[2]).[6] But it is not clear when the rest of the books of the old Testament were first received into the canon. As for the Prophets – *Isaiah* and the others – since they predicted things which were to happen only during the captivity or after it, their writings could not be taken as

---

[4] The correct reference is Deuteronomy 13.1–3, 6.
[5] Reference given by Warrender.
[6] Reference given by Warrender.

Prophetic right away, by the condition cited above from Deut. 18.21–2, by which the *Israelites* were bidden only to take as a Prophet someone whose predictions were confirmed by events. And that is actually why, after the fulfilment of the prediction, the *Jews* accepted as prophetic writings, i.e. as *Word of God*, the writings of those whom they had put to death at the time when they were actually prophesying.

13. Now that we have ascertained what the *laws* of the *old Agreement* were, and what was originally accepted as *God's Word*, we must next carefully inquire what man or men had the authority to determine whether the writings of Prophets who arose later should be accepted as *God's word* (i.e. whether events answered to their predictions or not), and what man or men had authority to *interpret the laws which had already been accepted and God's written word*. The question must be examined for each different period and development of the Commonwealth [*Respublica*] of Israel.

It is clear that while *Moses* was alive this authority lay wholly with him. For if he had not himself been the *interpreter of the laws and the Word*, that function would have belonged necessarily either to *individuals* as private persons or to a congregation or *Synagogue* of several persons, or to the *High Priest*, or to other *Prophets*. But first, it did not belong to private persons or to a congregation of such persons; this rests on the fact that they were not consulted, in fact they were forbidden by the gravest threats from *hearing God* otherwise than through *Moses*. For it is written: *but let not the priests and the people pass the limits, or ascend to the Lord, lest perchance he shall kill them. And Moses went down and told them everything* (Ex. 19.24–5). Then it is clearly and explicitly stated that neither individuals nor a congregation should claim that God has spoken through them and consequently that they have *the right to interpret God's word* themselves, in the account of the sedition of *Core*, *Dathan*, and *Abiron* and the two hundred and fifty leading men of the Synagogue. When they contended that the Lord spoke through them no less than through *Moses*, this is the argument they put: *Let it be enough for you that the whole multitude is of holy men, and the Lord is in them; why do you raise yourselves above the people of God?* (Num. 16.3).[7] What God thought of this point may be seen from

---

[7] This remark is addressed to Moses and Aaron.

the fact that (*Core, Dathan* and *Abiron*) *descended living into hell* and *a fire came out from the Lord and killed the two hundred and fifty men* (*ibid.*, v.33, 35).

Secondly, it is clear that this Authority did not lie with the high Priest Aaron from a similar dispute which he and his sister *Miriam* had with *Moses*. The question was whether God spoke through *Moses* only or also through themselves, i.e. whether they as well as *Moses* were *interpreters of God's word*. This is what they said: *Did the Lord speak through Moses and not also through us?* (Num. 12.2). But God rebuked them, and made a distinction between *Moses* and the other *Prophets*, saying, *If there shall be any Prophet among you, I will appear to him in a vision, or speak to him through a dream; but my servant Moses is not of this sort*, etc. *For I speak to him face to face, and he does not see God through riddles and figures, so why were you not afraid*, etc.? (*ibid.*, v.6–8). Finally, we may infer that in *Moses*'s lifetime the *interpretation of God's word* was not in the hands of any other Prophets whatever, from the fact we have already cited of his pre-eminence over all the others; and from natural reason, since the Prophet who carries the commands of God must also interpret them; and there was no other *Word of God* at that time except the one that had been made known through *Moses*. And also from the fact that at that time there was no other Prophet that prophesied to the people but the 70 elders who prophesied by the spirit of *Moses*. *Joshua* too, *Moses*'s assistant at the time and later his successor, believed they should not have done it until he found out that it was done with *Moses*'s consent; this is clear from the actual text of scripture: *God came down through a cloud*, etc., *taking of the spirit that was in Moses, and giving it to the seventy men* (Num. 11.25). And after it had been reported that they were Prophesying, *Joshua* said to *Moses*: *My Lord, forbid them.* But *Moses* replied: *Why are you jealous on my behalf*, etc.? Since therefore *Moses* alone was the *messenger of God's word*, and there was no *function of interpretation* in the hands of *private persons* or of a *Synagogue* or of a *Priest* or of other *Prophets*, the only conclusion available is that *Moses* was the sole *interpreter of God's word*, and also held sovereign power in civil matters; And that the struggle of *Core* and the other conspirators against *Moses* and *Aaron*; and of *Aaron* and his sister against *Moses* was not started for the safety of their souls but from ambition for kingdom over the people.

14. In the time of *Joshua*, *interpretation of the laws and of God's Word* was in the hands of Eleazar, the high *Priest*, who was also the King, absolute under God. This is the inference first from the actual *agreement* in which the Commonwealth [*Respublica*] of the *Israelites* is called a *Sacerdotal Kingdom*, or, as cited at 1 Peter 2.9, a *Royal Priesthood*, which could not be said unless Royal power were understood to be in the hands of the *Priest* by the initiative and *agreement* of the people. This does not contradict what was said before, where it was not *Aaron* but *Moses* who had the kingdom under God. For where one man lays down the form of a future commonwealth [*respublica*], he inevitably governs the kingdom which he has set up for his time (whether it is to be a *Monarchy*, an *Aristocracy* or a *Democracy*); and for the time being he has all the power which he will assign to others for the future. And in the actual calling of *Joshua* to the control of affairs, it is explicitly said that *Eleazar* the Priest held not only the *Priesthood* but also *sovereign power*; this is how it is put: *Take Joshua, the son of Nun, etc., and he shall stand before Eleazar the priest, and the whole multitude, and in the sight of all you shall give him precepts and a share of your glory, so that the whole Congregation of the sons of Israel may hear. Whatever is to be done, Eleazar the priest shall consult the Lord for him. At his word he shall go out and come in, and all the sons of Israel with him* (Num. 27. 18–21). Here *to consult God as to what is to be done*, i.e. *to interpret God's word*, and to give commands in God's name in all things, belongs to *Eleazar*; but *to go out and to come in at his word*, i.e. to obey him, belongs to *Joshua* and to *the whole people*. Note also that the phrase *a share of your glory* plainly indicates that *Joshua* did not have authority equal to *Moses'*. None the less it is clear that even in the time of *Joshua* sovereign civil power and authority to interpret God's word both belonged to the same person.

15. After the death of *Joshua* comes the period of the *Judges*, which lasts till King *Saul*; it is clear that throughout this period the right of the Kingdom instituted by God stayed with the Priest. For there was a *Priestly kingdom* based on an *agreement*, that is, a Kingdom of God through a Priest. And it had to be like this until the form was changed by the people itself with God's consent, and that did not happen until God gave his consent to their request for a king, and said to Samuel: *Listen to the people in all that they say to you; for they have not rejected you, but me, so that I may not reign*

over them (1 Sam. 8.7). And thus *by right* sovereign civil power belonged by God's own design to the high Priest. In fact that power was in the hands of the Prophets (who were raised up by God outside the ordinary course of things); and the Israelites (a people avid of Prophets) submitted to them for protection and arbitration, because they had a high regard for Prophecy. And the reason for this was that by the institution of the Priestly Kingdom of God, although there were penalties laid down and Magistrates to give judgment, still the right to inflict punishment depended on private initiative. And it was up to the disunited multitude of the people and to individuals either to punish or not as they were prompted by private inclination. This was why Moses did not condemn anyone to death on his own authority; but when anyone was to be put to death (whether it was one man or several men), he relied upon divine authority to rouse the crowd against him or them, saying, *Thus saith the Lord*. This was appropriate to the nature of a particular kingdom of God. For God truly reigns where the laws are obeyed for fear of God, not of men. And if men were as they should be, that would be the best form of commonwealth. But to rule men as they are, there must be power[8] (which comprises both right and strength) to compel. That was also the reason why from the beginning God through *Moses* laid down laws for the Kings to come (Deut. 17.14); and *Moses* predicted in his last words to the people, *I know that after my death you will do wickedly and turn aside from the way that I taught you* (Deut. 31.29). When, in accordance with this prediction, another generation arose *that did not know the Lord and the works that he had done for Israel, the children of Israel did evil in the sight of God and served Baalim* (Judges 2.10[–11]), meaning that they rejected God's rule, i.e. the government of the *Priest* by whom God ruled, and afterwards when they were defeated by their enemies and reduced to slavery, they no longer looked for God's will from a *Priest* but from Prophets. The Prophets therefore gave judgment in Israel *de facto*, but *by right* the *Israelites'* obedience was due to the *high Priest*. Hence although the *Priestly Kingdom* was without strength after the deaths of Moses and *Joshua*, it was still not without *right*. That *interpretation of God's Word* belonged to the same Priest, is clear from the fact that after the consecration of the

---

[8] 'Power' here translates *potentia*.

tabernacle and ark of the covenant, God no longer spoke on Mount *Sinai* but in the tabernacle of the Covenant, from the mercy-seat which was between the Cherubim, which none might approach but the Priest. If then one looks at the *right* of the Kingdom, both *sovereign civil power* and the *authority to interpret God's Word* were together in the hands of the Priest; but if you look at the *fact*, they were both in the hands of the Prophets who judged the Israelites. For as *judges* they had civil authority; as *Prophets*, they interpreted God's word; and so in every way from that time on right up to today those two powers have been inseparable.

16. When kings were appointed, there is no doubt that *civil Authority* was in the hands of the Kings. For when the Kingdom of God by Priests had come to an end at the Israelites' request and with God's consent, the right by which the kings governed was grounded in the people's actual cession. (Jerome actually comments on this in speaking of the books of *Samuel*. Samuel, he says, demonstrates that the old law was abolished by the death of *Eli* and the killing of *Saul*. The Oaths of the new Priesthood and the new government in the case of *Zadok* and *David* are further evidence.) The Priest could only rightly do what God ordered, but the King could rightly do whatever each man could rightly do in himself. For the *Israelites* ceded to him the *right* of *judging* all of them and of *making War* on everyone's behalf; and these two things contain all the *right* that one man can transfer to another. *Our* King, they say, *will judge us, and go out before us, and fight our wars for us* (1 Sam. 8.20). Thus *judgements* were in the hands of the Kings. But to *give a judgement* is simply to *apply laws* to facts by *interpretation*; therefore *interpretation of laws* also belonged to them. And because, apart from the *law of Moses* no other written Word of God was recognised until the captivity, the Authority to *interpret God's Word* was also in the hands of the Kings. Moreover, since the Word of God is to be accepted as law, even if there had been another Word of God written apart from the *law of Moses*, its interpretation too would have been in the Kings' hands, because interpretation of the *laws* was theirs. Admittedly, when *Deuteronomy* (in which the *law of Moses* was contained) was rediscovered after being lost for a long time, the Priests did consult the Lord *about that book* (2 Kings 22.13); but it was not by their own authority but on the instruction of *Josiah*, and not directly but through the Prophetess *Huldah*. From this it appears that the

authority to admit *books* as *God's Word* did not lie with the *Priest*. However it does not follow that such authority lay with the Prophetess either; because there were others who judged whether the Prophets should be taken as true Prophets or not. Why did God give the whole people marks and signs by which to distinguish true from false Prophets, those marks being the outcome of their predictions and their conformity with the Religion Moses founded, if they might not be used as marks? The authority then to admit books as God's Word lay with the King, and thus that book was approved and accepted by authority of King *Josiah*, as appears from 2 Kings 23.1–3, where we are told that he summoned the orders of the Kingdom, that is, the *Elders, Priests and Prophets* and *all the people*, and in their presence *he read the book* and *encouraged them to perform the words of this covenant*, i.e. he ensured that this Covenant was recognized as the *covenant of Moses* i.e. as *God's Word*, and was once again accepted and confirmed by the *Israelites*. Thus in the time of the Kings too, civil authority and the power to *distinguish God's Word* from the word of men and to *interpret God's Word* was wholly in their hands. The Prophets had not been sent with authority but in the form and with the right of spokesmen or preachers; those who heard them judged them; and if in fact those who did not listen to them when they were giving clear instruction on easy matters were punished, it does not follow that the Kings were obliged to do whatever they said should be done in the name of God. For although *Josiah*, a good King of Israel, was killed because he did not listen to what God said by the mouth of *Nechao*, King of Egypt, i.e. he rejected what was actually good advice even though it did seem to come from an enemy, yet no one will say that *Josiah* was obligated by any bond of law human or divine to believe the *Pharaoh Nechao*, the King of Egypt, when he said that *God had spoken to him*.[9] As for the possible objection, that Kings rarely have enough learning to fit them to interpret the old books in which God's Word is contained; and for that reason it is not reasonable that this task should depend on their authority, the same objection can be made against Priests and all mortal men, for they can all make mistakes; and though Priests might be better equipped by nature and training than other men, still Kings are perfectly capable

---

[9] Cf. 2 Kings 23.29.

of appointing interpreters under themselves. Thus, even though Kings may not personally interpret God's Word, the task of interpretation can still depend on their authority; and to deny that authority to Kings, because they cannot perform the task themselves, is the same as saying that the authority to teach Geometry should not depend on Kings, unless they themselves are Geometers. We read that the Kings prayed for the people, blessed the people, consecrated the temple, instructed Priests, and removed Priests from office and appointed others. They did not indeed offer sacrifices, because that was the traditional right of Aaron and his sons. But it is clear that throughout the period from King *Saul* to the captivity in Babylon, Priesthood was, as in *Moses*' time, a ministry, not a magistracy.

17. After the return from slavery in Babylon, the *Priestly kingdom* was restored to the form it had had from the death of *Joshua* to the beginning of the Kings by the renewal and sealing of the *covenant*, except that it is not expressly said that the returning *Jews* gave the *right* of government [*imperii*] to *Ezra* (under whose guidance they ordered their state [*status*]) or to any one else but God himself. The reformation seems rather to have been no more than vows and promises on the part of individuals to observe the provisions of the book of the law. Nevertheless (and perhaps not by the people's intention) as a result of their renewal of the *agreement* at that time (for the *agreement* was the same as the one made on mount Sinai), that state was a *Priestly Kingdom*, i.e. supreme authority, civil and sacred, was united in the Priests. But although after this, right down to the time of our Saviour *Jesus Christ*, there was so much trouble from the ambition of contenders for the Priesthood and the intervention of foreign princes, that one can hardly gather from the histories of those times where that authority lay, this much is incontrovertible that during that period authority to *interpret God's word* was not separate from supreme civil authority [*potestas*].

18. It is easy to see from this how the Jews had to treat the commands of their princes in the whole period from *Abraham* to *Christ*. For just as in merely human Kingdoms one must obey the subordinate magistrates in everything, except when their orders entail the crime of treason, so in God's Kingdom obedience had to be given to the princes *Abraham*, *Isaac*, *Jacob*, *Moses*, and the *Priest* and the *King*, each in his time, except when their orders entailed

the *crime of treason against God*. The crime of treason against God comprised, first, *denial of divine providence*; for this was to deny that *God is King by nature*; and, second, *Idolatry*, or the worship not of *other* gods (for there is only one God) but of the gods *of other peoples*, that is, the worship of the one God, but under other *names*, *attributes* and *rites* than those instituted by *Abraham* and *Moses*. For this was to *deny that the God of Abraham* was their King by the *agreement* which they, like *Abraham*, had entered into. In all other matters obedience was due; and if the King or Priest who held sovereign power ordered any other thing that was contrary to the *laws*, that was an offence by the holder of sovereign power, not by the subject; whose duty is to carry out the orders of his superiors, not to dispute them.

Chapter XVII
On the Kingdom of God by the new Agreement

1. Prophecies of the dignity of Christ. *2. Prophecies of the* humility *and* passion of Christ. *3. Jesus is THE CHRIST. 4. The* Kingdom of God *by the* new Agreement *is not the Kingdom of Christ as Christ, but as God. 5.* The Kingdom of God by the new agreement *is a heavenly Kingdom, and begins on the day of judgement. 6. Christ's régime in this world has not been* power *but* counsel, *or a régime of teaching and persuasion. 7. What the promises of the* new Agreement *are on both sides. 8.* No laws *were added by* Christ *except the institution of the sacraments. 9. Repent, be baptized, keep my commandments, and similar formulae are not* laws. *10. It is for the civil authority to define what the sin of injustice is. 11. It is for the civil authority to determine what makes for the peace and defence of the commonwealth. 12. It is for the civil authority to judge (when need be) which definitions and which inferences are true. 13. It belongs to the office of* Christ *to teach morals, not as theorems but as laws; to remit sins; and to teach all those things of which there is no science properly so-called. 14. The distinction of temporal from Spiritual. 15. In how many ways Word of God is understood. 16. Not everything contained in holy scripture belongs to the Canon of the Christian faith. 17. The word of a legitimate interpreter of the holy scriptures is the Word of God. 18. The authority to interpret the scriptures is the same as the authority to decide controversies of faith. 19. Several meanings of church. 20. What a* Church *is, to which rights, actions, and similar personal qualities are attributed 21. A* Christian Commonwealth *is the same as a* Christian Church. *22. A number of* commonwealths *do not make one* Church. *23. What* Ecclesiastics *are. 24. The* choice of Ecclesiastics *is a matter for the* Church, *their* consecration *for the* Pastors. *25. Authority to remit sins to the repentant, and to retain them to the unrepentant belongs to* Pastors; *but the authority to judge repentance belongs to the* Church. *26. What* Excommunication *is, and the persons on whom it cannot fall. 27. The* interpretation of scripture *depends on the authority of the* commonwealth. *28. A* Christian commonwealth *should interpret the scriptures through Ecclesiastical Pastors.*

1. In the *old Testament* there are many plain prophecies about our Saviour *Jesus Christ*; who was to restore the *Kingdom Of God* by a

new *agreement*; some of them predict his Royal *dignity*, some his *humility* and *suffering*. Among the prophecies of his *dignity* are these: God, blessing Abraham, promises him a son, Isaac, and adds, *And the Kings of the peoples shall spring from him* (Gen. 17.16). Jacob blessing his son *Judah* says, *The sceptre shall not be taken from Judah* (Gen. 49.10). God to Moses: *I will raise up for them*, he says, *a prophet like you from the midst of his brothers, and I will put my words in his mouth, and he shall tell them all that I shall instruct him. And I will take revenge upon anyone who refuses to hear the words which he shall speak in my name* (Deut. 18.18[-19]). Isaiah: *The Lord himself shall give you a sign. Behold a virgin shall conceive and shall give birth to a son, and his name shall be called Emmanuel* (Isa. 7.14). Isaiah again: *A little child has been born to us, and a son has been given to us, and a princedom has been put upon his shoulders, and his name shall be called Wonderful, Counsellor, mighty God, Father of the age to come, the Prince of Peace* (Isa. 9.6). And again: *A branch shall grow from the Root of Jesse, And a flower shall rise from his Root, the spirit of wisdom shall rest upon him, etc. He shall not judge by the sight of his eyes nor reprove by the hearing of his ears, but he will judge the poor in justice, etc. and he shall strike the ground with the rod of his mouth, and the breath of his lips shall slay the wicked* (Isa. 11.1–5). Moreover, almost the whole of *Isaiah*, chapters 51–6 and 60–2 is a description of the advent and works of the *Christ* to come. Jeremiah: *Behold the day shall come, says the Lord, and I will make a new Covenant with the house of Israel and with the house of Judah*, etc. (Jer. 31.31). Baruch: *This is our God*, etc. *After this he was seen on earth, and kept company with men* (Bar. 3.36, 38). Ezekiel: *I will raise up over them one who shall pasture them, my servant David, and I will make with them an Agreement of peace* (Ezek. 34.23). Daniel: *I was seeing in a vision of the night, and behold, as it were the son of man was coming with the clouds of heaven, and he went up to the ancient of days, and he gave him power and honour and kingship, and all peoples and tribes and tongues shall serve him, and his power shall be an eternal power* (Dan. 7.13). Haggai, *Still a little time, and I will shake heaven and earth, both the sea and the dry land, and I will move all the nations, and the desired of all nations shall come* (Haggai 2.7,8). Zechariah under the image of *Jesus* the high Priest, *I will bring my servant from the East*, etc. (Zech. 3.8), and again, *Behold the man, the East is his name* (Zech. 6.12). And again: *Exult greatly, daughter of Sion, raise a shout of joy, daughter of Jerusalem, Behold your King and Saviour* (Zech. 9.9). Under the influence of these and other prophecies, the Jews expected a *Christ*, a King to be sent by God, to redeem them and what is more to rule all the nations. In fact a prophecy had spread throughout the Roman empire (which even the emperor Vespasian interpreted, though wrongly, as support for his own project) that *from Judaea would come one who would rule the world.*[1]

2. The following are among the prophecies of *Christ's humility and suffering*: Isaiah: *He himself bore our weaknesses and carried our sorrows; and we thought of him as a leper, as stricken of God and humiliated* (Isa. 53.4), and a little after: *He was offered up because it was his will, and did not open his mouth; as a Sheep he will be led to the slaughter, and as a lamb before its shearer, he will be mute,* etc. (ibid. 7), and again: *He was cut off from the land of the living; because of the crime of the people I have struck him,* etc. (v.8), and: *therefore I will assign him many men, and he shall divide the spoils of the brave, because he surrendered his soul to death and was numbered with the wicked, and he himself bore the sins of many, and prayed for the transgressors* (v. 12). And Zechariah: *Himself a poor man, riding on a donkey and on a colt, the foal of a donkey* (Zech. 9.9).

3. In the reign of *Tiberius Caesar* our saviour JESUS of Galilee, son (as was thought) of *Joseph*, began to preach, proclaiming to the Jewish people that the Kingdom of God for which they were waiting was at hand; and that he himself was the *King*, i.e. THE CHRIST; he expounded *the Law*; he took into his service *twelve Apostles* and *seventy disciples*, following the number of the princes of the tribes and of the seventy elders (in imitation of *Moses*); he *taught* the *way of salvation* through himself and through them; he purged the Temple; and did great signs and fulfilled all that the prophets had foretold about the *Christ* to come. He was hated by the Pharisees (whose teaching he had criticized as false, and their sanctity as pretence) and by the people because of them; he was accused of aspiring to kingship, and was Crucified. By recounting his genealogy, birth, life, teaching, death and resurrection, and by comparing what he did with what had been foretold, the Gospels show that

---

[1] Cf. Suetonius, *The Twelve Caesars*, Vespasian 4.

he was the true CHRIST and *King* promised by God, and sent by God the Father to renew the *new agreement* between themselves and God; and all Christians agree.

4. From the fact that CHRIST was sent by God the Father to make a *covenant*[2] between himself and the people, it is clear that even if Christ is equal in nature to his Father, yet he was inferior as far as the right of the Kingdom goes, for properly speaking such a task is not Royal but Vice-regal, as was the régime of Moses. For the Kingdom was not his but his *Father's*; and CHRIST himself indicated as much, when he was Baptized as a subject and openly professed, in his teaching on prayer, *Our Father* etc. *thy Kingdom come.* And when he said, *I will not drink*, etc., *until that day when I shall drink the new drink with you in the Kingdom of my Father* (Mat. 26.29); also St. Paul: *Just as in Adam all die, so in Christ all shall be made alive; but each one in his own order; the first-fruits are Christ; then those who are Christ's, who believed at his coming; and then comes the end, when he shall hand over the Kingdom to God and the Father* (1 Cor. 15.22–4). However it is also called *Christ's Kingdom.* The mother of the sons of Zebedee made a request to him in these words: *Say that these two sons of mine may sit one on your right hand and one on your left hand in Your Kingdom* (Mat. 20.21). And the thief on the cross: *Lord, remember me when you come into Your Kingdom* (Luke 23.42). And St. Paul, *Know this and understand that no fornicator* etc. *has an inheritance in the Kingdom of Christ and of God* (Eph. 5.5). Elsewhere: *I testify before God and Jesus Christ, who is to judge the living and the dead through his coming and his Kingdom* (2 Tim. 4.1) and, *The Lord has freed me from every evil work and will make me safe in his heavenly Kingdom* (v.18). It is not surprising that the same Kingdom is attributed to both, since both *Father* and *Son* are the same *God*; and the *new Agreement* about the *Kingdom of God* was not put forward in the name of the FATHER, but in the name of the FATHER, SON and HOLY SPIRIT, as *one God*.

5. The Kingdom of God, which CHRIST was sent by God the Father to restore, does not begin until his second coming, in fact from the day of judgement, when he is to come in majesty in the

---

[2] *Foedus*, which might also be translated 'treaty'.

company of the Angels. For the Apostles were promised that in the Kingdom of God they would judge the twelve tribes of Israel, *You who have followed me, in the regeneration*[3] *when the son of man sits in the seat of his majesty, shall also sit judging the twelve tribes of Israel* (Mat. 19.28). This promise can only be fulfilled on the day of judgement; hence CHRIST is not yet seated in the seat of his Majesty. And the time when CHRIST was on earth is not called a Kingdom but a *regeneration*, i.e. a renovation, or restoration of the Kingdom of God, and a calling out of those who are to be received into the kingdom to come. And when it is said, *When the son of man shall come in his majesty, and all the Angels with him, then will he sit upon the seat of his majesty, and all the Nations will gather before him, and he will separate them from each other, as a Shepherd separates the sheep from the goats* (Matt. 25.31), the inference is clear: there will be no physical separation of God's subjects from his enemies, but they will live mingled together till the future coming of CHRIST. This is corroborated by the comparison of the Kingdom of Heaven to wheat mixed with tares and with the net that catches every kind of fish. But a crowd of men made up of subjects and enemies living indiscriminately together can not properly be called a Kingdom. Besides when the *Apostles* asked our Saviour, whether he would restore the Kingdom to Israel at the time when he ascended into Heaven, they clearly evinced their belief that the Kingdom of God had not yet come at the time of his ascension. And then there are CHRIST's Words, *My Kingdom is not of this world*, and, *I will not drink*, etc., *until the Kingdom of God comes*, and *God did not send his son into this world, to judge the world, but that the world might be saved through him*; and, *If anyone shall not hear my words and keep them, I do not judge him; for I did not come to judge the world, but to save the world.* And, *Man, who appointed me as judge or arbitrator between you?* The very name *heavenly Kingdom* points in the same direction. The same conclusion comes from the words of the prophet Jeremiah when he says of the *Kingdom of God* by the *new Agreement, Man shall no longer teach his neighbour and his brother saying, Know the Lord; for all shall know me, from the least to the greatest, says the Lord* (Jerem. 31.34). This cannot be meant of a Kingdom of this world. The

---

[3] Translating as if the comma were before *in regeneratione* and construing that phrase with the following temporal clause.

Kingdom of God, therefore, which CHRIST came into this world to establish; which the Prophets foretold; and of which we speak when we pray, *Thy Kingdom come* (if, as was predicted, it is to have its subjects physically separated from its enemies, if it must have judgement and majesty) will begin at the time when God shall separate the sheep from the goats; when the Apostles shall judge the twelve tribes of Israel; when CHRIST shall come in majesty and glory; and when, finally, all shall know God without needing to be taught, i.e. at the second coming of CHRIST, or on the day of the last judgement. If the Kingdom of God had already been restored, no reason could be given why, having completed the work for which he was sent, CHRIST should come again, or why we should pray: Thy Kingdom come.

6. Although the *Kingdom of God* which is to be established through CHRIST by a new Covenant will be a Heavenly Kingdom, we must not therefore think that those who entered into that Agreement with faith in CHRIST would not need also to be governed on earth, so that they would persevere in the faith and obedience which they promised in the agreement. For the Heavenly Kingdom and the promised country would be irrelevant unless we were to be guided to it. To be guided you have to be given directions about the way. When *Moses* had introduced the *Priestly Kingdom*, he ruled and guided the people himself, through the whole period of their journeying right up to the entrance of the promised land even though he was not a Priest. By the same reasoning it is our Saviour's task (for God wished him to be like *Moses* in this respect), insofar as he was sent from the Father, to govern the future citizens of the Heavenly commonwealth even in this life, so that they may be able to win through and enter that Kingdom, even if it will not properly be his but the Father's. The Régime under which CHRIST rules his faithful in this life is not properly *a Kingdom, or government* [*imperium*], but a *Pastoral office* or *right to teach*, i.e. God the Father has not given him authority to *give judgements* about *mine* and *thine* as he has to the Kings of the Earth, nor to *compel* by *penalties* or *make laws*, but he has given him authority to reveal to the world and to *teach the way* and *the knowledge of salvation*, i.e. the authority to *preach* and to *explain* to men what they should do to enter into the *kingdom of heaven*. That CHRIST has not received from the Father the authority to *give judgement* in questions of *Mine* and *Thine*, i.e. in any *questions of right*, between non-believers is well brought out

by his own words quoted above: *Man, who appointed me as judge or arbitrator between you?* and is confirmed by reason. For CHRIST was sent to *strike an Agreement* between God and men; no one is obliged to give obedience until after he has entered into an agreement; hence no one would be obliged to accept his verdict, if he had given judgement on questions of *right*. But in fact, trials of legal matters, whether between believers or unbelievers, have not been entrusted to CHRIST in this world. This is apparent from the fact that that right belongs without question to *Princes*, so long as God does not restrict their authority; and he does not do so this side of the day of judgement, as appears from St. Paul's words in speaking of that day: *Then comes the end* (he says), *when he shall hand over the King-dom to God and the Father, when he shall cancel every Principate and authority and power* (1 Cor. 15.24). Secondly, the words of our saviour in rebuke of James and John when they said:[4] *Do you want us to command that fire descend from heaven and consume them?* (meaning the *Samaritans* who refused to offer him hospitality on his way to *Jerusalem*); he said:[5] *The son of man has not come to destroy lives but to save them*; and the words: *Behold I send you forth as sheep in the midst of wolves; Shake off the dust*, and so forth. Also the words:[6] *God did not send his son into the world to judge the world, but that the world might be saved through him.* And the words:[7] *If anyone hears my words and does not keep them, I do not judge him, for I have not come to judge the world*, etc., show that he had not been given auth-ority to condemn or punish anyone. It is true that one reads,[8] *The Father does not judge anyone, but has given all judgement to the Son*, but that can and should be understood of the day of judgement, and so does not contradict the previous passages. Finally, he was not sent to make new laws, and therefore did not have the office and mission of a *legislator* – and neither did *Moses* – but introduced and promulgated his Father's laws (for it is God, not *Moses* or CHRIST, who was King by the agreement). This is the inference of his words,[9] *I have not come to abolish them* (meaning the *laws* pre-

---

[4] Luke 9.54.
[5] Luke 9.56.
[6] John 3.17.
[7] John 12.47.
[8] John 5.22.
[9] Matthew 5.17.

viously given by God through *Moses* which he interprets immediately afterwards) *but to fulfil them.* And, *he who abolishes one of the least of these commands and teaches men to do so, will be called least in the Kingdom of Heaven.* CHRIST *therefore did not* have royal or governmental [*imperatorium*] authority entrusted to him by the Father, but only the authority to advise and teach; and he indicates as much himself when he calls his *Apostles* not hunters but fishers of men, and when he compares the Kingdom of God to a grain of mustard and to yeast lying hidden in flour.

7. First God promised to *Abraham* numerous descendants, possession of the land of *Canaan*, and the blessing of the nations on his descendants, on condition that he and they served God. Then to the descendants of *Abraham* by the flesh he promised a *Priestly Kingdom*, an utterly free régime, in which they would not be subject to any human power on the condition that they served the God of *Abraham* with the worship which *Moses* taught them; lastly, he made a promise to them and to all nations of a *Heavenly Kingdom* which should be eternal, on condition that they served the God of *Abraham* with the worship which JESUS taught them. For by the *new agreement*, i.e. the *Christian agreement*, men contracted *to serve the God of Abraham with the worship which JESUS taught them*; and God contracted *to forgive their sins and bring them into the Heavenly Kingdom.* What *the Heavenly Kingdom* will be, we have discussed in article 5 above; but the usual names for it are sometimes the *Kingdom of Heaven*, sometimes the *Kingdom of Glory*, sometimes *eternal life.* Men's part of the contract, namely to serve God in the way CHRIST taught, has two elements: *obedience to God* (that is what serving God is); and *Faith* in JESUS, i.e. to believe that JESUS is THE CHRIST promised by God; for that is the only reason why we should follow his teaching rather than someone else's. *Repentance* very often takes the place of *obedience* in the holy scriptures because CHRIST everywhere teaches that God accepts the will to act as the act itself, and *repentance* is an infallible sign of an obedient heart. This understood, it will be evident from many passages of holy scripture that the terms of the *Christian Covenant* are as we have said, namely, on the part of God, to forgive men their sins and give eternal life, on the part of men to repent and believe in JESUS CHRIST. First, the words, *The Kingdom of God is at hand, repent and believe the Gospel* (Mark 1.15) contain the whole agreement. So do the

following: *Since it is so written, and since it was necessary that* CHRIST *would Suffer and rise from the dead on the third day, and that Repentance be preached in his name and Remission of sins to all the nations, beginning from Jerusalem* (Luke 24.46–7); and these too: *Repent and be converted, that your sins may be wiped out, so that when the times of refreshment come*, etc. (Acts 3.19). But sometimes one element is stated expressly, the other implied, as here: *He who believes in the son has eternal life; he who does not believe in the son shall not see life, but the wrath of God remains upon him* (John 3.36), where faith is expressed and repentance is implicit. And in the Preaching of CHRIST: *Repent, for the Kingdom of God is at hand* (Matt. 4.17), where *Repentance* is expressed, and *faith* is implied. But the elements of the *new contract* are most clearly and formally laid out in the passage where a certain Prince, as if seeking the price of the Kingdom of God, asks our saviour: *Good master, What shall I do to gain eternal life?* (Luke 18.18). CHRIST first puts before him one part of the price, namely to keep the commandments, or *obedience*; and when he replied that he had already performed this part, CHRIST adds the second part, saying, *One thing is missing; sell all that you have, and give it to the poor, and you shall have Treasure in heaven, and come, follow me* (v.22). This was of *faith*. He therefore not having that much faith in CHRIST and the Treasures of Heaven, went away sad. The same agreement is contained in these words, *Whoever believes and is Baptized shall be saved, but whoever does not believe shall be condemned* (Mark 16.15–16). Here *Faith* is expressed, and *Repentance* in those who have been baptized is assumed. And in this: *Unless one is reborn of water and of (the) holy spirit, he cannot enter the Kingdom of God* (John 3.5), where *to be reborn from water* is the same as regeneration, i.e. conversion to CHRIST. The requirement of *Baptism* in the last two passages quoted and elsewhere is to be taken to mean that *Baptism* is required for the *new agreement* in the same way in which *circumcision* was for the *old Agreement*. Circumcision was not of the essence of the *old agreement*; it served as a reminder of it, as a ceremony and a sign (which was omitted in the desert); similarly baptism was not taken as the essence of the making of the new covenant, but as a reminder and a sign; and provided the will is there, it may be omitted in case of necessity as an actual act; but *Repentance* and *Faith*, which are of the essence of the agreement, are always required.

8. In the *Kingdom of God* after this life there are to be *no laws*; both because there is no place for laws where there is no place for sin, and because laws are given to us by God to direct us to heaven, not in heaven. Let us now therefore look into the laws which CHRIST put forward as the Father's laws (he did not authorize them himself because he refused to take legislative authority upon himself, as was shown above in article 6). We have a passage in scripture where he captures all the *laws God* had given down to that time in two precepts: *You shall love the Lord your God with all your heart and with all your soul and with all your mind; this is the first and greatest command. And the second is like it: you shall love your neighbour as yourself. The whole of the Law and the Prophets depends upon these two commands* (Matt. 22.37–40). The first of these had been given before in as many words by *Moses* (Deut. 6.5). The second even before *Moses*; for it is a natural law, and has its beginning with rational nature itself. The two together are a summary of all laws. For all the laws of natural divine worship are contained in the words, *You shall love God*, and all the laws of divine worship due by the *old agreement*, are contained in the words, *You shall love your God*, i.e. God as peculiarly the king of *Abraham* and his seed; and all natural and civil laws in the words, *You shall love your neighbour as yourself.* For he who loves God and his neighbour has a heart of obedience to the laws of God and man. And God requires no more than an obedient heart. We have another place where CHRIST *gives interpretation of laws*, namely the whole of chapters 5, 6 and 7 of St. Matthew. All these laws are found either in the *decalogue* or in the *moral law*, or are contained in the faith of Abraham; e.g. the law on not divorcing a wife is contained in the *faith of Abraham*; for the phrase, *the two shall be one flesh* was not first taught by CHRIST or by *Moses* but was handed down from *Abraham*, who was the first to tell of the creation of the world. Thus the laws which CHRIST summarizes in one place and expounds in another are precisely the laws to which all who recognize the God of *Abraham* are bound. Apart from these, we read of no law taught by CHRIST except the institution of the Sacraments of *Baptism* and the *Eucharist*.

9. What then shall be said of precepts of this kind: *Repent. Be baptized. Keep the commandments. Believe the Gospel. Come unto me. Sell all that thou hast, give to the poor, follow me, and so on?* One must say that they are not *laws* but a call to *faith*, like the call of

Isaiah: *Come, buy wine and milk without money and without price* (Isa. 55.1). And those who do not come when called, are not offending against any law, but only against good sense; they will not be punished for unbelief, but for their previous sins. Hence St. *John* says of the unbeliever, *the wrath of God remains upon him*; he does not say, *the wrath of God shall come* upon him. And, *he who does not believe is already judged, because he does not believe*; he does not say, *he will be judged, but he is already judged*. In fact, one cannot form a conception of the *forgiveness of sins* as a benefit of *faith*, without also accepting the contrary that the punishment of sins is a penalty [*damnum*] of *unbelief*.

10. Our Saviour prescribed no distributive laws for subjects of Princes and citizens of commonwealths. That is, he gave no rules by which a citizen could know how to distinguish what is *his own* from what is *another's*, nor what were the appropriate formulae, words or circumstances for *giving, passing, entering upon* and *possessing* a thing, so that it would be regarded as rightly belonging to the *recipient, entrant* or *possessor*. The only inference possible is that individual citizens should get those rules from the commonwealth, i.e. from the man or council which holds sovereign power in the commonwealth; and that this is the case not only among unbelievers, where CHRIST himself denied that he was a judge and *arbitrator* between them, but also among Christians. It follows therefore that what he was teaching by the laws: *You shall not Kill, you shall not commit Adultery, you shall not Steal, you shall honour your Parents*, was simply that citizens and subjects should absolutely obey their Princes and sovereigns in all questions of *mine, thine, his, other's*. For not all killing is forbidden by the precept *You shall not kill*; for he who said *You shall not kill* also said: *Whoever works upon the sabbath, let him be killed* (Exod. 35.2). Nor every killing without trial; for he said, *Let each man kill his brother and friend and neighbour* (Exod. 32.27), and twenty-three thousand men were killed. Nor every killing of an innocent man; for Jephtha vowed, *Whoever shall come out* etc., *I will offer him as a burnt-offering to the Lord* (Jud. 11.31), and God accepted his vow. What then is forbidden? Only this, that one may not kill anyone whom one has no right to kill, i.e. let no man kill unless it is *his* [*suum*] to do so. CHRIST's law therefore on killing, and thus on every kind of assault and on establishing penalties, commands one to obey the commonwealth alone.

Similarly, the precept, *Thou shalt not commit Adultery*, does not forbid all sleeping together outside of marriage, but only sleeping with *another man's* woman; but who is *another man's* woman, is for the commonwealth to say and is to be decided by the rules the commonwealth makes. Thus this precept commands man and woman to keep the faith which they have given each other, under the commonwealth's regulation. Similarly, not every entrance upon property is forbidden by the precept *Thou shalt not Steal*, nor every stealthy removal of property, but only of another person's property; the citizen receives just one command, not to enter upon or surreptitiously remove anything which the commonwealth forbids one to enter upon or surreptitiously remove; and in general not to call anything *murder*, *adultery* or *theft* unless doing it is against the civil laws. Lastly, since CHRIST gave the order to honour parents, but did not prescribe the ceremonies, titles and kind of obedience appropriate for honouring them, it is understood that they are to be honoured inwardly and by the will as kings and lords of their children, but externally only so far as the commonwealth allows; it will assign *each person his own honour* (as it will assign other things too). And as the nature of justice consists in giving every man his due, it is also clear that it is the responsibility of a CHRISTIAN commonwealth to determine what justice is, and what injustice or an offence against justice is. And responsibility of the commonwealth is to be taken to mean responsibility of the holder or holders of the commonwealth's sovereignty.

11. Further, as our Saviour did not declare any rules about the governance of the commonwealth apart from the laws of nature, i.e. apart from the command of civil obedience, no citizen may privately determine who is an ally or public enemy of the commonwealth, nor when to make war or alliance, peace or truce; nor may he decide what is for or against the interest of the commonwealth in the matter of who are to be citizens, and who should have what authority, nor what doctrines, morals, and public pronouncements are useful, and what unions of which men. All this kind of thing is to be learned, as needed, from the commonwealth, i.e. from the sovereign rulers.

12. Moreover, the building of fortifications, houses and churches; the moving, carrying and lifting of heavy weights; safe passage of the Seas; the construction of Machines for every purpose of life;

investigation of the face of the Earth, of the courses of the stars, the seasons of the Year, the calendar and the nature of things; knowledge of natural and civil laws; and the sciences which go under the name of Philosophy; all these are necessary for living and for living well. These things we must learn (because CHRIST has not taught us) by reasoning, i.e. by drawing out consequences from our starting point in experience. But men's reasonings are sometimes correct, sometimes mistaken, and accordingly their conclusions and what they hold to be true are sometimes truth and sometimes error. Now even errors about these Philosophical questions sometimes do public mischief, and give scope for great seditions and injuries. Whenever, then, a controversy arises about these matters which threatens the common good and social peace, there must be someone to give a judgement of the reasoning, i.e. whether the inference is good or not, so that the controversy may be stopped. CHRIST gave no rules for this purpose; and indeed he did not come into this world to teach *logic*. The only thing left therefore is that the judges of such disputes be precisely those whom God had already instituted by nature, namely those appointed in each commonwealth by the sovereign. Moreover, if a controversy arises about the accurate and proper meaning of words or terms in common use, i.e. about definitions, which needs to be settled to preserve public peace or the distribution of right, it will be the commonwealth's responsibility to settle it. For men devise such definitions in their reasoning when they become aware of the variety of concepts which those terms are used to signify at different times and for different reasons. But the decision on the question, whether a person has reasoned rightly or not, is for the commonwealth. For example, suppose a woman gives birth to a deformed figure, and the law forbids killing a human being, the question arises whether the new-born is a human being. The question then is, what is a human being? No one doubts that the commonwealth will decide – and without taking account of the Aristotelian definition, that a Man is a rational Animal. These are subjects (namely, *law*, *politics* and the *natural sciences*) on which CHRIST says that it was not his business to give instruction or to teach anything but this one thing, that in all disputes on these topics individual citizens should obey the laws and decisions of their commonwealth. Yet one must remember that as God CHRIST could rightly have commanded, as well as taught, whatever he wished.

13. The sum of our saviour's task was to teach the way of salvation and of eternal life and all the means thereto; and one of the means to salvation is *justice, civil obedience* and *observation* of all *natural* laws. These can be taught in two forms. One is as Theorems, through natural reason, deducing natural right and natural laws from human principles and human contracts; doctrine so taught is subject to the scrutiny of the civil powers. The other is in the form of laws, by divine authority, revealing that such-and-such is the will of God; this form of teaching is only appropriate to one to whom God's will is supernaturally known, i.e. to CHRIST. Secondly, it was a part of CHRIST's office to forgive the sins of the repentant; for that was crucial to the salvation of men who had already sinned, and could be done by no one else. For remission of sins does not naturally follow upon repentance (as a matter of desert), but depends (as a free gift) upon a supernatural revelation of God's will. The third element of CHRIST's office was to teach all the commands of God – about worship or the dogmas of faith – which cannot be known by natural reason but only by revelation; as, that he is CHRIST; that his *Kingdom is not of this world, but of heaven; that there are rewards and punishments after this life; that the soul is immortal; and how many sacraments there are and what they will be*, and so on.

14. From what has been said in the last few articles, it is not difficult to distinguish between things *spiritual* and things *temporal*. For as things spiritual means things which have their foundation in the authority and office of CHRIST and could not be known if CHRIST had not taught them, and all the rest are things temporal; it follows that the definition and authoritative pronouncement on what is *just* and what is *unjust*, the settlement of all disputes about *measures of peace* or *public defence*, and the scrutiny of doctrines and books in every *rational science belongs to temporal right* [*jus*]. But the scrutiny of things which depend solely on CHRIST's word and his authority and are *mysteries of faith* belongs to *spiritual right* [*jus*]. As our Saviour did not teach us the distinction between what is *temporal* and what is *spiritual*, its definition is a question of reason, and belongs to the *temporal authority*. For although St. Paul distinguishes in many passages between *things spiritual* and *things carnal*, and applies *spiritual* to things which are of the *spirit*, namely, *wisdom, discourse of knowledge, faith, the ability to cure disease, working of miracles,*

Prophecy, discerning of spirits, knowledge of tongues, interpretation of utterances (Rom. 8.5, 1 Cor. 12.8–9), all things which are supernaturally inspired by the *holy spirit* and which *animal man* cannot understand, but only he who knows the mind of CHRIST (1 Cor. 2.14–16);[10] and the good things of fortune he calls *carnal things* (Rom. 15.27) and men who are merely men he calls *carnal* (1 Cor. 3.1–3); yet he has not defined or given rules by which we may know what proceeds from natural reason and what from supernatural inspiration.

15. Since therefore it is settled that sovereign authority to judge and decide all disputes in *things temporal* was committed to, or rather not taken from, Princes and those who hold sovereign power in each commonwealth, we must next see to whom he committed similar authority in *things spiritual*. As that can only be known from the *Word of God* [*Verbum Dei*] and the *tradition of a Church*[11] [*Ecclesiae traditione*], we must next ask what the *Word of God* is, what it is to *interpret* it, what a *Church* is, and what is the *will* and commandment of a *Church*. Omitting the occasional use of *Word of God* in holy scripture for *Son of God*, the phrase is used in three senses. First and most properly, for what God has spoken; in this sense the Word of God is what God spoke to *Abraham* and *the Patriarchs*, to *Moses* and *the Prophets*, or our Saviour to his disciples and anyone else. Secondly, whatever has been said by men on the orders or by the influence of a holy spirit; in this sense we recognize that the holy scriptures are the *Word of God*. Thirdly – in fact, most commonly in the New Testament - *Word of God* signifies the teaching of the Gospel, whether it is a word about God or a word about the Kingdom of God through CHRIST. As when CHRIST is said to have preached the *Gospel of the Kingdom* (Matt. 4.23), when the Apostles are said to preach the *Word of God* (Acts 13.46), when the Word of God is called the *Word of life* (Acts 5.20), the *Word of the Gospel* (Acts 15.7), the *Word of Faith* (Rom. 10.8), the *Word of truth*, which is interpreted as the *Gospel of salvation* (Eph. 1.13). Also when the *Word of the Apostles* is mentioned. St. Paul says, *If anyone does not obey our word*, etc. (2 Thess. 3.14). Such passages can only be under-

---

[10] Hobbes wrongly refers here to 2 Cor. 2.14–16.

[11] Since there is no article in Latin, *Ecclesia*, which is normally translated as 'a Church' might also be rendered 'the Church', here and in many other passages. The same is true of *Verbum Dei* ('a/the Word of God').

stood of *Gospel teaching*. Similarly when the *Word of God* is said *to be sown, to grow and to multiply* (Acts 12.24 and 13.49), this is difficult to understand of the actual voice of God or of the Apostles, but easy to understand of the teaching. And in this third sense, the *Word of God* is all the *doctrine of the Christian faith* which is taught from the Pulpits in our day and contained in the books of Theologians.

16. Because we recognize holy scripture as inspired by God, all of it is thereby Word of God in the second sense. Then countless passages in scripture have the phrase in the first sense. And as the greatest part of scripture is concerned with the prediction or prefiguration, before CHRIST's incarnation, of the Kingdom of heaven, or in Spreading and expounding the gospel of the Kingdom after his incarnation, holy scripture is also the *Word of God* in the third sense, where *Word of God* is taken as *Word about God*, i.e. as *Gospel*, and hence as canon and rule of all *Gospel teaching*. But as there is a good deal of *Politics*, *History*, *Morals*, and *Physics* to be read in scripture, and many other things that have nothing to do with the *Mysteries of faith*, those passages, although they contain true teaching, and are a canon of such teaching, still cannot be a canon of the mysteries of the Christian Religion.

17. And indeed it is not the voice and letter of *God's Word* which is the canon of Christian doctrine, but its true and genuine meaning; for the mind can only be governed by the scriptures if they are understood. For scriptures to become a canon, then, they must have an interpreter. One of two things follows: either the word of the interpreter is the Word of God, or the Word of God is not the canon of Christian doctrine. Of these the latter must be false; for a rule of doctrine which cannot be known by any human reasoning but only by divine revelation can only be divine. For when we admit that someone does not know whether some doctrine is true or not, it is impossible to take his verdict on this doctrine as the rule. Therefore the former is true: the *word of the interpreter* of the scriptures is the *Word of God*.

18. An interpreter for whose opinion we have so much respect that we accept it as *God's Word*, is not just anyone who translates from the Hebrew and Greek tongues into Latin for his Latin audience, and into French for his French audience, and for others into their own native language: this is not interpretation. For it is univer-

sally true of language that although it rightly takes first place among the signs by which we disclose our ideas to others, it cannot do the job on its own; it needs the help of a context [*multarum circumstanti-arum*]. A living voice has interpreters right there in the time, the place, the expression, gesture and purpose of the speaker, and even, when necessary, the speaker's own explanations of his meaning in other words. To recover these lost aids to interpretation in writings of an age long gone, requires no common intelligence, and cannot be done by anyone, however intelligent, without great learning and an expert acquaintance with antiquity. To interpret the scriptures therefore it is not enough to know the language in which they are written. Nor can just anyone who writes commentaries on the scriptures be a canonical interpreter of them. For men can make mistakes; they can also twist scripture to their own ambition or force it against its natural meaning to serve their prejudices; from which it would follow that a wrong opinion would have to be taken as the *Word of God*. Even if this could not happen, still, as soon as these commentators have passed away, their commentaries will need glosses, and as time goes by the glosses will require theses and the theses will need new commentaries, endlessly; and consequently there is no way that the canon or rule of Christian doctrine by which controversies of religion are to be settled can consist in any kind of written interpretation. The only alternative left is that a canonical interpreter should be one who has the legal responsibility to put an end to disputes as they arise by explicating *God's Word* in actual judgements; his authority is to be as strongly upheld as the authority of those who approved scripture itself as the canon of faith in the first place; and he should be both *interpreter of scripture* and *supreme judge* of all *doctrines*.

19. Now for the word *Church* [*Ecclesia*]: in origin it has the same meaning as the Latin word *Concio* or assembly of citizens, just as *Ecclesiastes* means the same as *concionator*, that is, one who addresses an assembly. In this sense we read in the Acts of the Apostles of a *lawful Ecclesia* and a *disorderly Ecclesia* (Act. 19.32, 40), the former for a duly summoned assembly, the latter for a riotous concourse of the people. And in fact *Ecclesia of the Christians* in holy scripture sometimes does mean an assembly, but sometimes it means the Christians themselves even if they are not actually congregated, since they may enter a meeting and communicate with the congre-

gation. For example, *Say to the Church* (Ecclesia, Mat. 18.17) is meant of a congregated *Church*; for otherwise it is impossible to *say* something to a *Church*. But he *laid waste the Church* (Acts 8.3) involves the non-congregated sense. *Church* is sometimes also understood as those who have been Baptized, or who profess the Christian Faith, whether they are inwardly Christians or only pretending; as when we read of something said or written to a *Church*, or said, decided or done by a *Church*. Sometimes it is used only of the *elect*, as when *the holy and immaculate Church* is spoken of (Eph. 5.27). But the elect are not properly called a *Church* while they are still striving; but a *Church to be*, in that day, that is, in which, set apart from the wicked, they will triumph. Again *Church* can sometimes be taken for all Christians together collectively, as when Christ is called *the head of the Church* and *head of the body of the Church* (Eph. 5.23, Col. 1.18), sometimes for its parts, as, *the Church at Ephesus, the Church which is in his house, the seven Churches*, etc. Finally when *Church* is used of a group actually congregated, its meaning varies with the different reasons for congregating: it sometimes means those who are congregated for deliberation and judgement, in which sense it is also called assembly and Synod; sometimes those who meet in a house of prayer to worship God, which is the sense in which it is used at 1 Cor. 14.4, 5, 23, 28, etc.

20. But in the sense in which its own *personal rights* and *actions* are attributed to it, and in the sense in which the sentences, *Say to the church, he who shall not obey the church*; and all such phrases must be understood, *Church* is to be so defined that we may understand by that word: *a crowd [multitudo] of men who have entered into a new agreement with God through Christ* (i.e. a crowd of people who have undergone the Sacrament of Baptism), *and a crowd which may be rightly summoned into one place by someone, at whose summons all are obliged to attend either in person or through others*. For if a crowd of men cannot assemble as a group when necessary, it must not be said to be one *person*. For a Church cannot speak or decide or give audience except as a group. As for things said by individuals (and, as they say, there are as many opinions as there are heads), each is a comment of one man not of a church. Moreover if a group is formed which is unlawful, it will not be recognized as a group. No one present at a seditious gathering will be bound by a decision of the rest, especially anyone who disagrees with it; and therefore such

a *Church* can decide nothing; for a crowd is said to decide something when each one is obligated by the decision of the majority. One should add therefore to the definition of a *Church* (at least to a *Church* to which we attribute *personality*) that it not only may meet, but may do so of right. Moreover even if there is someone who may rightly summon them, if those who are summoned have the right not to come (which can happen among men who are not subject one to another), that *Church* is not one *person*; for by the same right by which those who meet at a time and place at which they are summoned are one *Church*, those who get together at another spot of their own choosing are another Church. And any number of *co-believers* is a *church*; and consequently, there will be as many *churches* as there are different opinions, that is, the same crowd of men will be *one church* and *several churches* at the same time. Hence a *church* only exists where there is a definite and recognized, i.e. legitimate, authority by which individuals are obliged to attend the meeting either in person or through others. And it becomes *one* and capable of the functions of a *person*, not because it has uniformity of doctrine, but because it has unity of authority to summon Synods and assemblies of CHRISTIans; otherwise it is merely a crowd, and several distinct *persons*, however much they agree in belief.

21. It is a logically necessary consequence of what has been said that a *commonwealth* [*civitas*] and a *church* [*ecclesia*] of the same *Christian* men are exactly the same thing under two names, and that for two reasons. For the *material* of the *commonwealth* and of the *church* are the same, namely the same Christian men. And the *form* which consists in the legal authority to summon them is also the same; for it is common ground that individual citizens are obliged to come to the spot to which they are summoned by the commonwealth. And what is called a *commonwealth* in being made up of *men*, is called a *church* in being composed of *Christians*.

22. Another consequence is that *if there are several Christian commonwealths, they cannot all at the same time be a church which is one as a person*. They can become one by mutual agreement, but only on condition that they become one commonwealth. For they can only meet at a specific, appointed time and place. Persons, times and places of meeting are matters of civil law; and neither citizen nor foreigner may rightly set foot in any place without permission of the commonwealth which has dominion over it. And what can

only be rightly done with the permission of the commonwealth, is done, if done rightly, by authority of the commonwealth. The *universal Church* is certainly one *mystic Body* whose head is CHRIST, but in the same manner in which all men who together recognize God as ruler of the world are one Kingdom and *one commonwealth*, but that commonwealth is not *one person* and they do not have a united action or a common policy. Moreover when CHRIST is said to be *head of the body of the Church*, it is quite evident that that was said by the Apostle of the elect, who so long as they are in this world are only potentially a *Church*, and will not be one in fact, until they are separated from the wicked, and meet as a congregation at the day of judgement. The *Roman Church* was once very extensive, but it never passed the bounds of the empire; it was not therefore *universal* except in the sense in which this was said of the *Roman commonwealth: the victorious Roman now possessed the whole world*,[12] when it did not actually have a twentieth part of it. After the civil empire split into pieces, the individual commonwealths that came from it were so many *Churches*; and the authority which the Roman *Church* had over them could only depend wholly on their authority; and though they had shaken off the Roman Emperors, they were still content to have Roman Teachers [*Doctores*].

23. Those who exercise a public function in a *Church* [*Ecclesia*] may be called *Ecclesiastics*. One of their functions was *Service* [*Ministerium*], the other *Superintendence* [*Magisterium*]. The function of Ministers was to serve tables, supply the temporal needs of the *Church*, and (at a time when they had abolished all private property, and were maintained from the common stock) to give individuals their shares. The *Superintendents* were called, according to their rank, some *Apostles*, some *Bishops* [*Episcopi*], others *Presbyters* [*Presbyteri*] i.e. older people or seniors; not however to distinguish their age by the name *Presbyter*, but their *office*. For *Timothy* was a Presbyter, though a young man; and the age-name was used to signify the job, because it was usually *older people* who were given the tasks of Superintendence. The *Superintendents* were given different names because they had different functions, some being *Apostles*, others *Prophets*, some *Evangelists*, others *Pastors* or *teachers*. The *Apostles'* work was universal; the *Prophetic* task was to declare their own

---

[12] Petronius, *Satyricon* 119.1.

revelations in *Church*; the *Evangelical* to preach or to be envoys of the Gospel to unbelievers; the *Pastoral* task was to teach, strengthen and govern the minds of those who already believed.

24. In the *Choice of Ecclesiastics* two things had to be taken into account: *selection* of persons and consecration or appointment, which is also called *ordination*. CHRIST himself *chose* and *ordained* the first twelve *Apostles*. After CHRIST's ascension, *Matthias* was appointed to fill the place of the traitor *Judas*; the *Church* (which at that point was a congregation of about 120) selected two men: *for they put forward two, Joseph and Matthias*; but God himself gave his approval by means of the lot only to *Matthias*. And St. Paul calls these twelve the first and the great *Apostles*, and also the *Apostles* of the circumcision. Later two other *Apostles*, *Paul* and *Barnabas*, were added, ordained, admittedly, by the Teachers and Prophets of the *Church at Antioch* (which was a *particular Church*) by laying-on of hands, but selected by order of the Holy Spirit. That they were both *Apostles* is settled by Acts 14.13.[13] St. Paul himself makes clear, that they received their *Apostolate* by being set apart for the work of God by the Prophets and Teachers of the Church at Antioch on orders from the holy Spirit; for he distinguishes himself from them as an *Apostle set apart for the Gospel of God* (Rom. 1.1). If the further question is asked: *by what authority* did it happen that what those Prophets and Teachers said proceeded from a holy spirit was accepted as a command of the holy Spirit? the reply must be: *by the Authority of the Church at Antioch*. For Prophets and Teachers have to be examined by a *Church* before they are accepted; for St. John says: *Do not believe every spirit, but try the spirits to see if they are from God, since many Pseudo-Prophets have gone out into the world.*[14] By which *Church* but the one to which that Letter was addressed? Likewise Paul criticizes the *Churches of Galatia* for Judaizing (Gal. 2.14), even though they seemed to be doing it on the authority of *Peter*; for he tells them that he had criticized *Peter* in these words: *If you though a Jew live like a Gentile, how can you compel Gentiles to Judaize?* And just below he puts the question directly to them, saying: *I want to learn this one thing from you, have you received the spirit from works of the law or from the hearing of*

---

[13] 14.13 by the Vulgate numbering; 14.14 in the King James version.
[14] 1 John 4.1.

faith? (Gal. 3.2). It is clear from this that what he faults in the *Galatians* is *Judaizing*, even though it was the *Apostle Peter* who had compelled them to Judaize. Since therefore it was not for *Peter*, nor therefore for any man, to determine which teachers the *Churches* would follow, the selection of their own Teachers and Prophets also rested upon the Authority of the *Church at Antioch*. But since the holy Spirit set apart the *Apostles Paul* and *Barnabas* for himself through the laying-on of hands by the Teachers who had been selected in this way, it is evident that the consecration and laying-on of hands of the highest Teachers in any *Church* belongs to the Teachers of the same *Church*. And at that time *Bishops*, who were also called *Presbyters*, although not all Presbyters were Bishops, were ordained both by *Apostles* (for when *Paul* and *Barnabas* taught in *Derbe*, *Lystra* and *Iconium*, they appointed *presbyters* throughout the individual Churches, Acts 14.22),[15] and by other bishops. For *Titus* was left in *Crete* by *Paul* to appoint *presbyters* throughout the cities (Tit. 1.5). And *Timothy* was instructed: *Do not neglect the grace of God which is in you, which was given to you through prophecy with the laying on of hands of the board of presbyters* (1 Tim. 4.14). And he was given rules about the selection of *presbyters*. But this can only be understood of the ordination of those who were chosen by a Church. For no one could appoint a teacher in a Church without the permission of the Church. For the *Apostles'* own task was to teach, not to command. And although the candidates of the *Apostles* or *presbyters* could not be refused because of the high prestige of their backers, they were still considered to be chosen by *authority of a Church* because they could not be chosen against the *will of the Church*. Similarly the ministers who are called *Deacons* were *ordained* by the *Apostles* but *chosen* by a *Church*. For when seven *Deacons* were to be chosen and ordained, the *Apostles* did not choose them, but said: *Look carefully, brothers, for seven men among you of good reputation*, etc., and they *chose Stephen*, etc., and *they set them before the Apostles* (Acts 6.3, 6). It is therefore incontestable that by the custom of the *Church* under the *Apostles*, while the *ordination*, or *consecration*, of all Ecclesiastics which is done by prayer and the laying-on of hands, *was the business of the Apostles and Teachers*, the *selection* of ordinands was the business of *a Church*.

---

[15] Vulgate numbering.

25. On the power of *loosing and binding*, i.e. of *remitting* and *retaining sins*, there can be no doubt that it was given by Christ to the *Pastors* of the future, in the same way as to the *Apostles* of the present. The whole of the power to *remit sins* which Christ himself had was given to the *Apostles*. *As my father sent me*, says *Christ, so I also send you* (John 20.21), adding, *Whose sins you remit, they are remitted, and whose you retain, they are retained* (v.23). But there is a doubt what it is to *loose* and to *bind*, to *remit sins* and to *retain* them. For, first, to *retain the sins* of one who has been Baptized for the remission of sins and is truly penitent, seems to be contrary to the Agreement of the new Testament, and could not therefore be done by Christ, much less by the Pastors. And to *remit the sins* of a non-penitent seems to be contrary to the will of God the Father, by whom *Christ* was sent to convert the world and bring men into obedience. Then if individual Pastors were allowed to *remit* and *retain sins* in this way, all fear of Princes and civil Magistrates, and all civil government with it, would be subverted. For *Christ* said, and in fact, nature herself also dictates: *Do not fear those who kill the body, but cannot kill the soul; but rather fear him who can destroy both soul and body in Gehenna* (Matt. 10.28). And no one is so stupid that he would not choose to listen to those who can *remit* and *retain sins* rather than the most powerful kings. On the other hand one must not suppose that *remission of sins* is simply exemption from the penalties of the *Church*; for what evil does excommunication hold beyond the eternal punishment that follows from it; or what would be the good of being accepted into the *Church*, if there was salvation outside it? One must therefore hold the view that *Pastors have the power to truly and absolutely remit sins*, but only *to the penitent, and to retain them* but only *to the impenitent*. But as men think that repentance is nothing other than for the individual to condemn his own actions, and change the intents which seem to him to be *sins* and blameworthy, a belief has arisen that there can be repentance before confession of sins in men's presence; and that repentance is not an effect but a cause of confession; hence the difficulty of those who say that the *sins* of the penitent have already been remitted in Baptism, and that the *sins* of the impenitent cannot be remitted at all, is contrary to Scripture, and against the Words of *Christ* in saying, *Whose sins you remit* etc. To solve this problem, one must first recognize that true acknowledgement of sin is itself repentance;

for one who knows that he has sinned, knows that he has made an error, and it is impossible to want to be in error; therefore he who knows that he has sinned, would wish he had not done so, and that is repentance. Then where it is doubtful whether the act in question is a sin or not, one should reflect that repentance does not precede confession of *sins*, but follows it. For there can only be repentance of acknowledged Sin; the penitent must therefore acknowledge the thing done and come to know that it is sin, i.e. that it is contrary to law. If anyone believes that what he has done is not contrary to law, it is impossible for him to repent it. Therefore acts have to be measured against laws before repentance. But it is useless to measure actions against law without an interpreter; for it is not the words of the law but the meaning of the legislator which is the rule of actions. Now an interpreter is certainly a man or men; for no one can be the judge of whether an action of his was a sin or not. Therefore the action whose sinfulness is in question has to be told to a man or men. This is a confession. And once the interpreter of the law has judged that the action is a sin, if the sinner accepts the judgement, and decides within himself not to do it again, that is repentance. And in this way it is either not true repentance, or it follows, and does not precede, confession. Now that we have clarified this, it is not difficult to see what the power of *loosing* and *binding* is. For there are two elements in remission: one is the *judgement* or *condemnation* by which the act is judged to be a sin, and the second is either *remission of sin* (when the convicted person acquiesces in the judgement and obeys, i.e. repents), or (if he does not repent) *retention*. The first of these, i.e. the judgement whether it is a sin, is for the *interpreter of law*, i.e. the *supreme judge* to decide; the second, remission or retention of sin, belongs to the Pastor; and that is precisely the *power of binding and loosing* which is in question. That this was the real intention of our Saviour in instituting this kind of power, appears from St. Matthew, 18.15–18. Addressing his disciples, he says: *If your brother has sinned against you, go and show him his fault between you and him alone.* (Note in passing that *if he has sinned against you* is the same as *if he has done you a wrong* [*injuria*];[16] hence *Christ* is speaking of things in the jurisdiction of a *civil court*.) He adds, *If he will not listen to you* (i.e. if he denies

---

[16] Italics added by the translator.

having done it, or if he admits that he did it but denies that it was wrong to do it), *take with you one or two more. And if he will not listen to these, tell the Church.* Why *the Church,* except to get their judgement whether it was a sin or not? *And if he will not listen to the Church,* i.e. if he does not accept the sentence of the *Church,* but continues to insist that what the *Church* has judged to be a sin was not one, i.e. if he does not repent (for it is certain that one does not repent of an action which one does not believe to be a sin), *Christ* does not say, *Tell the Apostles,* because he wants us to know that the definitive verdict as to whether it was a sin or not, is not left to them but to the *Church*; he says, *Let him be to you as a Gentile and a publican,* i.e. as one who is outside the *Church,* unbaptized, i.e. as one whose *sins* are *retained.* For all Christians were baptized for remission of *sins.* Since it could be asked, who had this great power of taking away the benefit of baptism from the impenitent, *Christ* shows that the very persons to whom he had given the power to baptize penitents for the remission of sins and to make Christians out of Pagans, also have the authority to retain the sins of those whom the *Church* judges to be unrepentant, and to make Pagans out of Christians again; for he immediately adds these words: *Amen I say to you, whatever you bind on earth shall be bound also in heaven, and whatever you loose upon earth shall be loosed also in heaven.* From this it can be understood that the *power of loosing and binding* or of *remitting and retaining sins,* which is also called the *power of the keys,* is the same as the power given in another passage in these words: *Go and teach all nations, Baptizing them in the name of the Father and of the Son and of the holy Spirit* (Matt. 28.19). And just as Pastors cannot refuse Baptism to anyone whom the *Church* thinks worthy of it, so they cannot *retain* the *sins* of one whom the *Church* believes should be absolved; nor can they *remit* the *sins* of one whom the *Church* pronounces contumacious. Judgement of sin belongs to the *Church,* but the *Pastors' task is to expel* them from the *Church* when they have been *judged,* or to accept them into it. So St. *Paul* to the *Church at Corinth: Surely,* he says, *you judge those who are within?* yet he himself decreed that a fornicator should be separated from the *Church, I myself,* he says, *absent in body but present in the spirit,* etc.

26. The act of retention of sin is what the *Church* calls *Excommunication,* and St. *Paul, delivering to Satan.* The word *Excommuni-*

cation, meaning the same as ἀποσυνάγωγον ποιεῖν (*to expel from the Synagogue*), seems to be drawn from the Mosaic law, by which those who had been judged Leprous by a Priest were ordered to live apart outside the camp, until they were clean again in the judgement of the priest, and had been purified by certain rites (which included washing the body) (Lev. 13.46). As time went on, the Jews developed a practice of not accepting converts to *Judaism* from the *Gentiles*, unless they were first *washed*, on the ground that they were unclean; and of *expelling from the Synagogue* those who disagreed with its teaching. By analogy with this ritual, converts to *Christian*ity (whether Jews or Gentiles) were only received into the *Church* by *Baptism*; and those who disagreed with the *Church* were deprived of its *Communion*. They called it *being delivered to Satan*, because everything outside of the *Church* was included in *Satan's* Kingdom. The purpose of such discipline was that, deprived for a time of grace and the spiritual privileges of the *Church*, they would be made humble for salvation. And the secular effect was that the *excommunicate* was not only barred from assemblies or Churches, and from participation in the Mysteries, but was also avoided by other individual Christians as dangerous to touch, even worse than a Pagan. For the Apostle allowed *mingling with pagans*, but with these he even forbade *taking food together* (1 Cor. 5.10–11). This being the effect of *excommunication*, it is evident in the first place that a *Christian commonwealth cannot be excommunicated*. For a Christian commonwealth is a Christian Church, as was shown above at article 21, and is co-extensive with it; and a *Church* cannot be *excommunicated*; for either it will excommunicate itself, which is impossible; or it *will be excommunicated* by another *Church*, which will be either a *universal* or a *particular Church*. As a *universal Church* is not a *person* (as shown in article 22) and does not therefore do or make anything, it cannot *excommunicate* anybody. And a *particular Church*, by *excommunicating another Church*, achieves nothing and changes nothing; for there cannot be *excommunication* of people who do not form a *common* group; and if some *Church*, say, the *Church at Jerusalem*, had *excommunicated* another *Church*, say, the one at *Rome*, it would have *excommunicated* itself as much as the other. For in depriving someone else of communion, one is also depriving himself of communion with that person. Secondly, it is evident that *no one can excommunicate at one time all the citizens of an independent* commonwealth [*civitas absoluta*], or bar them from the use of religious buildings or the public worship of God. For they cannot be *excommunicated* from a *Church* which they themselves constitute; for if they really did that, there would be no more *church*, but there would be no more *commonwealth* either, and they would be dissolved of their own free will; which is neither *Excommunication* nor *interdiction*. But if they are *excommunicated* by another *Church*, they have to be viewed by that *Church* as pagans. But by *Christ*'s teaching, no *Christian church* can ban *pagans* from congregating and *communicating* with one another in the manner determined by their commonwealths, especially if they meet to worship *Christ*, even if it is done in singular fashion with unusual ritual; and hence they cannot ban *excommunicates* either, who are to be treated as Pagans. Thirdly, it is evident that *a prince who holds sovereign power cannot be excommunicated*. For by *Christ*'s teaching neither a single subject nor several together can ban public or private places to their Prince, even if he is a Pagan, or refuse him entry to any gathering or prevent him from doing whatever he wants in his dominion. For in any commonwealth it is the crime of treason for any individual citizen or any number of citizens together, to claim for themselves any Authority whatever over the whole commonwealth; but those who claim Authority over the holder of sovereign power are claiming Authority over the commonwealth itself. Besides, a sovereign Prince, if a Christian, has this further quality, that the commonwealth whose will is contained in his will, is the very thing which we call a *church*; and therefore a *church* only excommunicates when it excommunicates by authority of the Prince. But the Prince does not *excommunicate* himself and therefore cannot be *excommunicated* by his subjects. It is indeed possible that a group of rebellious citizens or traitors may declare a sovereign Prince *excommunicated*, but not *by right*. Much less may a Prince be *excommunicated* by a Prince; for this would not be *excommunication*, but rather a declaration of war by insult. For a *Church* which is put together from the citizens of two independent commonwealths is not one *Church*, because (as was said above in article 22) it does not have the power of duly meeting in a single group [*coetus*]; and therefore the members of one *Church* are not obliged to obey the other, hence cannot be *excommunicated* for disobedience. Someone might say that as Princes are members of the *universal Church*, they can also be *excommuni-*

cated by the authority of the *universal church*, but this will not do, because a *universal church* (as said in article 22) is not *a single person*, of which it could be said that it has *done, decreed, decided, excommunicated, absolved*, or engaged in any other such personal activities; nor does it have a ruler on earth who may give the order for it to meet and deliberate. For to be a ruler of a *universal church* and to be able to call it to meeting is the same as to be ruler and lord of all Christians throughout the world, and God alone has this privilege.

27. It was shown above (article 18) that the Authority to *interpret* holy *scripture* does not consist in the interpreter's freedom to expound and explain to others, in writing or orally, the meaning he finds in it, but in the fact that no one else has the right to act or teach against his version; so that *interpretation* in the sense under discussion is the same as the *Power* [*Potestas*] of definition (in all disputes which holy scripture should settle). We must now show that that authority [*authoritas*] belongs to individual *churches*, and depends on the authority of the holder(s) of sovereign power, provided they are Christians. For if it does not depend on civil authority, it has to depend either on the judgement [*arbitrium*] of individual citizens or on an outside authority. But it cannot depend on the judgement of individual citizens: that can be seen from the inconveniences and absurdities it would give rise to. The chief of these is that it would not only be the end of all civil obedience (contrary to *Christ*'s command), but would mean the dissolution of all society and peace among men (contrary to the natural laws). For as individuals interpret holy scripture for themselves, i.e. each man makes himself judge of what pleases God, and what displeases him, they cannot obey their Princes until they have decided for themselves whether his orders conform to scripture or not. And so either they do not obey or they obey at their own discretion, i.e. they obey themselves not the commonwealth. And that is the end of civil obedience. Again, since each man is following his own opinion, the disputes which arise must inevitably be innumerable and insoluble, and that would be the occasion (for by their nature men take disagreement as an insult) first of resentment and then of quarrelling and war; and all society and peace would perish. Moreover we have as an example the procedure God willed should be followed for the book of the law under the old law. This was that it should indeed be written, and publicly used, and be the Canon of divine teaching,

but that disputes arising from it should be settled by the Priests alone, not by individuals. Finally, it is a command of our Saviour, that in cases of offences committed by individuals, they should *listen to the Church*. Hence it is the task of a *church* to settle disputes; and therefore it is for a *church*, not for individuals, to interpret holy scripture. And authority to *interpret the Word of God*, i.e. to settle all questions about God and Religion, has nothing to do with any outsiders whatsoever. To see this, the essential point to grasp is the importance of that Authority in the citizens' minds and in their civil actions. It is a plain fact known to everyone that men's voluntary actions follow by natural necessity the beliefs they hold about good and evil, rewards and punishments; this is why they inevitably tend to offer obedience to those on whose will depends (they believe) their happiness or utter misery for eternity. Men expect eternal happiness or damnation at the will of those who determine what doctrines and actions are necessary for eternal salvation, and so will obey them in everything. This being so, it is quite obvious that citizens who believe themselves obliged to comply with an external Authority for doctrines necessary for salvation, do not constitute a commonwealth in themselves but are subjects of that foreigner. Hence, if a sovereign Prince ceded this great power in writing to another person, the document would not be valid, even if in the cession of power he were recognized as retaining the civil government; nor would he succeed in transferring anything essential to maintaining and properly running the government. For, by chapter II, article 4, no one is said to *transfer a right* unless he has given *an appropriate sign of his will to transfer* it; but anyone who has publicly indicated his *intention to retain* power, cannot have given an appropriate sign of transfer of the essential instruments of power; a document of this kind therefore will not be a sign of intention but of ignorance in the contracting parties. Secondly, one should reflect on how absurd it is that a commonwealth or its sovereign should commit to an enemy the governance of its citizens' consciences. For those who have not grown together into unity of person are, as shown above at v.6, in a state of enmity with each other. Never mind that they are not always fighting (for enemies too make truces); hostility is adequately shown by distrust, and by the fact that the borders of their commonwealths, Kingdoms and empires, armed and garrisoned, with the posture and appearance of gladiators, look across at each other like enemies, even when they are not striking each other. Finally is it not unreasonable of you to demand something which by the very grounds of your demand you admit belongs to someone else? I am an interpreter of holy scripture to you who are a citizen of a foreign commonwealth. On what grounds? By what agreement between you and me? By God's authority. How is it known? From holy scripture; there's the book, read it. No point, unless I interpret it for myself; and so interpretation is my right, and that of all other individual citizens; which we both deny. The only solution is that in every *Christian Church*, i.e. in every *Christian commonwealth*, the *interpretation* of holy scripture, i.e. the *right to settle* all *disputes*, should depend on and be derived from the Authority of the man or group of men in whose hands lies the sovereignty in the commonwealth.

28. There are then two kinds of disputes. One is about *spiritual matters*, i.e. about questions of faith whose truth cannot be examined by natural reason. Among these are questions about the *nature and office of* CHRIST, about *future rewards and punishments*, about the *resurrection of the body*, about the *nature and offices of Angels*, about *Sacraments and external worship*, and so on. The other kind of dispute is about questions of human knowledge, whose truth is drawn out by natural reason and Syllogisms from human agreements and definitions (i.e. from the meanings of words accepted by common use and consent); this kind includes all questions of *right* and *Philosophy*. For example, when the question is asked in *law* whether a *promise* and an *Agreement* exists or not, that is simply to ask whether such words, uttered in such a manner, are called a promise or an agreement by the common use and consent of the citizens; and if they are so called, it is true that an agreement has been made, otherwise it is false. That truth therefore depends on men's consent and agreements. Similarly, in Philosophy when the question is asked whether the same thing can be wholly in several different places at the same time, the settling of the question depends on a knowledge of men's common consent about the meaning of the word *Wholly*; for if it is the case that when men say a thing is wholly somewhere, they signify, by common consent, that they understand that none of it is elsewhere, it is false that the same thing is in several places at the same time. Thus that truth depends on men's consent and on the same grounds so does truth in all other questions of *right*

and *Philosophy*. And those who take the view that anything can be settled from obscure passages of scripture contrary to the common consent of men on the names of things, are favouring the abolition of the use of language and of all human society with it. For one will sell a field, and say that the whole field consists of one turf, and claim the rest was not sold and keep it. In fact he is abolishing reason itself, which is nothing other than examination of the truth formed by such consent. The commonwealth need not settle questions of this kind by interpretation of holy scripture because they do not belong to the *Word of God* in the sense in which the Word of God is understood as the *Word about God*, i.e. as *Gospel teaching*; nor is the holder of *Sovereign Power over the Church* obliged to engage *Teachers of the Church* to make judgements of this kind. But to decide questions of faith, i.e. questions *about God*, which are beyond human understanding, one needs God's blessing (so that we may not err, at least on essential questions) and this comes from CHRIST himself by *laying on of hands*. For our eternal salvation we are obliged to accept a supernatural doctrine, which because it is supernatural, is impossible to understand. It would go against equity if we were left alone to err by ourselves on essential matters. Our Saviour promised this Infallibility (in matters essential to salvation) to the *Apostles* until the day of judgement, i.e. to the *Apostles* and to the *Pastors* who were to be consecrated by the *Apostles* in succession by the *laying on of hands*. As a Christian, therefore, the holder of sovereign power in the commonwealth is obliged to interpret holy scripture, when it is a question about the *mysteries of faith*, by means of duly ordained *Ecclesiastics*. And so in *Christ*ian commonwealths judgement of *spiritual* and *temporal* matters belongs to the civil authority. And the man or assembly which holds sovereign power is the head of both the *commonwealth* and the Church; for a *Christian Church* and a *Christian commonwealth* are one and the same thing.

Chapter XVIII
On what is necessary for entry into the Kingdom of Heaven

1. The alleged difficulty of a conflict between obeying God and obeying men, to be removed by making a distinction between things necessary, and things not necessary, to salvation. 2. All things necessary for salvation are contained in faith *and* obedience. *3. The sort of* obedience *that is required. 4. What Faith is, and how it is to be distinguished from* profession, *from* knowledge, *and from* opinion. *5. What it is to* believe in CHRIST. *6. Proof from the intention of the Evangelists, that only one Article, that JESUS IS THE CHRIST is necessary for salvation. 7. Proof from the preaching of the* Apostles. *8. From the easiness of the Christian religion. 9. From the fact that it is the* foundation *of faith. 10. From the explicit words of* CHRIST *and the Apostles. 11. The faith of the old Testament is contained in that Article. 12. How* faith *and* obedience *work together for salvation. 13. In a Christian commonwealth there is no conflict between the commands of God and of the commonwealth. 14. Most of the doctrines about Religion which are matter of controversy today are concerned with the right to rule.*

1. It has always been an acknowledged truth that all authority in *secular* matters derives from the authority of the holder of sovereign power, whether that be a man or a group of men. It is clear from what has just been said that in *spiritual* matters it depends upon the authority of a *Church*; it will also be clear that every *Christian commonwealth* is a *Church* endowed with this kind of authority. From which even the dullest may conclude that in a Christian commonwealth (i.e. in a commonwealth where sovereignty is held by a Christian Prince or Christian group) *all power, both secular and spiritual, is united under Christ*; and therefore they must be obeyed in all things. On the other hand, because *one must obey God rather than man*, a difficulty has arisen as to how obedience can be safely offered if an order is given to do something which CHRIST forbids. The reason for the difficulty is that God no longer speaks to us in a living voice through CHRIST and the *Prophets*, but by the holy scriptures, which are understood differently by different people. Men know very well what kings and the congregated *Church* command, but they do not know whether *what* they command is against God's

orders or not. Their obedience wavers between the penalties of *temporal* and *spiritual* death; they attempt to sail between *Scylla* and *Charybdis*; and often fall foul of both. There will be none of these quandaries if one makes the right distinction between what is and what is not necessary to salvation. For if a command of Prince or commonwealth is such that it can be obeyed without loss of eternal salvation, it is unjust not to obey, and the Apostle's instructions are applicable: *Servants, obey your earthly Masters in all things. Children, obey your parents in all things* (Col. 3.20, 22), as well as the command of CHRIST: *The Scribes and Pharisees sit in the Seat of Moses; observe everything therefore that they say to you and do it* (Matt. 23.2). On the other hand, if they have ordered you to do things which are punishable by eternal death, it is crazy not to die a natural death rather than to obey and die eternal death. And CHRIST's words are applicable: *Do not fear those who can kill the body but cannot kill the soul* (Matt. 10.28). We must therefore see what all those things are which are necessary to salvation.

2. All things *necessary* to salvation are comprehended in the two virtues of *Faith* and *Obedience*. If the latter could be perfect, it would be enough in itself to save one from damnation; but because we have all for a long time now been guilty of wilfulness against God in Adam, and have also actually offended for ourselves, *obedience* without *forgiveness of sins* is not enough. Forgiveness, and the admission to the Kingdom of heaven that goes with it, is rather the reward of *Faith*. Nothing else is required for salvation. For the kingdom of God is closed only to sinners, i.e. to those who have not given the *obedience* due to God's laws; and not even to them, if they believe the *necessary articles* of the Christian faith. As soon as we see what obedience entails, and what the necessary articles of the Christian *faith* are, it will immediately be apparent what we should do at the command of commonwealths and Princes, and what we should decline.

3. By *obedience* in this passage is meant not the *act*, but the *will* and *the resolve*, with which we set ourselves to try henceforth to obey as much as we can. In this sense the word *obedience* is equivalent to *Repentance*. For the virtue of *Repentance* does not consist in the pain which accompanies the memory of a crime, but in a turn to the right direction and a determination not to offend again; without this the pain is called the pain of Despair not of Repentance. Those who

love God cannot fail to want to obey the Divine law and those who love their neighbour cannot fail to want to obey the moral law, which consists, as was shown above in chapter III, of the prohibition of *pride, ingratitude, insult, unkindness, unmercifulness, wrongs* and such offences by which we hurt our neighbours. Therefore *Love* too, or *Charity*, is equivalent to the word *obedience*; *justice* (which is a steady determination to give everyone his due) is also equivalent. It is already evident that *Faith* and *Repentance* are sufficient for salvation. It is evident, first, from the actual covenant of Baptism; for when at *Pentecost Peter's* converts asked him, *What shall we do?* he replied: *Repent, and let each one of you be Baptized in the name of Jesus for the forgiveness of sins* (Acts 2.38). Thus the only thing that had to be done to obtain Baptism, i.e. entry into the Kingdom of God, was to *repent* and *believe* in the name of JESUS. For the kingdom of heaven is promised by the Agreement made in Baptism. It is evident also from CHRIST's words in reply to the Prince, who asked him what he must do to have eternal life: *You know the commands, do not kill, do not commit adultery*, etc., which were a matter of *obedience*; and: *Sell all that you have, come and follow me*, which was of *faith* (Luke 18.20, Mark 10.21). And from the saying, *The just* (not anyone, but the *just*) *shall live by faith*; for *justice* is the same disposition of the will as *Repentance* and *Obedience*. And from the words of St. Mark, *As the time is fulfilled, and the kingdom of God is at hand, repent and believe the Gospel*; which indicates quite plainly that to enter into the Kingdom of heaven the only necessary virtues are *repentance* and *faith*. The *obedience* therefore which is *necessarily* required for salvation is nothing other than the *will* or *effort to obey*, i.e. to act according to the laws of God, i.e. the moral laws which are the same for all, and the civil laws, i.e. the commands of rulers in *temporal* matters, and the *Church* laws in *spiritual* matters; these two kinds of laws are different in different commonwealths and Churches, and are known by promulgation or public judgements.

4. To know what *Christian Faith* is, one must first define *Faith* in general and distinguish it from the other mental acts with which it is commonly confused. Taking *Faith* in the universal sense, an *Object of Faith*, i.e. *the thing which is believed*, is always a *proposition* (i.e. an affirmative or negative assertion) which we allow to be true. But as propositions are allowed for different reasons, it happens that such allowances are given different names. Sometimes we allow

propositions which, however, we do not accept in our own minds. We may do so for a time, until, in fact, we have examined their truth by seeing what would follow from them, and that is called *assuming*. We may also allow a proposition simply as such, perhaps from fear of the laws, and that is to *profess* or *confess* by external signs; or from the automatic deference, which men give out of politeness to those whom they respect, and to others from love of peace, and this is to *concede* in the simple sense. But propositions which we accept as true, we always concede for some reasons of our own. The reasons are drawn either from the *proposition* itself or from the *person of its proponent*. They are drawn from the *proposition itself* by calling to mind what things the words [*nomina*] which make up the proposition are used to signify by common consent; in this case, the assent which we give is called *Knowing* [*Scire*]. But if we cannot recall what is really meant by those words, but now it seems to mean one thing, now another, then we are said *to have an opinion* [*opinari*]. For example, it may be proposed that *two and three are five*, and one may recall the order of the number words, that it has been determined by the common consent of speakers of the same language (as by a kind of agreement necessary for human society) that Five is the name for as many units as are contained in Two and Three taken together; if one then assents that it is therefore true that *2* and *3* together are the same as *5*, that assent will be called *knowledge* [*scientia*]. To know that truth is simply to recognize that it was made by ourselves. For those who made the decision and the rule of language that the number ** is called *Two*, *** *Three*, and ***** *Five*, are also responsible for the fact that the proposition, *Two* and *three* taken together make *Five* is true. Likewise, if we remember what it is that is called *Theft* and *wrong*, we shall *know*, from the words themselves whether it is true that *Theft is a wrong*, or not. *Truth* is the same as *true proposition*, and a *proposition* is *true* in which the *consequent term*, which logicians call the *Predicate*, embraces in its extent the *Antecedent term* which they call the *subject*; and *to know the truth* is the same as *to remember* that it was made by ourselves by the actual use of the terms. Plato was not far off when he said long ago that *knowledge is memory*. And it sometimes happens that though words [*voces*] have fixed meanings defined by decision [*ex constituto*], they are so distorted in popular usage from their proper meanings by a particular passion for ornament or even deception, that it is very difficult to recall to memory the concepts for the sake of which they were attached to things, and it needs a keen judgement and intense labour to overcome the difficulty. It also happens that a large number of words [*voces*] have no proper fixed and constant sense of their own, and are not intelligible in themselves but only by the force of other signs used with them. Thirdly, certain names are of things that are inconceivable; there are therefore no concepts of the things for which they are the names. And for this reason it is pointless to look at the names themselves for the truth of the propositions which they make. In these cases as we examine the truth of a proposition by pondering the definitions of the words, we sometimes think that it is true and sometimes false as we feel more or less sanguine about finding its truth. Either of these two separately is called *Opining* [*Opinari*], and even *believing* [*credere*], both together are called *doubting* [*dubitare*]. But when the reasons for which we assent to a proposition are drawn not from *the actual proposition* but from the *person of its proponent*, because we judge him to be expert enough not to be deceived and we see no reason why he would want to deceive us, our assent is called *Faith* [*Fides*], because it arises from *reliance* [*fiducia*] on someone else's knowledge not our own. And when we believe someone's reliability, we are said to *believe him* or *believe in him*. From what has been said the difference between *Faith* and profession is apparent: for the former is always combined with internal assent, not so the latter. The former is an internal mental conviction, the latter is external obedience. Also the difference between *faith* and *opinion* appears; for the latter rests on our own reason, the former on someone else's reputation. Finally, the difference between *faith* and *knowledge*: the latter proceeds by cutting a proposition into small pieces, then chews it over and digests it slowly; the former swallows it whole. It contributes to knowledge to explain the words in which the subject of inquiry is put forward; in fact, this is the one and only way to knowledge, *the way of definitions*. But it is harmful to *faith*. For things put forward for belief which are beyond human understanding never become clearer by explanation, but to the contrary, become more obscure and more difficult to believe. A man who goes about to demonstrate the *mysteries of Faith* by natural reason, is like a sick man who tries to chew some health-giving but bitter pills before swallowing them; the result is that he throws them up straight away, whereas, if he had swallowed them whole, they would have made him better.

5. We have seen then what it is to *believe*. Now what is it to *believe in* CHRIST? Or, what proposition is the object of *faith in* CHRIST? For when we say *I believe in* CHRIST, we indicate *whom* we believe but not *what*. *Believing in* CHRIST is nothing other than believing that JESUS *is* CHRIST, namely the ONE who, according to the predictions of *Moses* and the *Prophets* of Israel, was to come into this world to *inaugurate the Kingdom of God*. This appears very well from the words of CHRIST to Martha: *I am*, he says, *the resurrection and the life, he who* BELIEVES IN ME *shall live, even if he has died, and everyone who lives and* BELIEVES IN ME, *shall not die for ever. Do you believe this?* She says to him, *Yes, Lord, I have believed that* YOU ARE CHRIST, *the son of the living God, and have come into this world* (John 11.25–27). In these words we see that BELIEVE IN ME is explained by BECAUSE YOU ARE CHRIST. To *believe in* CHRIST then is nothing other than to believe JESUS himself when he says that he is CHRIST.

6. As *faith* and *obedience* combine together for salvation, and both are *necessary*, we have shown above (art. 3) what that *obedience* is and to whom it is due. We must now ask which *Articles* of *faith* are required. And I say that no other Article of faith (*) is required of a Christian man as *necessary* for salvation but this one, that JESUS IS CHRIST. But one must distinguish, as above in art. 4, between *faith* and profession. The *profession* of several dogmas may be *necessary* (if so ordered); for it is a part of the *obedience* due to the laws, but we are not now inquiring into the *obedience necessary* for salvation, but about *faith*. The first proof is from the aim of the authors of the Gospels, which was to establish that one article by describing the life of our Saviour. We shall see that that was the aim and intention of the writers of the Gospels, if we look carefully at the History itself. St. Matthew begins with his Genealogy and shows JESUS to be of the race of *David*; Born of a Virgin (ch. 1); adored by the *Magi* as king of the Jews; sought to be killed by *Herod* for the same reason (ch. 2); his Kingdom preached both by himself and by *John the Baptist* (ch. 3, 4); he taught the laws, not as the Scribes but as one who had authority (ch. 5–7); he cured diseases miraculously (ch. 8, 9); he sent out *Apostles* as heralds of the Kingdom into every part of Judea to preach the Kingdom (ch. 10); to the messen-

gers from John who asked whether he was the Christ or not, he replied that they should report what they had seen, namely miracles, which were the privilege of CHRIST alone (ch. 11); he gave proof and proclamation of his Kingdom by arguments, Parables and signs before the Pharisees and others (ch. 12ff. to 21); he was hailed as King when he entered Jerusalem (ch. 21); he maintained against the Pharisees that he was the Christ; he warned others of *Pseudochrists*; he displayed the nature of his Kingdom in parables (ch. 22–25); he was arrested and charged with saying that he was a King; and the title inscribed on his cross was: THIS IS JESUS KING OF THE JEWS (ch. 26, 27); finally after his resurrection, he said to the *Apostles*, that *all power was given to him in heaven and on earth* (ch. 28). All this is intended to make us believe that Jesus was the Christ. This then was the aim of St. Matthew in writing his Gospel; the aim of the other Evangelists was the same as his. As St. *John*, for his part, explicitly says at the end of his *Gospel: These things have been written, so that you may know that Jesus is (the) Christ, the Son of the living God* (John 20.31).

And I say that no other article of faith but this one] *I have thought it worthwhile to explain this assertion more fully despite the fact that I have given it enough support in my text; I recognize that its novelty may displease a large number of theologians. First then when I say that the article that* Jesus *is the* Christ *is the only one necessary to salvation, I am not saying that only faith is necessary to salvation; I also require Justice, or the obedience due to God's laws, i.e. the will to live rightly. Secondly, I do not deny that the profession of many other articles may also be necessary to salvation providing their profession is commanded by a Church; but since Faith is internal and profession is external, I say that the former is strictly Faith, and the latter is a part of obedience; consequently, the article by itself is sufficient for internal Faith but not for the profession of a Christian. Finally, if I had said that true and internal Repentance for sins was alone necessary for salvation from the point of view of justice, it ought not to be taken as a paradox, since we understand that Repentance contains justice, obedience and a heart restored to every virtue. In the same way, when I say that Faith in one article alone is enough for salvation, it is not so surprising since this one article includes so many others. For these words* Jesus is Christ *signify, that Jesus is the one whom God had promised by the prophets to send into the world to inaugurate the Kingdom, i.e. that Jesus is the Son of God, creator of heaven and earth, born of a virgin, who died for the sins of those who would believe in him, that he is the Christ, i.e. the King, that he came back to life (for otherwise he would not reign) to judge the world and reward believers' works; for otherwise he cannot be a King; likewise that men will rise again: for without this they will not come to judgement. Thus this one single article contains the whole of the Apostles' Creed, but I thought that it should be summarized in this way, because I saw that both Christ and his Apostles admitted a large number of men to the Kingdom of God on account of this one article alone without the others which are derived as consequences from it; e.g. the thief on the Cross, the Eunuch baptized by Philip, the two thousand people gathered into the Church by St. Peter. If anyone is troubled because I do not hold the view that all those who do not give internal assent to whatever articles are defined by the Church (without speaking out against them, but conceding them if ordered to do so) are damned for eternity, I do not know what I am to do for them. For the plainest testimonies of holy scripture which follow prevent me from changing my mind.*

7. Secondly, the Apostles' preaching proves the same point; for they were heralds of the Kingdom, and Christ sent them out to preach only the Kingdom of God (Luke 9.2, Acts 17.6). What they did after Christ's ascension may be gathered from the charge against them: *They dragged,* says *St. Luke, Jason and some of the brothers before the Leading men of the commonwealth, shouting that these are the men who are upsetting the commonwealth, and they have come here and Jason has taken them in, and they are all acting against the decrees of Caesar, saying that Jesus is another King* (Acts 17.[6]–7). And the subject matter of the Apostles' sermons appears from these words: *he opened up the Scriptures* (meaning the old Testament), *and showed that the Christ had to suffer, and rise again from the dead, and that JESUS IS THIS CHRIST* (Acts 17.2–3).

8. The third piece of evidence is found in the passages which stress how easy are the things required by Christ for salvation. If a necessary requirement of salvation were internal mental assent to the truth of each and every proposition about the Christian faith which are today either disputed or differently defined by the different Churches, nothing would be more difficult than the Christian

religion. How then would it be true, *My yoke is easy, and my burden is light?* (Matt. 11.30), and, *the little ones believe in him* (Matt. 18.6). And, *it pleased God through the foolishness of Preaching to save those who believed* (1 Cor. 1.21), or how would the thief hanging on the cross be sufficiently instructed for salvation, whose confession of faith was limited to these words *Remember me when you come into your Kingdom?* Or how could St. Paul himself have so swiftly turned from an enemy to a Teacher of Christians?

9. Fourth is a proof from the fact that that article of *faith* is a foundation and does not itself rest on any other foundation. *If anyone says to you: look, here is Christ, or there is Christ, do not believe them: for false Christs will arise, and false prophets, and they will give great signs,* etc. (Matt. 24.23). It follows from this that on the basis of the faith of this article we must reject belief in signs and wonders. *Though we or an Angel from heaven, says the Apostle, should preach a Gospel other than the one that we have Preached to you, let him be Anathema* (Gal. 1.8). On the basis of this article then we would have to refuse to believe the Apostles and Angels themselves (and there-fore the Church too, I think) if they should teach against it. *Dearly beloved,* (says St. John) *do not believe every spirit, but try the spirits whether they are of God, since many False-prophets have gone out into the world; a Spirit of God is known by this: every spirit that confesses that JESUS CHRIST HAS COME* in the Flesh from God, etc. (1 John 4).[1] Thus the Article is a criterion of spirits, by which the authority of Teachers is accepted or rejected. It cannot be denied that all who are Christians today learned from Teachers, that there was a JESUS, who did all these things by which he was recognized as the Christ; but it does not follow that they are relying on teachers or on a Church for that article; rather they are relying on Jesus himself. For that Article came before the Christian *Church,* even if all the rest came later. And the *Church* is founded on the Article, not the other way around (Matt. 16.18). Besides the article *Jesus is Christ* is so fundamental that all the rest are said by St. Paul to be built upon it. *No one can lay any other foundation but the one that is laid, which is Jesus Christ* (i.e. *Jesus is Christ*). *And anyone who builds on this foundation, Gold, Silver, precious Stones, Timber, Hay, Straw, etc., the work of each one will be made manifest. Anyone whose work lasts*

---

[1] 1 John 4.1–2.

will receive his pay; anyone whose work burns, will suffer a loss, but he will be safe (1 Cor. 3.11, 12 etc.). It is clear from this that by foundation is meant this Article that JESUS IS CHRIST. For Gold, Silver, Hay, Straw, etc., which signify doctrines, are not built upon the person of *Christ*. It is also clear that false doctrines can be erected on the foundation, but those who teach them need not be damned.

10. Finally, it can be shown very plainly from very many passages of scripture, whoever may interpret them, that that article is the only indispensable tenet of *internal faith. You search the scriptures because you think that in them you have eternal life, and it is they that give testimony of me* (John 5.39). Christ means the scriptures of the old Testament alone, for the new Testament was not yet written. Now there is no other Testimony about Christ in the old Testament except that an eternal King would come, who would be born at such and such a place of such and such parents, and would teach and do such and such things, and these would be the signs by which he would be recognized. All these things testify to this one thing that JESUS who would be born thus and would teach and do such things was (the) CHRIST. No other Faith therefore was required for eternal life but this article. *Everyone who lives and believes in me shall not die for ever* (John 11.25). But to believe in Jesus (as explained in the same passage) is the same as to believe that JESUS IS CHRIST. He who believes this therefore will not die forever, and consequently this article alone is necessary for salvation. *These things have been written that you may believe that* JESUS IS CHRIST the Son of God, and that believing you may have life in his name (John 20.31). Therefore he who so believes will have eternal life, and therefore has no need of other *faith. Every spirit that confesses that Jesus Christ came in the Flesh is of God* (1 John 4.2), and, *Every spirit that believes that* JESUS IS Christ, is born of God (1 John 5.1), and, *Who is it that overcomes the world but one who believes that* JESUS IS the Son of God (1 John 5.5). If then – in order to be *of God, born of God* and to *overcome the world* – there is no need to believe anything else, than that JESUS IS CHRIST, that one, single article is sufficient for salvation. *Look, there is water, what prevents me from being baptized? and Philip said: if you believe with all your heart, you may. He replied: I believe that Jesus Christ is the Son of God* (Acts 8.36–37). If when that article is indeed believed with the whole heart, i.e. with internal faith, it is enough for Baptism, it is also enough for

salvation. Beside these passages, there are countless others, which say the same thing, clearly and explicitly. In fact whenever we read that our Saviour praised anyone's faith or said, *Your faith has saved you*, or that he healed anyone because of his *faith*, the proposition believed was precisely this, JESUS IS CHRIST, either directly or by inference.

11. No one can believe that *Jesus is Christ* who does not also believe *Moses* and the Prophets since he knows that by *Christ* is meant the King who was promised by God through *Moses* and the *Prophets* as *King* and *saviour* of the world, nor can he believe them if he does not believe that *God exists and governs the world*. Thus it is necessary that faith about God and the old testament be included in this faith of the new Testament. In the kingdom of God by nature the crime of treason against God's Majesty involved only Atheism and denial of divine Providence; in the kingdom by the old Agreement, it also covered Idolatry. In the kingdom by the new agreement we now also add *Apostasy*, or renunciation of the article, that *Jesus is the Christ*, after it has been accepted. One must not of course speak out against any other doctrines that have been defined by a legal Church; that is the sin of disobedience, and obedience is necessary to salvation. But we have demonstrated at length just above that they need not be believed with *internal faith*.

12. *Faith* and *Obedience* play different roles in effecting the salvation of a Christian; *obedience* contributes *power* or *capacity*, *faith* contributes the *act*. And each is said to justify in its own way. For *Christ* does not forgive sins for everyone, but only for those who *repent*, or *obey*, i.e. for the just (I do not say the *innocent*, but the *just*; for *justice* is the will to obey the laws and is compatible with a sinner; and the will to obey, in Christ's eyes, is obedience). *The just man* (not everyone) *shall live by faith*. *Obedience* therefore *justifies* because it *makes just*, in the way in which *Temperance* makes *temperate*, *Prudence prudent*, and *Chastity* makes *chaste*, that is to say, essentially. And it puts a man in the position of being capable of pardon. Again *Christ* did not promise to condone the sins of all the just but only of *those who believe that he is Christ*. Faith therefore *justifies* in the sense that the judge is said to *justify* the man he *acquits*; namely by a *verdict* that makes him safe in *fact*. In the latter sense of justification (for it is an equivocal word) *faith alone* justifies, and in the former sense *only obedience*; but neither justice alone nor faith alone *saves*, but both together.

13. From what has been said so far it will be easy to perceive the duty of Christian citizens towards their sovereigns. As long as sovereigns profess to be Christians, they cannot command their subjects to deny Christ or to treat him contemptuously; for if they did give such a command, they would be professing that they were not Christians. For it has been shown, both by natural reason and from holy scripture, that citizens should obey the Princes and rulers of the commonwealth in all things, except in what is contrary to God's commandments; and in a Christian commonwealth God's commandments on *temporal matters* (i.e. matters which are to be investigated by human reason) are the laws and beliefs of the commonwealth, published by those to whom the authority to make laws and judge disputes has been committed by the commonwealth; in *spiritual matters* (i.e. those which are to be settled through holy scripture) God's commandments are the laws and doctrines of the commonwealth, i.e. of the Church (for a Christian Church and a Christian commonwealth are the same thing, as shown in the last chapter, article 20), published by duly ordained Pastors, who have received authority to do so from the commonwealth. It therefore plainly follows that in a Christian commonwealth *obedience* is owed to sovereign rulers in all things, both *spiritual* and *temporal*. And it is beyond dispute that in all *temporal matters* a Christian citizen owes the same obedience also to non-Christian rulers; but in *spiritual matters*, i.e. in things relating to the mode of worshipping God, he must follow some *Church of Christians*. For it is a Presumption of Christian faith that in supernatural matters God speaks only through Christian interpreters of holy scripture. But what follows? Are princes to be resisted when they are not to be obeyed? Of course not! This is contrary to the civil agreement. What then must one do? Go to Christ through Martyrdom. If anyone thinks this a harsh thing to say, it is very certain that he does not believe with his whole heart that JESUS IS THE CHRIST, *the Son of the living God* (for he would long to be dissolved and to be with Christ),[2] but is using a pretence of Christian *faith* to try to slip out of his Agreement to obey the commonwealth.

14. Someone may be surprised that, apart from the article that JESUS IS THE CHRIST, which is necessary to salvation on the basis of internal faith, all the other articles pertain only to obedience, which

---

[2] Cf. Philippians 1.23.

can be given even if one does not inwardly believe all that is set forth by a Church (provided that he desires to believe it, and makes external profession whenever necessary); the result of all that is that there are so many dogmas about today which are said, one and all, to be of *faith* in the sense that one cannot enter the Kingdom of Heaven without believing them. But he will be less surprised if he reflects that in many disputes a conflict about a human Kingdom is involved, in some cases about profit, in some about intellectual reputation. The question about *Church properties* is a question about the *right of government*; for as soon as one knows what a *Church* is, one knows immediately who should have government of Christians. For if every Christian commonwealth is the Church which Christ himself teaches that every Christian subject of that commonwealth should listen to, then every citizen is obliged to obey his commonwealth, i.e. the man or men who have sovereign power over them, not only in *temporal* but also in *spiritual matters*. But if every Christian commonwealth is not that Church, then there is some other, more universal Church which one should obey; all Christians therefore should obey it, as they would obey Christ if he came to earth. And it will give its orders either through a monarch or through an assembly. The question therefore is one of the *right of government*. The question *about infallibility* has the same point; for anyone who was truly and inwardly believed by the whole human race to be incapable of error, would be certain of both temporal and spiritual power over the whole human race, unless he refused it himself; for if he says that he must be obeyed in *temporal matters*, he is given the right so to govern precisely because people believe that he does not err. The privilege of interpreting the scriptures also has the same point. He whose business it is to settle the disputes that can arise from different interpretations of scripture, has also the business of settling all disputes absolutely. Having this he also has authority over all who acknowledge the scriptures as the Word of God. This is also the point of the dispute about the *power of remitting and retaining sins*, or about *the authority to excommunicate*. For anyone in his right mind will obey absolutely in all things a person by whose judgement, he believes, he is to be saved or damned. This is the point of the power of *authorizing* [*religious*] *societies*; for they depend on the man by whom they exist, and he has as many subjects as he has monks even in a commonwealth of enemies. This is the point of the question about the *judge of legal marriage*. For the one who has the right to make that judgement also has the trial of cases about inheritance and succession to all the goods and rights not only of private individuals but also of sovereign Princes. And in a certain way, *Celibacy of the Clergy* also has the same point. For celibates are less attached than other men to the rest of the commonwealth. And besides, it is no negligible disadvantage to Princes, that they must either do without the Priesthood (which is a great bond of civil obedience) or not have a hereditary kingdom. *Canonization of saints* has the same point; the Pagans called it Deification. For he who can attract other people's subjects with such a reward can induce those who are avid for such glory to dare and do anything. For what else but honour in the eyes of posterity were the *Decii*[3] and the other Romans looking for when they devoted their lives, and a thousand others who have thrown themselves into unbelievable dangers? Disputes about *Purgatory* and *indulgences* are about profit. Questions about *free-will, justification, the manner of receiving Christ in the sacrament* are Philosophical questions. There are also questions about rites which are not recent innovations but survivals of the past in a Church not sufficiently purged of Paganism, but there is no need to go through more. Everyone knows that it is the nature of men to hurl abuse and anathemas at each other when they disagree over questions of *Power, Profit* or *Intellectual Preeminence*. It is no wonder therefore if when men grow warm in dispute, almost any dogma is said by one or the other to be *necessary* for entry into the Kingdom of heaven, so that those who do not accept it may be damned not only for their obstinacy (which is true according to the doctrine of the *Church*), but also for their lack of *faith*; and that is what I have shown above to be false on the basis of several very plain scripture passages; to which I now add this one from St. Paul: *One who eats,*[4] *should not reject one who does not; one who does not, should not criticize one who does. For God has accepted him. One man thinks one Day is better than another, another man values all days alike: let each be filled with his own conviction* (Rom. 14.3,6).[5]

THE END

---

[3] Cf. for example, Livy, VIII. 9.
[4] I.e. meat offered to idols.
[5] Romans 14.3, 5.

Index

Cambridge Texts in the History of Political Thought

Titles published in the series thus far

Aristotle *The Politics* and *The Constitution of Athens* (edited by Stephen Everson)

Arnold *Culture and Anarchy and Other Writings* (edited by Stefan Collini)

Astell *Political Writings* (edited by Patricia Springborg)

Augustine *The City of God against the Pagans* (edited by R. W. Dyson)

Austin *The Province of Jurisprudence Determined* (edited by Wilfrid E. Rumble)

Bacon *The History of the Reign of the King Henry VII* (edited by Brian Vickers)

Bakunin *Statism and Anarchy* (edited by Marshall Shatz)

Baxter *A Holy Commonwealth* (edited by William Lamont)

Beccaria *On Crimes and Punishments and Other Writings* (edited by Richard Bellamy)

Bentham *A Fragment on Government* (introduction by Ross Harrison)

Bernstein *The Preconditions of Socialism* (edited by Henry Tudor)

Bodin *On Sovereignty* (edited by Julian H. Franklin)

Bolingbroke *Political Writings* (edited by David Armitage)

Bossuet *Politics Drawn from the Very Words of Holy Scripture* (edited by Patrick Riley)

The British Idealists (edited by David Boucher)

Burke *Pre-Revolutionary Writings* (edited by Ian Harris)

Christine de Pizan *The Book of the Body Politic* (edited by Kate Langdon Forhan)

Cicero *On Duties* (edited by M. T. Griffin and E. M. Atkins)

Conciliarism and Papalism (edited by J. H. Burns and Thomas M. Izbicki)

Constant *Political Writings* (edited by Biancamaria Fontana)

Dante *Monarchy* (edited by Prue Shaw)

Diderot *Political Writings* (edited by John Hope Mason and Robert Wokler)

The Dutch Revolt (edited by Martin van Gelderen)

Early Greek Political Thought from Homer to the Sophists (edited by Michael Gagarin and Paul Woodruff)

The Early Political Writings of the German Romantics (edited by Frederick C. Beiser)

The English Levellers (edited by Andrew Sharp)